MODERN MANAGEMENT SERIES

Modern Marketing and Sales Management

Edited by

M.K. Singh
Anant Mahadevan

DISCOVERY PUBLISHING HOUSE
NEW DELHI-110002

First Edition 1995
Reprinted: 2013

This edition is published by special arrangement with Discovery Publishing House and is licensed for sale in South East Asia.

ISBN 81-7141-069-3

Printed at: Dynamic printers, Delhi

Preface

It would appear that the complexity of the modern world, more than any other factor, has taken a quantum leap into the realms of organised confrontation. One is not referring to the Group of 77, GATT or the EEC, or, for that matter, the nebulous world of South-South Cooperation. Confrontation, for our present purpose, connotes the invisible array of forces as sent into the field by the growing multinational corporations, opposed to the rather bedraggled and war-weary veterans of the Small Business Enterprise. The confrontation arises only because both have overriding ambitions—the former to develop into global empires of the economic kind and the latter to expand into the ever-growing but just-beyond-reach international markets. Both have two common denominators—they employ people and they have to sell their products and services.

This volume brings together the strategies and perceived goals of marketing and selling products and services, of both the developed and the developing worlds. The attempt in the choice of papers and articles, published and unpublished, is to present a balanced and intelligible mix of views, beliefs, principles and opinions which would be helpful in an understanding of the forces, both human and intangible, which constitute effective marketing and selling management. The volume has been compiled with the intention of pointing out to the professional marketing manager, especially the younger of them, the many facets of organised marketing and distribution which the increasingly competitive market has acquired.

In our efforts we have been assisted in generous measure by our many colleagues and friends, professional managers and expert consultants. They would be too numerous to list—suffice it to say that without their guidance these papers and articles would not have been brought together into a cohesive whole. Nonetheless, we feel it our bounden duty to acknowledge the fruitful discussions we have had with Prof. P. Sarveshwar and Dr. Arun Nimbalkar of the Institute of Corporate and Industrial Management, Bombay; Dr. S. Ganesan of the Textile Managers Association, Aurangabad; Shri K.R. Wadhawan of the Centre for Research in Management Sciences, Manila, and Smt. Urvashi Palekar, Documentation Officer, Institute of Corporate Management, Faculty of Economics, University of Lagos, Nigeria.

Excellent computer and secretarial support services were provided by S/Shri Sameer Kak, Arvind Goswami and Raghuraj T. We are grateful to them.

We have attempted to minimise all printing errors, but hasten to add that we alone are responsible for those that still remain.

M.K. SINGH
ANANT MAHADEVAN

Introduction

Management may be defined as the process of efficient functioning based on correct choices and actions. However, in the modern world which is increasingly dependent on large organisations, the most significant situations are those which require organisational management. This implies decision and action in a context which is characterised by organised group or collective activity and the goals or objectives towards which the group effort is directed.

These objectives are pursued by managers, who make decisions pertaining to the desired objectives and concerning relationships among resources—the people, money and machines, materials and methods which can be effectively deployed to attain those objectives. Managers then see that their decisions are carried out and that they have the desired effect. When necessary, they use *control actions* to redirect their resources toward the desired objectives. Since managers of large organisations cannot literally do each and every thing that is required as a result of the decisions that are made, organisational management is a process of *working through others* to achieve broad organisational objectives, such as profit or social welfare, or specific objectives such as the development of a new product with success potential or the efficient and time-bound construction of a power plant.

Management may thus be thought of as involving two major elements, *planning* and *control*. These two aspects of management apply to all areas of organised activity, such as the modern large firm represents. Planning involves decisions and actions concerning the future of the organisation. What type of business should be taken up? What kinds of manpower mix will be needed for effective functioning in the 1990s? What impact will increased leisure time have on the utilisation of the contemplated products?

Control involves decisions and actions related to the present organisations. How should production be scheduled to optimise machine-utilisation time? What should be the efficient allocation of workload among various levels of manpower? What mix of newspaper-radio-TV advertising would be best suited to the products?

Every manager is involved to some degree in both planning and control, but the jobs of many managers emphasise the control component. This is, in fact, true of many jobs which have the word 'planning' in their designation. The job of a production planning manager, for instance, is largely control-oriented as it stresses the present and the immediate future rather than the long-term future—which is an intrinsic aspect of correct planning.

Marketing managers make decisions concerning products and services to be offered by their organisations, prices to be charged, advertising and sales appeals to be employed, finances to be allocated to various promotional media and campaigns, personal sales effort to be expended, and a wide variety of other marketing variables which form a part of overall organisational management.

Despite the fact that marketing managers limit their efforts to marketing decision variables, and without engaging in a pointless discussion of the relative importance of marketing functions compared with other organisational functions such as production and finance, it should be pointed out that marketing decisions tend to be inherently involved in most of the strategic choices of the organisation. The moot question is: Which products or services should be distributed to which markets or market segments? Product and market choices are intrinsically marketing decisions. Thus, while marketing is indeed only one of the many and varied functions that must be performed if the organisation is to develop and prosper, it is the one function which most vitally affects the organisation's future because future success is primarily dependent on new generations of products and the developing markets which for the present are beyond the organisation's marketing abilities. Of course, marketing and sales management is equally important in determining the organisation's present performance. As the old marketing clichè goes, everything is cost until the product is sold.

The marketing manager is especially concerned with having on tap complete and high quality, also authentic, information since the job of planning and controlling the organisations marketing, promotion and sales activities involves a steady stream of complex choice situations. If marketing managers were able to make *informed* choices based on relevant information, they are more likely to experience good results and to move towards the task of achieving the goals and targets set by the organisation.

Another consideration which comes into play in marketing information is the degree of its reliability and credibility. Do the attitudes, expectations and intentions which survey respondents report really reflect their trend of underlying thoughts and beliefs? Is the respondent motivated to 'look good' or to appear to be sophisticated in responding to an attitudinal survey? Do panel members neglect to report everything that needs reporting about their purchase and usage of products? Do some respondents in a phone survey give an 'easy' answer about product end-use rather than take the pains to locate the particular end-use in their record? The answers to most of these questions about the reliability and credibility of marketing information is "Probably Yes."

The papers that are incorporated in the various chapters of this compilation constitute an effort to identify all workable, optimum approaches to the complex socio-economic business and function of marketing and sales management.

Contents

1

Toward a New Concept of Sales Management

LESLIE M. DAWSON

When efforts were being made several years ago to formulate a concept of physical distribution attuned to the modern business environment, this functional area of marketing was often referred to as *the most neglected*. Today it could be argued that the area of sales management is a prime contender for this *honour*. According to the Committee on Definitions of the American Marketing Association, sales management is:

> "the planning, direction, and control of the personal selling activities of a business unit, including recruiting, selecting, training, equipping, assigning, routing, supervising, paying and motivating as these tasks apply to the personal sales force."[1]

While this is no doubt a useful listing of the tasks in which the sales manager has typically become involved, it does not

Editors' Note: Reprinted from *Journal of Marketing*, April 1970, pp. 33-38; published by the American Marketing Association.

make clear the conceptual linkage of the sales management position to the general goals and efforts of the business organization.

This paper develops the thesis that (1) top business management has always tended to operate under *some* implicit concept of the sales management function; (2) this has been evidenced by the locus of emphasis in the prescribed duties and responsibilities of managerial strata existing between the top sales executive and field selling force; and (3) having already shifted several times in this century, it would appear that the locus of emphasis is about to shift again, thereby generating fundamental change in the nature of the sales manager's role.

A Historical Perspective

In general, the concept held by top management of the sales manager's role has always tended to be determined by the corresponding conception of the salesman's role. This role seemed to have been a function of the general tone of business' response to perceived dominant environmental forces. The process may be given a useful historical perspective by relating it to the well-known hypothesis that the dominant orientation of American business has passed through several distinct phases in this century.

The Production Era

Rapid technological change dominated the business environment in the late nineteenth and early twentieth centuries. Technological progress in the fields of agriculture, transportation, and communication occurred with a swiftness as to constitute revolutions rather than evolutions. In an environment which suddenly reflected both the technical capacity for mass production and the expanded markets to absorb the increased output, the natural response of business consisted of a production orientation. Management was preoccupied with increasing volume and improving plant efficiency. While it would be an overstatement to say that market considerations were ignored during this era, there is ample foundaton for Drucker's claim that "fifty years ago the typical attitude of the American businessman toward marketing was still: 'The sales department will sell whatever the plant produces.'"[2]

In the production-dominated era, the job of the salesman was not held in very high regard either by business management or the public at large. The salesman was viewed as the congenial, hail-fellow-well-met representative who built up good will for the manufacturer among the trade. This conception of the selling process as an art, not amenable to any type of scientific analysis, and of the sales job as one requiring a relatively low degree of skill and intelligence—an occupation which could naturally be expected to attract people of less than ideal character—led to a conception of sales management emphasizing *tight supervision and control.*

The Sales Era

The sales era of American business probably should be dated from the late 1920s. These years were marked by significant change in the dominant environmental forces affecting business. Unparalleled prosperity was the hallmark of the nation's economy in the post-World War I years from 1922 to 1929. Continued improvements in technology and labour efficiency propelled industrial output to a new plateau. Whereas population gained approximately 12 per cent during these years, industrial productivity almost doubled. As assembly lines proliferated, America fast became the world's first genuine mass-production society. The demand for consumer goods could not keep up with the rapid pace of the national product, which is one reason why accumulated funds flowed into various kinds of speculation. The crash of 1929 witnesed the beginning of a depression which cast an economic pall over the nation that was never fully lifted until the start of World War II. Thus, the dominant environmental forces during this period were, first, strains of consumption saturation at an unprecedented level of industrial productivity, and ultimately, an extended period of extreme economic depression. Both of these environmental pressures tended to evoke a similar response by business. This took the form of an increased concern with the development of a mass-distribution machinery to complement the now realized mass-production system.

The stature of the sales position increased in the eyes of top management during the sales era. The fallacy of the "better mousetrap" theorem as a workable guide to successful marketing was exposed. It became evident that something beyond congeniality was required for a salesman to sustain a consistently high volume. The term *scientific salesmanship* came into use to describe the application of sound management principles and basic behavioral science concepts to the selling process. Still, management's conception of the salesman reflected the basically company-oriented outlook of the period. His job was to generate sales, and a simple amount of product-market knowledge combined with a highly structured selling presentation was usually deemed sufficient to this end. Short-run sales volume was normally the measure of his success.

Top management's realization that the sales job required knowledge and skills beyond personality led to an emphasis on *broadened responsibilities* for sales managers. Definitions of sales management now commonly included responsibilities in such areas as recruiting, selecting, training, and compensating. The sales manager's role in overall marketing strategy and planning remained less definite. Significantly, the sales manager's performance in this era was generally measured by the *volume* produced by his selling force. Profit may not have been ignored altogether, but it was generally felt that sales volume data were easier to procure and more precise. The direct relationship between increasing sales volume and increasing profit was widely assumed.

The Marketing Era

Much has been said about the dynamic character of the business environment in the post-World War II years. The nation's economy not only recovered from the effects of the Depression, but also swiftly advanced well beyond the highest prewar levels. Postwar prosperity ushered in the age of the affluent society in the United States. The great technological surge produced by the war led to new processes and techniques which brought down traditional industry boundaries. Chemicals became the competitor to textiles; plastic of steel; and paper of glass. Rising costs and pricing constraints made the term *profit squeeze* prominent in the lexicon of business. The postwar consumer was not only better off economically, better educated, and more sophisticated, but also before long more saturated with goods. The notion of a limit to the *capacity to consume* became something more than a mere theoretical concern. As the American economy was rapidly transformed into one of abundance, the survival of the business enterprise became largely dependent upon its skill in determining, and flexibility in adjusting to, shifts in consumer tastes. An all-out commitment to market considerations became vital, and this was termed as the *marketing orientation* or the *marketing concept.*

The strategic role of the salesman as the direct link between seller and prospective buyer resulted in a virtual redefinition of the sales job in the marketing era. Numerous references have been made in the postwar literature to the death of the "old salesman" and his rebirth as the "new salesman." Several distinct attributes are supposed to differentiate the latter from his predecessor.

He is seen as a *manager of a market area* responsible for goal determination, forecasting, planning, and long-run market development. Such a managerial approach to territory cultivation is significant because "it is the difference between viewing salesmen as employees or as members of management."[8]

The new salesman is visualized as a *problem-solver*. In fact, the salesman's problem-solving abilities are recognized as often constituting the key to product differentiation, "He is a man capable of absorbing stacks of information churned out by the marketing department, and of applying it to his customer's problems. He goes forth armed with a tremendous amount of data on his customers' needs, their products, their corporate organizations, and their supply and delivery schedules."[4]

The new salesman functions as an *educator* in a technological age where effective communication across functional or disciplinary lines has become increasingly difficult. "The more effective are salesmen as educators, the more effective they will be as sales purveyors of the knowledge, concepts, and ideas contained in their sales proposals."[5]

He is an *empathizer* with a solid, often formal, grounding in the behavioral sciences which enables him to better recognize and cope with the personal need patterns of prospective buyers.

As the salesman's role has been redefined in the marketing era, a redefinition of the sales manager's role has also been necessary. For instance, the greater the degree to which firms have come to view salesmen as managers of a market area, the less emphasis has been placed on field supervision and control of salesmen's activities by sales management. In general, the redefinition of the sales management job in the marketing era has tended to increase the organizational importance of the job through new emphasis in two major areas:

The new sales manager, largely freed from day-to-day activity planning for salesmen, has become involved in creative *strategy development* at a higher marketing level. His job requires a total sales perspective wherein field sales activities are properly related to, and integrated with, other elements of the total marketing mix. "Perhaps the most important change in the scope and nature of the sales manager's job . . . is that he must become a planner, a strategy developer, as well as an operator."[6] Due to the major influence of the computer, the sales manager of the marketing era has taken on new *profit responsibilities*. Faster and more thorough analysis of sales data facilitates the measurement of profitability of individual salesmen, products, territories, and other components of the selling operation. The profitable selling operation, instead of the

high volume one, increasingly has become the criterion of successful sales management.

The 1970s and Beyond—The "Human Era"

There has been much recent speculation as to whether business will enter a new era as it moves into the last third of the twentieth century; for example, "the age of the computer" and the "era of social responsibility." It seems clear that the environmental forces which resulted in a greater focus on the market place will endure and intensify in the foreseeable future. Yet the tumultuous events ushering in the 1970s suggest that a market focus will not be sufficient in coping with a powerful new milieu of pressures emanating from the environment. The impact of computer technology on marketing management continues to grow. Not only has this often compelled the competitive firm to redesign operations and procedures, but also to deal with the human adjustments necessary in the integration of the computer in the organization system. Externally, demands mount for a deeper commitment by the business community to the solutions of the social problems which plague the United States and the world. Pressures on business leaders intensify for more action in such diverse areas as the war on poverty, pollution control, and the eradication of social injustice. Numerous recent initiatives by prominent corporations in such human need areas signify a response to such pressures and are suggestive of a possible movement beyond a *marketing orientation* to a broader *human orientation.*

A New Concept of Sales Management

It has been entirely consistent with the perspective of a marketing orientation that the sales management concept be characterized by emphasis on strategy development and profit responsibility. Both of these relate to market opportunity and the firm's search for greater profit return. But for the firm moving to a broader human orientation, the concept of the sales manager's job may be expected to reflect a very basic shift in emphasis and priorities. For such a firm the most congruous concept of sales management is one which revolves around the *total development of human resources*. Beyond the general thrust of a human orientation, three probable developments may be cited in support of this contention:

1. *Greater concern over personal development of salesmen.* Commensurate with the interest of progressive firms in achieving a greater measure of internal social purpose, it is clear that more attention is being paid by upper management to the capacity of all organizational roles to contribute to the self-actualization needs of organization members. Few positions require more attention in this respect that the field of personal selling. Several studies have indicated that it is lack of recognition and prestige which frustrates and demoralizes the salesman (even the *successful* salesman) more than any other job-related factor.[7] Relevant also are the widely accepted estimates that one-half of all young persons who enter the sales field are unsuccessful in the career, and that 20 per cent of nation's salesmen currently account for 80 per cent of the total sales of products and services. These indications of widespread failure and mediocrity constitute a human and economic waste of truly staggering proportion. While neither statistics nor management's concern with their impact on profits is new, what is new is the strong moral mandate for an end to this waste which a human orientation thrusts upon business management. Professional development is one part of the answer, but salesmen are whole men; thus their development within personal dimensions cannot be ignored and is likely to gain increasing attention.

2. *Greater use of computers in sales management.* The impact of the computer upon the sales management function has been the topic of recent discussion. As computer applications in maketing increase in quantity and sophistication, one plausible impact upon sales management will be the greater degree to which strategic decisions in the personal selling operation will become computer-assisted, if not computer-directed. Many of the most critical kinds of strategic and tactical decisions in the

personal selling area lend themselves ideally to computer analysis, particularly the simulation technique. Allocation decisions involving manpower or money, optimum sales force numbers, territorial assignments, and profitability analysis of component parts of the sales operation are all examples of key sales management decision areas which seem certain to become increasingly computer oriented. As firms move more toward the *total information system* concept, establishing procedures and routines for generating information inputs for computer analysis, the sales manager's contribution stands to be incidental or advisory. Rather than being dominated by the computer, it is far more likely that the computer's impact will be to free the sales manager from many of his present responsibilities for developing strategic decisions—thus enabling him to concentrate more fully upon his responsibilities for developing people.

3. More professionalism in the personal selling field. Continued progress may be expected in the movement to higher professional standards for the sales career; standards pertaining to education and competence in technical, behavioral, managerial, and quantitative areas. Increased professional competence of salesmen reduces the occasions calling for direct involvement of the sales manager with customers, distributors, or other elements within the market area. The greater the degree of professionalism of salesmen, the greater the degree to which the general goal framework established by top management may be translated, adapted, and implemented directly in the field; in effect bypassing the sales management strata.

These three trends converge in such a way as to shift the logical emphasis of the sales management function. The most plausible concept of sales management for the era of the human orientation is one which has at its core a mandate for the total development of the individual members of the selling force. This development concerns not only the elevation of the salesman to the highest possible level of *professional* competence and stature; but also the creation of those condition which will produce the highest degree of *personal* growth and fulfillment.

Table 1. Changing emphasis in sales management in this century

	Year			
1900	*1910 1920*	*1930 1940*	*1950 1960*	*1970*
Business response to perceived dominant environmental conditions	Production Orientation	Sales Orientation	Marketing Orientation	Human Orientation
Emphasis in management's conception of sales job	Personality Art	"Scientific Salesmanship"	Professionalism	Personal Fulfillment
Emphasis in sales management	Tight Supervision and Control	Broadened Responsibilities	Strategies and Profits	Total Human Resource Development

The New Concept and the Sales Manager's Job

The sales management concept built upon strategy development and profit responsibility focuses upon the market environment, as does the general perspective of the firm operating under a marketing orientation. The new sales management concept stresses the involvement of the sales manager in a broader environmental realm, just as the general involvement of the enterprise is so stressed under a human orientation. The impact of a sales management concept based upon the total development of human resources within the sales manager's job activities would be to require non-traditional approaches to some of the key traditional areas of sales management concern, and to involve the sales manager in some quite new areas of high priority concern. For example:

Recruitment and selection. Sales managers have experimented with a variety of testing devices in the search for predictor variables correlated to successful sales performance. Under the new concept, the search for such variables would be broadened (or deepened) beyond *success* to include also variables predictive of an individual's potential for self-fulfillment in sales work.

Training. Sales managers have had the responsibility of equipping salesmen with the knowledge and skills necessary for effective sales performance. But the term *training* would be inadequate to describe the design and implementation of educational experiences contemplated under the new concept. These would enable salesmen not only to develop in the various professional dimensions of their work, but also to mature in personal dimensions through better understanding of themselves and the web of their relationships to the organization, clients, and society in general.

Motivation. Sales managers have been concerned with the motivation of salesmen, as in the design of compensation plans or studies of salesmen's attitudes. Under the new concept, the search for motivating forces would probe beneath the superficial and into such areas as the complexity of self-image or basic feelings toward business values (e.g., the Protestant Ethic).

Image of selling. Sales managers would be more concerned with improving the image of personal selling both within and without the organization's bounds. This implies a concerted and creative communication effort of major proportions among nonmarketing groups within the corporation, channel members, community groups, on college campuses, and wherever else the message can be carried.

Ethical standards. Sales managers would be involved in establishing and promulgating a clearer picture of the ethical dimensions of the salesman's role. This implies that specific and unambiguous standards of ethical conduct need to be established pertaining to the salesman's relationship to prospects, clients, fellow employees, and other persons and groups with whom he interacts. What is envisioned here are not variations upon the *golden rule*, but instead meaningful guides to the resolution of moral conflict in personal selling which may constitute an obstacle to genuine self-fulfilment in sales work.

Social purpose in selling. Sales managers would become occupied with identifying and evaluating ways in which the selling force may contribute to the firm's search for greater external social purpose. This may occur, for example, when corporate sales manpower is applied in helping to solve problems of ghetto entrepreneurs. It may also occur when the problem-solving sales professional applies his ingenuity to solve an immediate customer problem in such a way as concurrently to make a positive contribution in a more significant social problem area such as pollution, safety, housing, or production cost. Certainly by virtue of size or nature of product line some organizations have a greater potential in this respect than others. But the perspective itself of the sales department as a microcosm of the larger organization, seeking ways to achieve greater social purpose concurrently with the search for profitable customer problem-solving opportunities, opens endless and fascinating possibilities. Beyond the gains to society of such a perspective, it constitutes the most fertile source of the sense of worth and accomplishment for salesmen so vital under a total development concept.

The individual circumstances of any firm will determine in large measure the requirements for the sales management position for that particular enterprise. Nonetheless, it has been the author's contention that a basic sales management concept has always tended to exist in business, evidenced by the locus of emphasis in the sales manager's responsibilities. Table I illustrates the pattern of historical change relative to sales management in this century. This table indicates that the prevailing sales management concept has been a matter of changing emphasis in responsibilities rather than complete redefinition of the sales manager's role.

Conclusion

As business tends to be more responsive to the accentuation of human values occurring in society, and perhaps to move from a marketing orientation to a broader human orientation, the most congruous concept of sales management is one focused upon the total development of the individual members of the selling force. This does not necessarily imply a lesser contribution to profitability by the sales manager than has been true in the past. It does, however, imply a more subtilized view of profits, particularly as to the distinction between the short-run and the long run. Aggressive sales management techniques may appear to boost short-run profit, but in the light of negative consequences on loyalty, enthusiasm, self-respect, and *esprit-de-corps* within the sales force, their effect on long-run profit can never be clear and may well be negative. Thus, in the long run, the total development approach may be desirable not only for humanistic reasons but also from a profit standpoint.

NOTES

1. William J. Stanton and Richard H. Buskirk, *Management of the Sales Force* (Home-wood, III. Richard D. Irwin, Inc. 1964), p. 7.
2. Peter F. Drucker, *The Practice of Management* (New York: Harper and Brothers, 1954), p. 38.
3. Eugene J. Kelley and William Lazer, "Basic Duties of the Modern Sales Department," in *Managerial Marketing Perspectives and Viewpoints*. Third Edition, Eugene J. Kelley, and William Lazer, eds. (Chicago. III. Richard D. Irwin, Inc, 1967), p. 540.
4. Carl Rieser, "The Salesman Isn't Dead—He's Different, "*Fortune* Vol. 66 (November, 1962), pp. 124-127, at p. 126.
5. Joseph W. Thompson, *Selling: A Behavioral Science Approach* (New York: McGraw-Hill Book Co., 1966), p. 118.
6. Hector Lazo and Arnold Corbin, *Management in Marketing* (New York: McGraw-Hill Book Co., 1961), p. 576.
7. See, for example, John L. Mason, "The Low Prestige of Personal Selling," *Journal of Marketing*, Vol. 29 (October, 1965), pp. 7-10, and F.W. Howton and Bernard Rosenberg, "The Salesman: Ideology and Self-Imagery in a Prototypic Occupation," *Social Research* Vol. 32 (Autumn, 1965), pp. 277-298.

2

Effective Sales Management in Developing Economies

T. A. A. LATIF

IN every field of human endeavour, there is a basic urge which activates a person and influences the tempo of his work. In a field like selling, this is significant, because, selling has to be approached as a vital function in the modern economy. Its importance, to my mind, consists in the fact that it is a wonderful agency best fitted to accelerate the process of social and economic change, For a developing country like India, highly developed marketing and selling organizations are among the major requisites in its institutional set-up and are potent forces towards the nation's economic and industrial growth.

The Process of Social Change

Over a hundred years ago, the institution of "salesman" was rather an 'unknown phenomenon.' Those brave men who had the courage to "go out and sell" were really the pioneers of the modern economy. When an individual starts a new industry, begins a business enterprise or starts on an old trade, he is incidentally contributing to the building up of a socio-economic order. No doubt, it has been the responsibility of the State to see how far these activities, broadly speaking, were socially purposive. In our country, it has been this basic criterion that has been the most important factor for the State in deciding the industrial and trade policy, and on that basic, encourage or itself take over particular industries and business or organize State trading.

In most of the industrially developed countries, selling had been long recognised as a key economic function; and this has given to the salesman or trader who makes available the products or services a comparatively greater role; to his personality a more colourful prominence and to his work a social purposiveness. Let us have a look at this distinctive personality and his work.

A Modern Economy — the Pioneers

The history of Sales Management tells us that it was the merchant adventurers of old who were the first salesmen—the fathers of the profession. In most countries it has been the result of the work of generations of the 'men in the business' who sold different products in the far-reaching corners of the world. What we might note here is that while the salesman was thus helping to lay the foundations of international trade, he was also laying down the broad principles of professional conduct for salesmen all over the world. It also helped to reshape the social pattern and put a new emphasis on old values. It is this point that needs to be marked out as the most vital contribution of salesmen to modern times.

New Fields

It is an obvious conclusion that the salesman as the ultimate representative of a business, can contribute tremendously towards the process of social change. So far as we in India are concerned, we have been late-comers in the race for economic and industrial development and the process of social change in the country has been invariably slow. But as the importance of industrial and business development grew and as the needs of the community become more widely felt, institutions like Salesmanship began to gain in importance and recognition. Today, there is before us a tremendous field for salesmen to extend their services to an ever-widening circle of men. The role of the salesmen lies in the fact that perhaps they constitute the most powerful agency to provide the much needed 'social capital' which can prepare the ground for industrial and economic growth.

A Thankless Job

The salesman, selling either a product or service, has been for a long time considered almost as 'not quite a welcome individual'. He was doing a job nobody appreciated. Few were prepared to take any serious notice of him in spite of the fact that even the most successful of them, with the costly conveniences he could command the envy of many. We thus see a long period during which the salesman has been a patient sufferer and a willing worker in the cause of raising the job to its right professional status. Though the job of selling has been 'one of the most exciting in the world', it has been one of the toughest of all throughout. The salesmen, whether of the product or service, was always asked to consider himself as a "fine man in a fine business." Ego Cultivation was a must for him. On it, he was told, depends his business turnover and so his success. So far as we in India are concerned, there is, of course a long way to go and progress and development which should normally take long periods, cannot just be pressed into service all of a sudden. But the one great single factor that gave the salesman the much required status was the recognition that his job is as productive as any other. And here again we can take a lesson from advanced countries like the USA where the salesman is considered an important person. It has been said on the basis of *ad hoc* enquiries that the American public would rate him higher than a merchant, a lawyer or even a member of the legislature.

Professional Ethic

Selling is as old as mankind. Though a prosessional body of men with the approach and "ethik" of business has been rather a late development, the technique of selling and the methods used to influence men to be the buyers, has been almost the same in most countries and perhaps in most periods. But if we examine it rather closely, we find that there have been shifts in the general approach or in the emphasis on certain points to suit changing times and changes in men's thinking. Towards this development, the salesman has been a patient worker. And that was an interesting phase in the growth of a profession. But what helped him most in his work was no doubt the continuous search for new markets and better techniques.

What type of personality was he? What was his reaction to the changing social trends? How did he feel about his own work? And how did he fit himself into his society? There are interesting questions to enquire into. But whatever might have been the importance which the salesman had in the social or professional ladder, there can be no denying that it is he who is ultimately the custodian on whom any industry has to repose its complete confidence. The story of Miller's character, (*Death of a Salesman*, Arther Miller) Willy Loman, leaves an undying image in our minds. Industry owes a great deal to his work and to his business methods.

Selling—A Socially Beneficial Calling

The history of salesmanship and sales management has thus been intimately connected with general economic history. Throughout this history, the stages in the growth of sales management and the philosophy of selling, represented the changes in society consequent on the changes in various stages of economic and social transformation. New concepts, new sales ideas and aids, new techniques all represented one or other element in the changing needs of a changing society. The history of salesmanship is an interesting saga of this evolution and change. What is remarkable has been the salesman's power of adapting his outlook and his technique in tune with the new demands. His role was that of in innovator. It is to this point that we should give the greatest importance. The growing importance of the selling and distributive function in a growing economy gives to the men in the sales field a particularly greater responsibility. For us in India, this is both an opportunity and a challenge. The historian must give to the salesman a unique place in business history because the work of the salesman in facilitating social transformation is going to be of tremendous importance for a country like ours in the early periods of planned economic development. Today he has to restart his professional conduct with a new conviction and a new understanding of his own dynomic role in an expanding economy. The schemes of training for salesmen and managers in industry, training in the technique of scientific selling, in market research, in international marketing, etc., all have to be so patterned as to facilitate the needs of industrial and economic growth. The sales force, to my mind, is the most powerful group that could push up the forces of economic and social transformation of a country; and selling, whether the product is shoes, tractors or cosmetics or any other, an honorable and socially beneficial calling. The salesman today is no longer a probationer. He has a front place in the ranks of the social and business elite.

One of the most remarkable facts in recent business history has been the emergence of the salesman as a powerful force for social and economic change. History tells us that popular reaction to the appeals of salesman has been different in different countries and in different portions it is being increasingly realised that a successful selling job requires that the technique cannot just be the same at all times. In our search for new markets and wider clientele, we have been incessantly on the look-out for new colourings to attract the overcareful buyer. The emphasis, of course, has not been uniformly the same everywhere. But there has been an acceptance of the idea that the work of successfully influencing the minds of men is a pretty hard task which requires on the part of the salesman an honest effort and enthusiasm enough. As a matter of fact, selling as a career became popular among young men even in the USA only after the First War years. The explanation for this is obviously the necessity to cater to the new situations and needs brought about by an increasingly complex economic system. As complexity in the economic and social system grew, the salesman as the front bencher among the personnel of an industry now began to assume a greater and more purposive role. Not only he had to work harder, but he had also to know more because, he had to be an educator before he could be a salesman. And even in a country like the USA, it is surprising to find that the people in the beginning were by and large unmindful of the services of salesman and the role they played in her economic growth.

In our country, the consumer market has been a particularly tough one. The reasons were not merely economic. The people had an instinctive understanding of tne salesman as somewhat of a mysterious personality practising a 'secret art'. It took years before they were able to understand the realities and the need for his services. It is interesting to find that in the USA, though the public image of the salesman was not clear in the beginning, public attitude towards salesman and selling was highly accommodating.

Panchsila of his own Pattern

There has not been at any time any sort of a definite set of ideas as to the 'how' of selling. The scientific selling technique as we know it today, was almost entirely his own creation and is a tribute to his imagination and inventive faculties. And here we find bim as one of the most highly endowed of all professional groups. In spite of the limitations of his professional circle, he appears as a versatile personality with a social awareness business acumen, emotional stability and financial security. His initial entry into the sales field has been represented as occasioned by a basic revolt or against mental dislike of the regular salaried job where there is normally little or no room for initiative or enterprise. His desire for a better life, greater facilities for himself and his children and some social life attracted him into the profession. More than that, there was his emotional desire for importance and recognition. He therefore saw in this a veritable field for the man with "courage", "vision", '"tenacity", "industry" and "competence". His entry into a business world of competitive co-existence with his *panchsila* is an interesting incident in business history.

Science of Selling

Unlike other business, for the salesman a knowledge of human psychology has been vital. It is the most important of all his tools. A knowledge of his product and what it does for the community is basic to him; to know intimately and understand correctly his clients is also 'must' for him. His whole approach, his diagnosis and findings decides his business performance and determines ultimately the frontiers of his business empire.

The philosophy of his creed is a philosophy of action. His job is entirely to capitalise on the theory and strategy of his calling. And he has always to be persuasive and convincing. It is exciting for students of business economics to look at his business methods and the practices of his calling. The old maxim that honesty is the best policy is as much true in his case as perhaps in diplomacy. The job of overcoming the force of buyer resistance has been both an art and a science.

New Markets

Business as carried on in most countries, is essentially competitive and should necessarily be done on a business basis. State management of certain industries and business in India and other countries has given to them a social purpose which has widened their appeal. This implies a new emphasis, greater responsibility of the personnel, wider markets and an added dignity. Selling today demands of the salesman an important personality trait—a capacity for understanding and adjustment. We hear it often said about the American salesman that he has a wonderful capacity to adjust his business philosophy to the demands of changing times and value or even to forget some, if it suits his business interest and to interpret the old in a new setting. And nobody has ever said that the American has been bad in his business or in his social obligations. The point that I would like to stress here is that in all business, the man in the field matters much. Today, his responsibility is much greater. And when we talk of market analysis and promotion, it means not just the increase in business figures; the salesman has to take up the major task of educating the people to a new social awareness. He has to create in them a new faith and a new hope. Creating popular response to a product or service is one part of his work; to my mind, it is more important work to make a larger number of people join, join willingly in contributing their share to the building up of an enduring social fabric.

The task of market development might mean that we have to borrow a few lessons from other countries. For the present, let us leave aside the question of its effectiveness and its applicability in our social situation. But there is one fact that nobody can dispute. That is, there certainly has not been that emphasis on the crucial role that salesmen had played in the economic growth of many countries, it was their patient work that helped to transform the American economy tremendously. We have to realise that. In the everyday life of the people, the salesman appears as the best agency for economic and social change. This points obviously to the value of the services of the salesman which we in this country have to bring home to the public.

In the present context of our industrial development, therefore, it should be the endeavour of our men in the field to bring home to our public the contribution that selling can make in the development of our economy. The next few decades are going to be the beginning of a new epoch of great industrial and economic activity. No doubt, we have always to remember that the socio-economic set-up and thinking of our people will largely determine the frontiers within which we have to work. In the task, therefore, of expanding the scope of business operations, we have to keep in mind the broad principles of selling and the salesman's place in a growing economy.

It is very much true that the public can learn best about new products or services from the salesman. To be respected as a good salesman, a good knowledge of the product or service is an essential attribute for a salesman. His ability to interpret the business services to the requirement of the individual and the community and his sense of service and business honesty will give him a favoured place in the annals of individual initiative and enterprise. What the people think that he can do for them is the all important thing. The people's attitude to the business and their ideas and experiences will shape the work of the salesman. And that is also at the same time the right opportunity for him to raise the standard of professional conduct, to help speed up social change, to contribute to economic development to create an educated, richer and happier people and above all, for himself to feel a thrill to be in the selling job. In the years of change and progress of the country, the salesman should find himself a more respected businessman.

Selection, Training and Control of Salesmen

It is stated that most of us operate in a protected market, that we can anyhow sell whatever we produce; furthermore, the Indian market at its present stage of development is relatively unsophisticated; and therefore what is the need for an elaborately chosen and rigorously trained salesman ? This is due to a misunderstanding of the role and function of marketing in the country's economy. It has to be sufficiently realised that production based economies can never be self-propelling in the long-run. The situation has been, however, gradually, changing. There is growing competition for one's wares, if not from direct competitors at least from substitutes, and for the limited discretionary purchasing power with the people. Most of us would have noticed that the Indian market is already, fairly sophisticated and is increasingly becoming so every day. A firm which neglects its marketing may get by today, but is seriously imperilling its future.

The salesman in any organisation occupies a key position. To a large and vital section of the public, he is virtually the company. Upon his performance depend the progress and growth of the company; on his reporting of what is happening depend many of top management's major policy decisions. It is, therefore, a matter of legitimate concern to marketing managers that salesmen should be properly selected and trained.

First of all, let us examine what is involved in selection—whether it is of a salesman or of a sales manager. Selection is the art of prediction. The selector's job is to forecast how well a gtven candidate will fulfil the demands and match the circumstances of a given job. We have two factors here, the job and the candidate. The first consideration in selection, and one which is most commonly overlooked, is a thorough study of the job. It is one's observation that too many salesman are recruited with very little idea of what the job demand. One cannot properly select a man for anything without a thorough, direct and first-hand knowledge of the demands and circumstances of the job. It is equally necessary not to think of general traits and descriptive adjectives. It is much more useful and, incidentally, much harder to think exactly what the selected candidate will in fact have to do than to talk of fact, drive, initiative, personality and the like.

At this stage we might make a distinction between job analysis which is a systematic analysis of the job and its material and psychological environment and job specification which is a list of attributes and qualities required in a candidate to perform that job satisfactorily. The point is that job specification should not be arrived at "in vacuo" but should logically emerge from the job analysis. If, for instance, we specify that we require a graduate, we must be sure that the demands of the job are such that a graduate is necessary.

There is no standard job specification for salesmen. It will vary from industry to industry and from company to company, depending on the product, on the market, on the distribution system and a host of other factors. It is, therefore, very difficult to generalise what sort of person should be selected. But two points are worth mentioning. First, there is a serious danger in recruiting what might be called the "over-qualified" man. In India, just because highly qualified people are available for a salesman's job, we are often tempted to recruit them. This has serious repercussions. It is not always appreciated that a candidate who possesses certain qualities which, however, desirable in themselves, are not demanded in the job, or who possesses certain necessary qualifications to a much greater degree than the job demands, may be no more successful than the candidate who does not measure up to the minimum requirements. It is therefore just as important to recognise that the job offers, let us say, little scope for initiative as that it calls for a knowledge of the Indian market; that it can be done by a person whose intelligence is not above average as that it involves close co-operation with the trade. In considering the limitations of the job, the link between successful performance and personal satisfaction in the work should not be forgotten. If the job demands a good deal less than the candidate is capable of giving, then a potentially valuable person can become a frustrated, dissatisfied and ultimately "unsuitable" employee.

Secondly, we perhaps should have another look at the image of the successful salesman. Many of us tend to think of the salesman as a smooth, clever fellow with an unusual gift of the gab. In some cases a certain proficiency in one-upmanship is not unwelcome: We have often heard at Sales selection boards, "he talks very well", "he knows the way around", "he can sell you anything." In practice, however, one finds that the best salesmen are good listeners, rather quiet individual eager to find out what the customer wants, and seldom employ high pressure tactics to sell something which the customer does not really want to buy. Therefore what techniques of selection one employs will depend on what one wants to find out about the candidate: Each selection technique has an advantage over the others in illuminating a limited area of the candidate's personality. If, for instance, one wants to find out about the candidate's intelligence, a test is used. This will give us more valid results than any other method of assessing intelligence. If one wants to find out about the candidate's ability to present facts in writing, one should perhaps give a written examination. If one wants to see how the candidate will behave and function, the interview as a method of selection is hard to beat. Usually a combination of two or three techniques is indicated in most cases. A technique which has only been rarely tried but is recommended, wherever practicable, is to test the candidate's selling aptitude in a real selling situation. This will tell us whether a particular candidate has the temperament and the resourcefulness to be trained into a good salesman and thus save a lot of wasted effort.

Training

Let us first take the case of the new recruit. It is obvious that he must be given some training before he can be sent out to the field. What should this training consist of ? Before salesmen are sent out to work independently, they must be given thorough training in the following areas:

1. *Organisation and Objectives*: Each recruit should understand why the Company operates as it does, what are the real objectives of its marketing and activities and how his own work fits into the overall picture.

2. *Product Knowledge*: This is sadly neglected in India. Product knowledge does not necessarily mean technical knowledge which may be required in the case of some specialist industrial salesmen. Product knowledge means such things as:

What are the sales features or selling points of each product ? In other words, what particular technical points the salesman should know in order to sell the product ? What are the applications of the product ? The salesmen must obviously understand this if all sales opportunities are to be grasped. How does the product compare with its competitors ? What are its plus points in comparison with other similar products in the market ?

Practice in demonstrating the use of product, etc. The salesman's primary job is to sell but he needs sufficient knowledge of the product to enable him to do this successfully. When exceptional circumstances arise, he should know what technical and other services in the company he can call upon.

3. *Sales Presentation*: A good sales technique is basically an orderly but persuasive method of selling. A new recruit will certainly need some training in presenting his arguments to a customer in a clear and logical manner. Whether sales techniques can be reduced to a set of cut and dried principles is a matter of opinion; I personally favour rigorous training in clear and logical thinking and in persuasive presentation to the individual salesman to work out according to his own genius and the circumstances of each case.

4. *Organisation of Work*: The objective here is to teach the fresh recruit how he should plan his daily work, so that good working habits are instilled in the trainee from the very start of his career.

5. *Correspondence and Reports*: All salesmen are not good at writing letters, inter-office memoranda, etc. Some guidance should be provided in the matter of courteous as well as lucid writing; also what reports are required and how they should be made out.

6. *Market Intelligence*: The trainee salesmen should be given a comprehensive idea of what the market for a product is, who are the competitors in the field and what opportunities he should grasp to his company's advantage. He should also be briefed as to what sort of market intelligence he should send back to headquarters, as this is an area where most salesmen tend to be weak.

7. *Espirit-de-corps and Morale*: Team spirit and high morale are the signs of a successful sales force. As the Chairman of a very large marketing company once mentioned "It is no use having a salesman who is not proud of his work." It is vital

that the initial training programme convince the recruit that he is a member of a happy, progressive team and that he should go to the market with enthusiasm.

The initial training of a new recruit, covering the above points, might consist of a full-time training course, preferably residential. Training is, a continuous process and the major part of the salesman's development will naturally take place in the field. Here the sales manager himself should take personal interest and responsibility, and not hand over the new recruit to a senior salesman or the sales supervisor.

What about the experienced salesman ? How can their interest be sustained, so that they do not become rusty of state ? In their case too, formal refresher course would be useful. Periodic sales conferences, visits by the sales manager and transfer to another territory are other means to keep the vitality of the salesman alive. The idea here is to continually expose the experienced salesman to new ideas and fresh challenges. The responsibility of training salesmen must lie fully on the shoulders of the sales manager, though technical advice on methods and techniques may be sought from the training department wherever this exists.

Promotion

Successful and experienced salesmen often tend to lose their enthusiasm and vitality if they do not see any prospects of promotion. The best salesman does not necessarily make a good sales manager; the American, strongly believe that the best salesmen should be promoted. It is, however, suggested that provision should never be made in the organisation structure for reasonable advancement of salesman in their own vocation. There should be some avenue of promotion available to a salesman. This could be done, for instance, by having two or three grades for salesmen.

What about the promotion of a salesman to sales manager? Here, we have to apply rigorous standards in the interest of the organisation. A salesman, merely because he is a good salesman, should never be promoted. The question is whether he will be able to manage other salesmen and carry out the administrative work involved in a sales management position. Will he be able to plan marketing strategy? Does he possess the capacity to analyse marketing data? It is, suggested that the pendulum should not be allowed to swing to the other extreme as, was happening in a few organisations. I have known of some poor salesmen being promoted on the basis that they have management potential, it being argued that a sales manager does not have to sell anyhow; he has got other salesmen under him to do that. This, is detrimental to the morale of the sales force. It also puts a severe limit on the training capacity of the sales manager. Whereas on salesman should be promoted unless he has a definite sales management potential, it must be recognised that he cannot be a good sales manager unless he is also a good salesman.

I am not in favour of laying down certain minimum conditions of age and service before a candidate can be considered for promotion. The most suitable person should get the promotion, irrespective of his age or seniority. I am also not in favour of an internal selection procedure for promotion whereby applications are invited from confirmed salesmen and interviews held.

It is a failure of management that we do not know our men well enough to be able to decide which one should be promoted. In my own experience. I have seen a lowering of morale confidence of some really good salesmen because they were repeatedly put up for promotion, interviewed by the selection panel and every time turned down.

When a Sales Manager decides to recruit salesmen he should make up his mind clearly on the following points:

1. What he wants to sell.
2. Where he wants to sell.
3. How he wants to sell.

Based on a study of these he should put down his own specifications of the type of salesmen he should look out for:

Ways of Recruitment

There are mainly two ways of recruitment—(1) through internal selection and (2) external, by advertisements.

Internal: Depending upon the product requirements, in some cases it may be possible to find the required salesmen within the organisation. For this category, one has to believe firmly that "Salesmen are not born, but made." The internal man already has a knowledge of the Company's policies—perhaps he knows the product fairly well and has the aptitude to sell. What is required then is only a systematic commercial and product training.

External: Advertisements will have to be inserted in the newspapers having a good coverage of the right type of people. The wording of the advertisement must be chosen in such a way that the job requirements are clearly specified. In many cases, it has been found advantageous not be have box numbers but to openly put down the name and address of the Company.

Selection

Having got the applications—internal or external—it is now necessary to sort them out. It is essential that the Sales Manager who needs salesmen for his products, finds time to go through each one of the applications very carefully. They can be grouped into categories like,

(a) Excellent (meaning, ideal for us).

(b) Good (meaning, that the candidate can be groomed).

(c) Mediocre (can be rejected).

Let us now see the main part of the selection job, *viz.*, the interview.

Interview

The candidate must be given a very courteous reception and made to feel free and at ease. His personality, way of dressing, general demeanour, self-confidence, etc., should be judged. The candidate should be asked set questions in the beginning to check on age, scholastic records, special aptitude, experience with past employers, type of work handled, remuneration, reasons for desiring change, etc. However, the questions and answers should be in the proportion of:

10 per cent talk by the Sales Manager, and

90 per cent talk by the candidate.

During the interview, we may come across engineers with product knowledge but not complying with the requirements of a salesman. It may be that the man does not have a good personality, a sense of humour, a cooperative attitude or a readiness to help. Parts/service men having continued customer-contacts and product-knowledge make good salesmen in some cases. However, there can be no hard and fast rule on these points. Each man will have to be judged on his own merit.

Training

The aim of any sound sales training should be to build up the salesmen as worthy ambassadors of the Company whom they represent. The training course should be well planned in such a way that it is more tightly packed rather than lay in a loose and leisurely way.

Product training/commercial training/visual aids, etc., must be interpersed. There should be sufficient breaks and question/ discussion sessions.

The following grouping of subject is a typical course input for a training programme:

1. Introduction of the Company.
2. Mutual introduction to encourage team spirit.

3. Past history and present activities of the Company.
4. Who is a Salesman?
5. What is a salesmen supposed to do?
6. How does the salesman do selling?
7. Administrative procedure—Call reports, Discipline, Loyalty, etc.
8. Who is a customer?
9. What are customers' objections and how to overcome them?
10. Product knowledge—theory, demonstration as well as knowing manufacturing operations.
11. Visit product installations.
12. Competition—How to face it?
13. Summing up, warning and a boost-up talk.

Control

Call reports about the day-to-day activities of a salesman are necessary and these must be prompt and regular. Based on the call reports, sales control cards should be maintained in the office entering them at the appropriate places. The cards, among other things should carry the name and address of the customer, people in charge of buying decisions, type of business, progress of transactions, when next call due, projects in the offing, dates by which orders are expected to be closed, etc. An intelligent use of the sales control cards will enable the business being well in hand.

Number of Calls

For selling any product through salesmen, it is essential to have a customer coverage plan. This can be done broadly on the lines indicated below:

1. Ascertain the territory to be covered.
2. Prepare a mailing list of customers, industry-wise.
3. Assess potential if customer in terms of either the product or sales value (this is particularly suitable for consumer goods or raw materials).
4. Categorise the customers as per potential.
5. Specify the numbers of minimum calls over a year to each one of the customers under each category.
6. Multiply the number of calls by the number of customers under each category.
7. The product of No. (6) gives the total number of calls required for the territory during the whole year.
8. Now calculate the number of working days in a year after deducting holidays, provision for casual absence, etc.
9. Divide the total number of calls by the total number of working days per year.
10. Put down what you think should be the minimum number of calls per day for a salesman.
11. Divide No. (9) by No. (10). The result will give the approximate number of salesmen, required for the territory.

Having appointed the minimum number of salesmen and having trained them ideally, it should be easy to maintain the sales control cards accurately, so that effective assistance is offered to the sales force. This type of sales control suits raw material or consumer goods selling very much. For other items, it should be adapted suitably. A regular inflow of call reports and a clear follow-up at the appropriate time as prompted by the sales control cards, enables the Sales Manager to practise "remote control". The Sales Manager should give all active guidance from the office or the headquarters and visit customers, with the salesman, whenever required.

The Sales Manager should also try and address personal communications to salesmen who perform well and encourage people who do not perform so well. It should be more a case of "guidance or direction" rather than control. The Sales Manager should keep the sales force together through a regular news bulletin containing results, good orders, interesting case histories. tough cases and how they were solved, etc.

Compensation and Performance Bonus

Salary plus commission appears to be the best. If the cost ratio can stand it, it will be a good idea to provide the salesman with a car under the Company's car loan scheme, giving him financial assistance, repayable over a period of three years. It will also be a good idea to arrange sales competitions offering cash prizes or higher training, with overseas principals if any, at Company's expense. In case of competitions, it is necessary to set out the rules very clearly to avoid complications or misunderstanding towards the end.

3

The Effect of Product Sales Quotas on Sales Force Productivity

LEON WINER

Sales quotas are sales volume objectives assigned to specific sales units, such as regions, districts, or salesmen's territories, usually expressed in terms of dollar sales volume. Sometimes, in order to achieve manufacturing efficiency or long-term goals, sales managers set quotas for specific products at challenging levels (i.e., levels that are higher than the level of sales expected to be achieved in the absence of such quotas). The underlying idea is that by setting challenging quotas and attaching significant rewards to their achievement it is possible to direct salesmen's efforts along desired paths.

However, it does seem that employment of product quotas should result in some loss of sales force efficiency. *If* salesmen respond to the reward system and are directed away from sales activities they would normally pursue, then the sales force is presumably using its time inefficiently. An apparently superior

Editors' Note: Reprinted from *Journal of Marketing Research*, May 1973, pp. 180-183; published by the American Marketing Association.

quota-setting procedure would take into account both manufacturing efficiency, long-term goals, *and* optimal use of sales effort.

In two articles, Farley and Davis and Farley have shown mathematically that management should set commission rates calculated at an equal percentage rate of gross profit on all products. Furthermore, to insure maximum profits, salesmen should be asked to specify "desired quota" on all products. If necessary, quotas and commission rates would then be negotiated until both management and salesmen are in agreement. This model is based on two assumptions which have several implications.

The first assumption is that salesmen always try to allocate their sales time among *products* in a way that will result in maximum income for themselves. This assumption implies that salesmen *can* manage their time in terms of products. An alternate possibility (that would gravely weaken the Davis-Farley model) is that salesmen can effectively manage their time only in terms of *customers.* Once a sales call is in progress, salesmen may find that it pays to sell *many* products, perhaps, *all* their products. Another implication is that salesmen are "economic" men (i.e., they seek to maximize income to the exclusion of other goals). An alternate possibility is that salesmen, like most people, have several goals and that at least occasionally they will not pursue the last dollar, but instead will choose to work fewer hours.

The second assumption of the Davis-Farley model is that centrally set quotas for products may lead to serious inefficiencies because of a lack of information about market opportunity. Davis and Farley seem to overlook the possibility that quotas set centrally at a challenging (higher than achievable without quotas) level may motivate salesmen to utilize their time more fully and more effectively for sales work.

Nevertheless, in spite of the questionable assumptions of the Davis-Farley model, the concepts of the model appealed sufficiently to the management of the Universal Products

Company (real company, fictitious name) to warrant serious investigation.

Company Background

The Universal Products Company is a manufacturer and marketer of electronic and electromechanical industrial equipment. The company's product line consists of approximately twelve items ranging in selling price from a few hundred dollars to about twenty-five thousand dollars. Almost all of Universal's sales are made directly to ultimate users by a sales force of over 1,000 salesmen, organized in 10 districts and 135 branches.

At the salesman level, product quotas are set only for two products: "Dataprinters" (priced at $1,000) and "Micromagnetics" (priced at $5,000). The reason given by Universal's management for imposing this "product discipline" is that it encourages salesmen to push these products which are considered essential to long-term company growth.

Salesmen at Universal are paid salaries ranging from $5,000 to $8,000 per year with a commission of 5 per cent of sales. On the average, this works out to a salary of about $7,000 plus commissions of about $9,000. Branch managers are paid on a 65 per cent salary and 35 per cent commission basis. Their total incomes average about $26,000 per year.

"Making quota" is defined as selling at least 100 per cent of the total quota assigned and at least 90 per cent of the quotas assigned for Dataprinters and Micromagnetics. The immediate reward for making quota is a bonus of 0.5 per cent of the salesman's assigned total quota. In addition, there is a very significant longer term reward: making quota is recognized throughout the company as an accomplishment of great importance. Several years of making quota are considered a prerequisite for advancement to the management level.

The Dataprinters Problem

Universal has been marketing Dataprinters for five years. However, many salesmen still complain that making quota in Dataprinters consumes inordinate amounts of the time they have available for facc-to-face customer contact. Privately, many salesmen grumble that if the company would only relax "product discipline" they would not only increase their own earnings, but would also make more money for the company as well.

Partly in response to these complaints, the company conducted several surveys of salesmen's activities. The results of four such surveys conducted over a two-year period were remarkably consistent. These studies revealed that, on the average, salesmen spent 60 minutes per day on "Videophonics" and 30 minutes per day on Dataprinters. Projecting these values to the entire sales force and relating them to annual sales of the two products showed that on the average each unit of Videophonics required 6 hours of sales time, while each Dataprinter required 12 hours of sales time.

Both of these products were priced at $1,000 and both yielded the same amount of commission per unit to the salesman. Based on these studies, it appeared that the complaints management was hearing were well-founded. Accordingly, a specific study aimed at the Dataprinter problem was requested.

Analysis of the Dataprinter Problem

The initial hypothesis formulated regarding this problem was as follows: Due to the pressure of product discipline, salesmen are "forced" to seek out Dataprinter prospective customers that require more sales time to be persuaded to buy, or are more likely to refuse to buy after time-consuming presentations than prospects for other products, such as Videophonics. It was further hypothesized that not all Dataprinter sales required 12 hours of sales time, but the "last" sales, the ones that salesmen *pursued* to make quota, were *so* time consuming that they raised the average to 12 hours.

Substantial amounts of "free" time. Then, *assuming that salesmen seek to maximize their incomes,* they would use this "free" time to sell other products. Presumably, these would be products with a more favourable sales volume to selling time ratio. In this way, salesmen would earn higher commissions and the company would make greater profits.

Interviews with Salesmen

The first test of the hypotheses consisted of a set of interviews with salesmen in the field. A stratified clustered sample of 100 men from 20 branches was selected, and 3 skilled interviewers traveled to these locations over a 10-day period.

During these interviews, salesmen were asked to what extent they would be willing to accept a higher total quota in exchange for a lower Dataprinter quota. In order to obtain projectable results the questions were formulated as follows:

"In each of the following groupings underline the *highest* total trade-off in your monthly quota you would be willing to accept:

Decrease in Dataprinter quota ($)	*Traded-off for*	*Increase in total quota ($)*
1a. 1 0.0		1.500
b. 2,000		3,000
c. 3,000		4,500
d. 4,000		6,000
2a. 1,000		2,000
b. 2,000		4,000
c. 3,000		6,000
d. 4,000		8,000
3a. 1,000		2,500
b. 2,000		5,000
c. 3,000		7,500
d. 4,000		10,000"

As the reader can see, the trade-off ratios offered were 1.5, 2.0, and 2.5 to 1.0 for three groups, in increasing order. After the results were collected and analyzed, the following summary was prepared:

Forty per cent of the men wanted some trade-off. Assuming each of the ratios used in the survey, and projecting the answers given, to the entire population gave the following results:

1.5 to 1	8,100,000 per year
2.0 to 1	10,800,000 per year
2.5 to 1	8,700.000 per year

At this point, serious consideration was given to implementing the trade-off concept—that is, permitting salesmen who wished to trade off Dataprinter quota for total quota to do so at the 2 to 1 ratio. This proposal was reconsidered because of the risk that sales results might differ considerably from survey results. Therefore, a controlled experiment was selected as the next step.

Setting up the Trade-off Experiment

In setting up the Dataprinter trade-off experiment, several important decisions were made:

1. To administer the test at the branch (as opposed to individual salesmen) level. The reason was that it was very difficult to visualize a nationwide implementation at the salesman level due to communication problems.

2. A "typical" district was selected rather than selecting branches throughout the United States to facilitate supervision of the test and to increase the probability that "test" and "control" conditions would be maintained for the desired time period.

3. Offices would be assigned to test and control groups on the basis of trade-off desired and the number of men in each office. The two groups would be made as nearly equal as possible.

To implement the test, a survey was taken among salesmen and branch managers in the district selected, the North Central District. The people surveyed were asked essentially the same questions that were asked on the first survey. To no one's surprise, their answers were quite similar.

The underlying hypothesis at this point was that salesmen in the test group would behave in accordance with the results of the survey. They would utilize their time more efficiently and would sell more, on the average, thansalesmen in the control group. In addition since they would be pursuing quotas which, to a large degree, they had selected themselves, there would be a greater proportion of 100 per cent quota-makers in the test group than in the control group.

Based on the results of the second survey, it was decided to go ahead with the experiment. The North Central District was divided into three groups: test, control, and no-change. The no-change group included the branches whose managers indicated that they wanted no trade-offs in the quotas assigned to their branches.

The test and control groups compared as follows:

	Test	*Control*
Number of branches	6	6
Number of salesmen	53	51
Managers' desired trade-offs (units/month)	29.5	28

Monitoring the Experiment

The original intention was to run the experiment for a full year. Consequently, the North Central District was monitored closely for an entire 12-month period. However, manpower and quota changes were made by the district manager during the test year so that for evaluation purposes, the test was considered valid only to the end of July.

At the end of this period, the finding was that the ***test group had done worse than the control group***. See the table for a

Trade-off Experiment, Summary of Sales Volume

	Total $ Sales per man-month (000's)	
Branch	***Test***	***Control***
1		**17.7**
2	**15.6**	
3		**15.1**
4	**14.0**	
5		**12.3**
6		**12.0**
7	**11.2**	
8	**11.0**	
9		**10.5**
10	**10.3**	
11		**10.0**
12	**9.4**	
Average	**11.9**	**13.4**

Statistical test

Man-months	**380**		**372**
Standard deviation	**11.0**		**11.0**
Difference between means		**1.5**	
Standard error of the difference		**.8**	
***t*-test**		**1.9**	

summary of test results. The difference between the two groups was significant at the 90 per cent confidence level using the *t*-test. Furthermore, the superior performance of the control branches cannot be explained in historical terms because in the previous year their performance had been worse than the performance of the test group. Year-to-year comparisons can

only be made for 3 test branches and 4 control branches because of geographical restructuring. These are branches 4, 10, and 12 in the test group and 3, 5, 6, and 11 in the control group. In the prior year, the three test branches had a *higher* average ranking than the four control branches.

Allowing salesmen to trade off had resulted in worse performance rather than better. The salesmen had *not* used the time freed up by trading-off to maximize either their own earnings or the company's profits. Salesmen were *not*, regrettably, "economic" men. What made the results even more disappointing was that total quota performance was *also* consistently worse for the test group, as shown in the following:

Percent of salesmen at or over 100 per cent of quota

	Test	*Control*
January	44%	57%
February	28	45
March	46	57
April	55	56
May	54	57
June	52	60
July	53	60

Conclusions

First and foremost, the conclusion was that implementing the trade-off concept would *not* lead to any desirable results. That much was obvious. The troublesome question was *why* had the control group outperformed the test group?

Many explanations were considered and most were rejected as being inconsistent with the facts. The only ones that survived critical review were the following:

1. Most Universal salesmen are not "dollar maximizers"; they are "quota achievers". If they are given a quota which

appears to be easily attainable, their motivation declines. In fact, it may decline so much that they will be less likely to make the easier quota than they were to make the more difficult quota. In reaching for a challenging (higher than achievable without quotas) quota for one product, salesmen will work more effectively and are likely to finish the year with higher sales in other products simply as a result of having made more sales calls and approached more prospects. The normative conclusion, on the basis of this study would be: (a) set product quotas at challenging levels (higher than achievable without quotas) for at least one product, (b) attach a great deal of significance to attainment of this quota, and (c) conclusions (a) and (b) hold if the sales force consists primarily of "quota achievers". If the sales force consists of "economic" men, the approach tested in this study may work.

2. Sales managers, when given a chance to trade-off, pass the trade-off along to salesmen who are likely to have particular difficulty in selling a high quota of a product that is hard to sell. They do *not* give the trade-off to the few men who are "dollar-maximizers." The managers' goal does not appear to be to maximize sales, but to minimize the amount of difficulty they may experience in managing their salesmen. The normative conclusion would be to design a reward system for managers that motivates them to maximize attainment of the company's objectives rather than permit them so much latitude that they minimize the need for training and other managerial responsibilities.

3. Another conclusion is that what salesmen say they will do, may differ from what they do ultimately.

4. The final conclusion is that the concept of trade-offs *may* have some theoretical merit as a way of achieving overall optimization. Unfortunately, its successful implementation depends on factors which, in our present state of knowledge, are difficult to estimate and probably vary considerably from one sales force to another. Additional research is needed in two areas: salesmen's value systems and salesmen's behaviour under various conditions and reward systems.

SALES FORCE PARTICIPATION IN QUOTA SETTING AND SALES FORECASTING

A company's outside sales force is potentially one of its best sources of market and sales forecasting information, especially under unique economic conditions which make historical data unreliable. Yet many sales managers do not use inputs from their salespeople for forecasting sales or establishing performance goals. Those who do solicit such information may have to modify these inputs up or down depending on such factors as the abilities of the men or women comprising the sales force, their knowledge of company plans, and potential deliberate distortion of data because the salespeople feel that their estimates will be used later in setting their quotas or in determining their level of pay. Thus, asking a sales force for future sales estimates and using these inputs in any fashion requires a degree of caution and a concern for just how to interpret that information.

This article reports the results of a study designed to investigate the extent of sales force participation in sales forecasting and quota setting in different kinds and sizes of companies. It also examines the experiences of sales managers in interpreting and using such data.

Current Status

Research conducted during the past decade shows that many firms use a forecast constructed from the inputs of the entire sales force as a part of their sales forecasting procedure. For example, the National Industrial Conference Board reported that the sales force composite was given heavy or moderate reliance by well over half of all manufacturers and service companies studied.[3]

One reason often cited for having salespeople participate in forecasting is to take advantage of the insight of those company representatives who are closest to the customer. Another is that greater commitment by salespeople to the forecast might result if they believed they had a voice in formulating it. For example, quotas based on these forecast inputs might be more acceptable to the sales force.

Newton's comprehensive study of the sales management practices of over one thousand companies found, however, that while more than 70 per cent of the responding firms used quotas for each salesperson, a relatively small proportion—less than 10 per cent—based these quotas on sales force estimates.[4]

An important factor affecting the determination of quotas is the type of compensation plan in effect for the sales force. If sales force compensation is tied to quota attainment, sales managers may be reluctant to let their salespeople participate in quota determination. Relationships between the type of compensation plan and the extent of sales force participation in sales forecasting and quota setting have not been clearly documented, however. Nor have any studies investigated the direction and degree of error in the quota estimates of salespepople. The present study sheds some light on these areas.

The Study

Variables Investigated

Five major variables were singled out for study:

A. Extent of sales force participation in forecasting. In this study, *sales forecasting* is defined as estimating future sales for a geographic area, product line, or list of accounts. *Participation in forecasting* is the existence of a company policy or practice of obtaining a sales estimate from salespeople at the sales manager's request. *Extent of participation* is defined as the degree of formalization of these policies or practices and is categorized into three groups; formal policy, informal policy, or no policy regarding sales force participation in the forecasting process.

B. Participation of salespeople in quota setting. A *quota* is defined as a revenue, profit, or unit volume goal assigned to a salesperson. *Participation in quota setting* is the submission to the sales manager of an independent estimate of what the salesperson believes his quota level should be.

C. Type of compensation plan for salespeople. Four types of compensation plans were identified for separate analysis:

1. Straight salary—fixed payments for a certain period of time.
2. Straight commission—payment amount varies in proportion to some type of performance, usually the amount of revenue obtained.
3. Commission with guaranteed draw—commissions that are guaranteed up to some minimum level.
4. Salary combinations—includes three major variations: salary plus commission, salary plus bonus, and salary plus bonus plus commission.

D. Direction of error of sales force quota estimates. This variable reflects the judgement of the sales manager regarding whether the quota estimates of his salespeople are too high or too low.

E. Degree of error of sales force quota Estimates. This variable reflects the sales manager's judgement regarding to what extent the estimates of his salespeople are too high or too low.

Data for variables *D* and *E* were also obtained from sales managers who do not ask their salespeople for quota estimates; in these cases the sales managers were requested to give their opinions about the direction and degree of error that would occur if their salespeople were asked for estimates.

Hypotheses

Although many relationships among these five variables could be investigated, this study focused on the following six.

Variables Compared	*Hypothesis Number and Statement*
A:B	1. The extent of sales force participation in the quota-setting process will be greater in firms where salespeople participate in the forecasting process.
A:C	2. The extent of sales force participation in the forecasting process will differ depending on the type of compensation plan in effect.
B:C	3. The extent of sales force participation in the quota-setting process will differ depending on the type of compensation plan in effect.
C:D	4. Whether the quota estimates of salespeople are judged to be too high or too low by their managers will depend on the type of compensation plan in effect.
C:E	5. The degree of error in the quota estimates of salespeople, as judged by their sales managers, will depend on the type of compensation plan in effect.
D:E	6. The degree of error in the quota estimates of salespeople will be greater when their quota estimates are too low than when their estimates are too high.

Each of these hypotheses was reformulated into its null counterpart so that it could be tested statistically using chi-square analysis. In addition, a number of secondary variables such as type and size of firm were investigated. These will be introduced and discussed in the following section.

Data Collection

The Sales and Marketing Executives-International chapters in San Francisco and Los Angeles granted permission to poll their members, and a cover letter from each chapter's president accompanied each questionnaire mailed to the members of that chapter in early 1974. The membership directories of both chapters were reviewed and edited before the survey was undertaken. Retired, academic, and consultant members were not polled. In addition, members who could not be identified as sales or marketing managers, general managers, or presidents were not included in the sample. The remaining 559 names were mailed a questionnaire.

Two hundred and two usable responses were received in postage-paid return envelopes provided with the questionnaire. This is an effective response rate of 36 per cent. Table 1 reports some descriptive characteristics of the respondents.

Table 1. Characteristics of respondent companies

Characteristic	*Percentage of respondents (n=202)*
Number of salespeople	
1-9	15
10-19	15
20-49	20
50 99	10
100 or more	40
	100
Sales volume	
Under $5 million	22
$6 to $19 million	24
$20 to $49 million	12
$50 million or more	42
	100
Dominant customer type	
Manufacturers	32
Consumers	15
Service	10
Wholesalers/retailers	33
Multiple	8
Other	2
	100

Results

Although the data suggested a number of relationships, only one of the six hypotheses was supported by the chi-square analysis. The study also revealed several other findings with regard to sales force participation in forecasting and the use of sales quotas.

Hypotheses

Hypothesis 1: Participation in forecasting and quota setting. A total of 86 per cent of the respondent firms reported a policy of sales force participation in sales forecasting, with 56 per cent having a formal policy and 30 per cent indicating an informal policy. Quotas for salespeople were used by 74 per cent of these firms; in the firms using quotas, 56 per cent request that their salespeople submit an estimate of what they believe their quota level should be.

The first hypothesis, that quota participation relates to forecast participation, is *supported* based on chi-square analysis of the data shown in Table 2. Firms with formal policies on sales force participation in forecasting are much more likely to ask salespeople to submit quota estimates than are firms with informal policies on participation in forecasting. Companies that do not involve their sales force in forecasting are the least likely to ask salespeople to submit an independent estimate of their quota level.

Hypothesis 2: Participation in forecasting and compensation plan. Straight-salary compensation plans were used by 21 per cent of the responding firms, while combination plans involving salary plus commission or bonus or both were employed by 52 per cent. Commission with some portion guaranteed in a drawing account was used in 10 per cent of the responding firms, and the remaining 17 per cent employed straight-commission sales forces.

The data in Table 2 used to test hypothesis 2 show that it *cannot be supported* at the .05 level. The data do suggest a mild

Table 2. Relationships among variables in the hypotheses tested

Hypotheses	*Variables*						*Chi-square value and probability*
		Participation in forecasting					
1	**Submission of a quota estimate**	Formal	Informal	None			
	Yes	73%	47%	5%			33.02
	No	27	53	95			p<.001
		100%	100%	100%			
		Compensation plan					
2	**Participation in forecasting**	**Straight Salary**	Salary Combination	Commission with Draw	Straight Commission	Total	
	Formal	64%	45%	61%	72%	56%	
	Informal	24	38	17	22	30	10.08
	None	12	17	22	6	14	p<.10
		100%	100%	100%	100%	100%	

(*Contd.*)

	Submission of a quota estimate	Straight Salary	Salary Combination	Commission with Draw	Straight Commission	Total	
	Yes	71%	48%	62%	68%	56%	6.04
	No	29	52	38	32	44	p<.15
		100%	100%	100%	100%	100%	

	Direction of error in quota estimate	Straight Salary	Salary Combination	Commission with Draw	Straight Commission	Total	
4	Underestimate	60%	44%	40%	50%	48%	1.41
	Overestimate	40	56	60	50	52	p<.75
		100%	100%	100%	100%	100%	

	Degree of error in quota estimate	Straight Salary	Salary Combination	Commission with Draw	Straight Commission	Total	
5	10% or less	80%	78%	80%	67%	76%	0.81
	More than 10%	20	22	20	33	24	p< 90
		100%	100%	100%	100%	100%	

6	Direction of error in quota estimate		
Degree or error in quota estimate	Underestimate	Overestimate	
10% or less	79%	73%	0.27
More than 10%	21	27	$p < .70$
	100%	100%	

relationship between forecasting participation and type of compensation plan, however, since the chi-square value could occur by chance only about 10 per cent of the time under conditions of no relationship between these variables. There appears to be a tendency for sales forces working under either straight salary or straight commission to participate more than other sales forces in the forecasting process.

Hypothesis 3: Participation in quota setting and compensation plan. The hypothesis that sales force participation in quota setting depends on the type of compensation plan in effect *cannot be supported* by the results shown in Table 2, since the probability of these results occurring by chance under conditions of independence is greater than .05.

However, a considerably smaller proportion of salary-combination sales forces submit quota estimates than the corresponding proportion under each other compensation plan. If compensation plans are compared two at a time rather than all at once, two of these pairwise comparisons are statistically significant at the .05 level (the commission-with-draw plan is not significantly different from the salary-combination plan primarily because its sample size is small), and these results would provide support for hypothesis 3.

Hypothesis 4: Direction of quota estimate error and compensation plan. The fourth hypothesis, that the type of compensation plan in effect will influence the direction of the sales force's quota estimate error, *cannot be supported* as shown by the results in Table 2. It appears that a sales manager's judgement of whether his salespeople will overestimate or understimate is not related to the type of compensation they receive. In fact, the proportions of salespeople who overestimate versus those who underestimate in the eyes of their managers are nearly equal regardless of the type of compensation plan under which they work.

Hypothesis 5: Degree of quota estimate error and compensation plan. Hypothesis 5 states that the degree of error in sales force quota estimates, as determined by their managers' judgement, will depend on the type of compensation plan in effect. As shown by the data in Table 2, this hypothesis *cannot be supported* because the chi-square value is very small. Overall, the degree of error is 10 per cent or less in three-quarters of the sales forces whose salespeople do participate in setting quotas, and the same general pattern exists regardless of the type of compensation plan.

Hypothesis 6: *Direction versus degree of quota estimate error.* The final hypothesis, that the degree of error in sales force quota estimates will be greater when salespeople underestimate than when they overestimate their quotas, *cannot be supported* as measured in this study. As table 2 shows, in approximately three-quarters of the sales forces the error is 10 per cent or less regardless of whether the direction of error is over or underestimation.

Other Findings Regarding Sales Force Participation in Forecasting

Respondents were asked whether they agreed or disagreed with a number of statements regarding sales force participation in forecasting. These statements were developed based on assumptions and beliefs often expressed in textbooks and by sales managers regarding the nature and consequences of sales force participation in forecasting. Each respondent could agree with any number of the statements. The results are shown in Table 3.

Some statistically significant relationships (at the .05 level) were found when the responses from these statements were crosstabulated with other variables in the study:

1. Those who thought their salespeople forecast low to earn more money had a significantly lower incidence of formalized policies for sales force participation in the forecasting process than those who did not agree with the statement (22 per cent versus 57 per cent respectively).

Table 3. Extent of sales managers' agreement with statements concerning sales force participation in forecasting

Percent of Respondents Agreeing	*Statement*
5	My salespeople typically forecast low so they can earn more money.
20	In general, my salespeople are inaccurate forecasters because they lack the information about the company's plans needed to accurately estimate their future sales.
24	In general, my salespeople forecast high because their optimism outweighs their business judgement.
16	In general, my salespeople are inaccurate forecasters because they lack the necessary insight into the economic factors that impact their customers' need for our products.
38	In general, my salespeople forecast just about right.

2. Those who agreed that their salespeople forecast just about right were much more likely to have a formalized forecasting participation process than those who did not agree with this statement (67 per cent versus 48 per cent).
3. **Managers of salespeople working under commission-only plans were more likely to agree that their personnel forecast high due to overoptimism than were managers using a salary-only plan for their sales force. Specifically, 38 per cent of the respondents with a commision-only plan agreed with this statement, whereas the corresponding percentages for commission with draw, salary combination, the straight salary were 35, 21, and 14, respectively.**

Other Findings Regarding Quotas

Salespeople in 74 per cent of the responding firms work under a quota plan of some kind. The presence of a quota plan was not

found to be associated with the type of customer or market served, but it was related to the number of salespeople in the respondent's firm as well as to the size of the company as measured by sales volume. Quotas are least likely to occur in smaller firms and most likely to occur in larger firms.

The base of the quota plan was sales volume alone in 48 per cent of the participating companies. Another 19 per cent used some measure of profitability, such as gross margin or profit contribution, as at least part of the quota base. An additional 13 per cent of the quota plans were based solely on unit volume, while the remaining 20 per cent used both sales volume and unit volume in some combination. No significant associations were found between any of the other variables studied and the base of the quota plan.

As mentioned in the discussion of hypothesis 1, 56 per cent of the respondents using quotas requested quota estimates from their sales force, and the data in Table 2 represent answers from this group of respondents. But the 44 per cent of the respondents using quotas who do not ask for quota estimates were requested to give their opinion of what they believed would happen if they did ask for such estimates. Table 4 presents a comparison of their answers with the answers from managers who do ask for quota estimates from their sales force.

On each of the two comparisons—direction of error—a larger proportion of managers who do not ask for estimates expect an underestimation as well as a higher degree of error than the corresponding proportion of managers who do ask for estimates. The differences in both these comparisons are significant beyond the .02 probability level. To test whether these differences could possibly be reflecting other relationships, the submission of quota estimates was cross-tabulated with each of the following: base of quota, number of salespeople in the company, dominant customer type, and company sales volume (and, of course, type of compensation plan as discussed in hypothesis 3). Chi-square tests showed no significant relationships between the submission of quota estimates and any of these variables.

Table 4. Responses on direction and degree of error in quota estimates by managers who ask for estimates vs. managers who do not

Direction and degree of error	*Experience of managers who do ask for quota estimates*	*Opinion of managers who do not ask for quota estimates*
Direction		
Underestimate	48%	67%
Overestimate	52	33
	100%	100%
Degree		
10% or less	77%	59%
More than 10%	23	41
	100%	100%

Note: Probability from chi-square test <.02 on each comparison.

Conclusions and Implications

This study sought to determine the extent of sales force participation in sales forecasting and quota setting, the relationships between such participation and company characteristics such as size of firm and type of sales compensation plan, and the extent of accuracy or error in the resulting estimates. Salespeople were asked to submit a sales forecast estimate in the vast majority—86 per cent—of the firms in this study. This rate of participation was essentially the same among different types of companies and among sales forces under various compensation plans. Thus, participation was not limited to markets of certain customer types, to particular compensation plans, or to selected company sizes. Sales force participation in sales forecasting is evidently practiced in most types of selling situations.

More than one-third of the respondents reported that their salespeople forecast just about right. Inaccurate forecast by salespeople were attributed to overoptimism by the salesperson, lack of information about his company's plans, and lack of economic knowledge and understanding as to how it affects his customers and territory, in that order. Only one respondent in 20 reported that his salespeople forecast low to earn more money. There was a significant relationship between the presence of formalized policies regarding forecasting participation by salespeople and the accuracy of sales force forecasts. Thus, formal procedures for guiding salespeople appear to aid the accuracy of results, and those procedures should incorporate giving the salesperson information regarding company plans as well as economic data and interpretations pertinent to each salesperson's market.

Quotas for salespeople were used in 74 per cent of the responding firms, and they were more likely to be used in larger companies than in smaller ones. Of the companies using quotas, 56 per cent ask their salespeople to submit an estimate of what each thinks his quota level should be. The extent of overestimation versus over estimation of quota levels in these firms appears to be about equal, and the degree of error in either direction is 10 per cent or less in more than three-quarters of the responding firms. Those managers who now use quotas but do not ask for quota estimates from their salespeople believe that their salespeople would, if asked, underestimate more often and be in error by a greater amount than what apparently takes place in similar firms in which salespeople are asked for quota estimates. Since participation in quota setting is often encouraged as a means of increasing a salesperson's involvement in his job, this evidence should prove encouraging to managers who have been reluctant to ask their salespeople for quota estimates.

NOTES

1. Davis, O. A. and J. U. Farley. "Allocating Sales Force Effort with Commissions and Quotas," *Management Science*, 18 (December 1971) Part II, pp. 55-63.

2. Farley, J. U. "An Optimal Plan for Salesmen's Compensation, "*Journal of Marketing Research*, 1 (May 1964), pp. 39-43

3. Stanely J. Pokempner and Earl L. Baily, *Sales Forecasting Practices*, Experience in Marketing Management, No. 25 (New York: National Industrial Conference Board, 1970), p. 10.

4. Derek A. Newton, *Sales Force Performance and Turnover* (Cambridge, Mass. : Marketing Science Institute, 1973), p. 145.

4

Time and Territorial Management for the Salesman

ROBERT F. VIZZA AND THOMAS E. CHAMBERS

Introduction

At least two factors lend to the importance of efficient time utilization by salesmen: the nature of time itself and the rising cost of salesmen's time. Time itself is nothing but a measured duration, and as such is simply a limited resource. However, it differs from every other resource in that it cannot be accumulated, but can only be used as it becomes available. Further, it becomes available constantly, and evenly, increment by increment. Managers plan for the use of most resources, and hold back additional amounts of those resources until they can be put to a planned use. Not so with time—it keeps coming at the executive in even doses, and if there is no plan for its use, it is wasted.

Editors' Note: This article was condensed by Joy Jaeckle Luna from an in-depth report prepared under the direction of the Research Committee of the Sales Executive Club of New York, 1971. The report has now been expanded and is available in programmed instruction format through R.F. Vizza Associates, 30 Marion St., Greenvale, N.Y. 11548.

Selling Time

The cost of a salesman's call has risen sharply in the last decade. In 1969 the average cost of a salesman's direct call on industry was $58.98, and the average cost of all industrial sales calls was $49.30[1] as compared to $22.33 in 1958. Cost per call includes direct costs only: salaries, commissions, bonuses, travel, and entertainment. Figure 1 indicates that this cost has risen much more than the Consumer Price Index. It is 185 points over the 1955 base, whereas the CPI is 37 points over the same base.[2] In a study on all types of sales calls, both industrial and consumer, the Sales Executive Club of New York fixed the cost per call at $41.07 in 1969 compared to $18.92 in 1959. The impact of direct sales costs on profits is considerable and any inefficiency in salesmen's time utilization is quite costly.

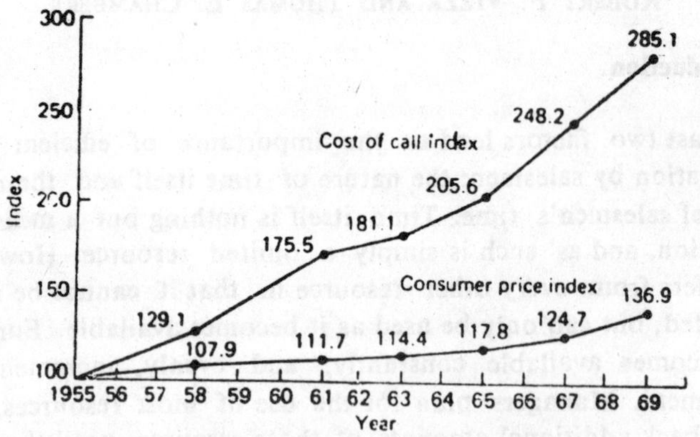

Base of each index—1955 value

Figure 1. Comparison of cost of call with consumer price index

Further, the amount of time a salesman spends in face-to-face selling contact with his accounts is diminishing. According to another study, "the average industrial salesman, in spite of the fact that he works more than a nine-hour day, is able to spend only three hours and fifty-two minutes in face-to-face selling. Traveling, waiting for interviews, and paperwork take up slightly over half of his day." A more recent survey indicated that industrial salesmen spend approximately "a third of their time in face-to-face selling."[3] Not only does this increase the cost per call, but it raises the serious question as to the effectiveness of the priorities being placed on salesmen's activities. It must be recognized that success in selling is a result of *what* a salesman does, in addition to *how* he does it. Much attention has been paid to the "how" of selling skills, *i.e.*, handling a sales call. Too little attention has been given to "what" a salesman spends his time doing.

Time and territorial management is defined as the planning, implementation, and control of those activities of the salesman required to realize the sales and profit potential of an assigned territory. The concept of territorial management is inextricably woven with time utilization. The terms "effectiveness" and "efficiency" will be used with the precise meaning. "Effectiveness" deals with accomplishing objectives, while "efficiency" refers to the costs involved in accomplishing these objectives.

A Model of Time and Territorial Management

Figure 2 describes the analytical tools used in effectuating successful management of a salesman's time and sales territory. Each major heading represents an essential element. The most important element in this definition is planning, for it provides a framework for the implementation and control of activities.

> *Planning* is a predetermined course of action that establishes goals and objectives, estimates the resources necessary to accomplish them, designs strategies for the best allocation and use of these resources, and controls activities to assure the realization of objectives.

Without a plan, a salesman's activities are not directed to accomplishing specific objectives, and control is impossible since there is no basis on which to evaluate the salesman's activities. Time utilization is optimized only when it results in the maximum contribution to the most desirable objective.

Implementation involves those activities required to call on accounts and cover the territory efficiently. As such it includes identifying decision makers to be called on in accounts, developing call schedules, planning and making the actual sales call, designing routing plans, and prospecting.

Control of these activities is essential to assure that they are contributing to the planned objectives. Informational inputs, including reports and records, provide the salesman with the critical data needed to evaluate actual performance against predetermined standards. Control over essential but unproductive non-selling activities is important in this phase. Finally, the self-discipline of time control is included in this area.

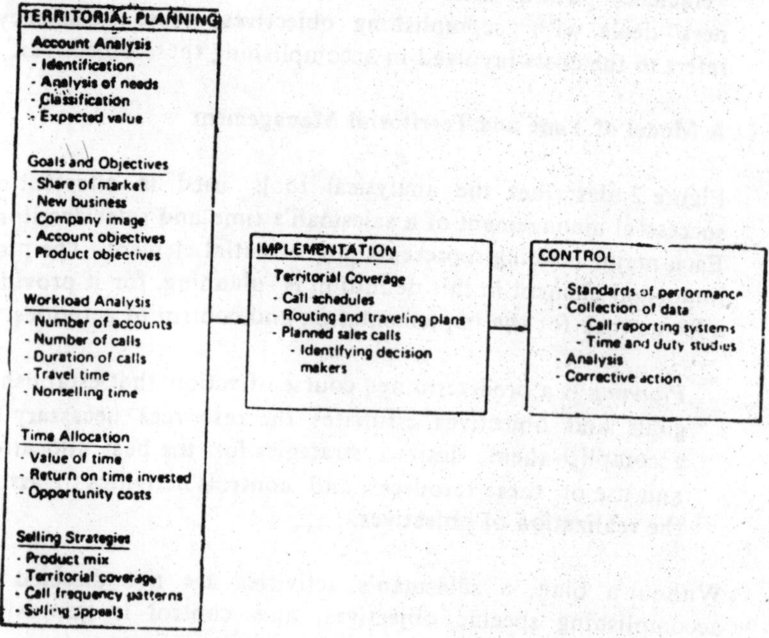

Figure 2. A model of time and territorial management for salesmen

Territorial Planning

The starting point in territorial planning is to conduct an audit of the territory to identify and determine the amount of potential in that submarket. The term "account" will be used here to include both existing customers and prospects.

The accounts must first be identified by name. Government data, company records of past sales in the territory, trade and professional association publications and membership lists, and directories of corporations are but a few of the many sources of information available to the salesman. These sources will generate a list of suspects rather than prospects. Quantifying the potential of these suspects through use of a market factor index or an input/output guide will give the salesman a rough idea of his *total* market potential. However, since a number of companies will share that total potential, the salesman must estimate his company's share of a particular account's potential.

The estimated share and probability of realizing that share of an account's potential depends upon many variables: (1) present share of that potential; (2) degree and kind of competition; (3) product, price, and service differentials with competitors; (4) relationships with the account. Assigning the estimated share and probability figures represents a judgemental decision by the salesman. Finally, some convenient system of account classification is necessary in order to group accounts by potential.

Goals and Objectives

An account analysis reveals the potential presented by the territory. As the manager of the territory, the salesman must next set goals and objectives for the realization of that potential. A goal differs from an objective in that it is more general and long range in nature; an objective is more specific and short range. A goal is accomplished by realizing a whole series of objectives. Goals for territorial coverage may be set in the following areas, as a minimum:

1. Share of market in the long-run
2. Company image in terms of its posture as a leader or follower in pricing, product superiority, service advantages, competitive position
3. New markets developed in terms of new uses and new users for existing products, and new product market penetration.

Objectives are derived from these goals and are usually set for annual periods. They should be set for:

1. Each account in the territory in terms of its expected value
2. Each product in the line with respect to its profitability and the contribution it makes to the sale of other products
3. A combination of these, *i.e.*, product sales objectives by customer.

The objectives should be measurable and, as such, will provide the standards to be used to evaluate and control performance. Further, objectives provide a criterion against which to evaluate each contemplated activity.

Workload Analysis

Having conducted an analysis of the accounts in the territory and established objectives, the next step is to estimate the resources required in terms of time and effort to realize these objectives. The variables to consider in a workload analysis are:

1. number of accounts to be covered
2. number of calls to be made
3. duration of each call
4. travel time required
5. non selling time factor.

Each account generates preparation and developmental activities which can be classified as non-selling activities, which are not included in the above analysis. In this regard, the selling job can be broken into three components: (1) order generating, involving making sales calls; (2) order processing; and (3) order servicing.

The latter two categories represent non-selling activities. A strict allocation of the time spent on these activities to the account responsible for generating them is hardly worth the time and effort that an analysis of this type would require. Therefore, a constant non-selling time factor per day can be estimated based on past experience.

A comparison is then made between time required and time available in order to measure the fit between the time demands of the territory and the total time resources of the salesman. Adjustments can therefore be made in advance. At this point, since the time resources of a salesman are limited, adjustments may have to be made in the objectives set for the territory. Limited resources act as a constraint on objectives, but a consideration of the amount available and any subsequent adjustment in objectives tends to make the objectives more realistic.

Resource Allocation—Return on Time Invested

Armed with an analysis of accounts in the territory, established goals and objectives, and an estimate of the time and effort resources needed to accomplish these objectives, the salesman can now allocate his resources so as to maximize the return he will realize on them. *Return on Time Invested*, or *ROTI*, is measured for a given account, as the ratio of gross margin to the salesman's direct selling costs.

This approach is meaningful in deciding on alternate uses of time. Comparing the ROTI of accounts suggests those accounts that represent greater profit potential. ROTI applied to all accounts will enable the salesman to allocate his time to those accounts in a way that will enable him to maximize his time utilization. These analyses are necessary to help a salesman decide which accounts are the more profitable to call on. In most cases, however, he must cover many lesser potential accounts in a territory. In either case, the salesman must estimate the amount of time he can afford to invest in that particular account.

Selling Strategies

Selling strategies are the ways in which the resources of the salesman are used to achieve objectives. Strategies develop answers to the following questions:

1. What products will be sold to whom?
2. How much of each product will be sold to each customer?
3. How will these products be sold, that is, what appeals will be used? Each salesman strives for his *differential advantage* over his competition and he seeks to capitalize on his advantages.
4. How should the territory be covered geographically?
5. What should be the balance between calling on existing accounts and prospecting?
6. Should the salesman concentrate on large potential prospects or small existing customers?

It is at this stage that the salesman works out a strategy of call frequency patterns for each account. The idea of a call *pattern*, however, adds the element of intervals between calls and is related to the selling strategy for a particular account. The salesman must recognize that there is an optimum number of calls that should be made on an account. As sales calls increase, sales increase to a point, but then level off. Calls beyond a certain point are wasted since they produce little in the way of additional sales.

Further, in terms of opportunity costs, when a salesman is calling on the plateau of the curve, his opportunity costs are high since he could be calling on an account whose curve is still climbing. This same analysis is true concerning the duration of each call. If we substitute "time per call" for "number of sales calls", the curve would be similar. At this point, the salesman develops a strategy for the number, duration, and interval between calls for each account so as to optimize his use of time and maximize his attainment of objectives.

Territorial Coverage

After a salesman develops his territorial plan, he must determine the most efficient and effective means of implementing it. Preparation of call schedules, routing and travel itineraries, and an effective sales call are three approaches that aid optimization of a salesman's actual selling time.

Call Schedules

A call schedule may be viewed as the sequential timing of the call efforts that go into a sales plan. It evolves directly from the call frequency patterns designed as a strategy for covering the territory. The call frequencies tell the salesman how often, for what duration, and at what intervals to call; call schedules tell him exactly *when* to call.

For the most part, it appears that call schedules are made out for one week in advance. As such, they serve as a work organizer and as an itinerary to inform management as to what the salesman expects to do for the next week and where he may be reached. In effect, a call schedule can be looked at as a pre-call report. It should indicate: day, date, and time of call; person/people to be called upon; and objective of the call. The call report, then, need only report the results of the call and future actions to be taken.

An efficient call scheduling system should also include a follow-up feature. It should enable the salesman to schedule the time of the next call or activity with the account, and provide a means that will bring the activity to the attention of the salesman at the appropriate future date. The time to schedule a future call on an account is at the completion of the previous call.

Routing and Travel Plans

Approximately one-fourth of a salesman's time is spent traveling, which is largely unproductive time. Obviously, any approach to improved time utilization looks to cut down on unproductive time in order to allow more time for face-to-face selling.

The first step is a routing pattern analysis. This is done by marking the location of accounts on a map. They should then be numbered based on the sequence of scheduled calls, that is, the account to be called on first numbered 1, etc. Lines are then drawn connecting the points in sequence and travel distance and time calculating between calls. Also, an average travel time per call should be calculated by dividing total travel time by total calls for each trip. The actual travel time per call is calculated and added to the call time when estimating return on time invested in any one account. For the purpose of travel planning, however, an average time estimate suffices since many calls are made in an area as fill-ins around a major call.

An analysis of the web represented by the lines on the map connecting calls will indicate whether or not the salesman is backtracking, criss-crossing, or otherwise wasting time traveling. The principle for efficient routing is simple—a straight line is most economical. Since this is not possible, we must try to straighten the travel lines as much as possible. Routing, therefore, must be done at the same time that call schedules are made up.

There are a number of routing patterns that have proven efficient in use:

1. Straight line—starting from the office, the salesman makes calls in one continuous direction to the end of his territory. He may make calls on the way back, along the same line, or return on another line. Thus he alternates "lines" on each trip.

2. Circular patterns involve starting at the home office and prescribing a circle of stops which is completed when the salesman returns to the office. There may be a series of different size circles covering the outer and inner portions of the territory, all with the home office as the common point.

3. A cloverleaf pattern is similar to the circular pattern, but instead of covering an entire territory, it circles a part of the territory. The next trip is an adjacent circle, and so on until the entire territory is covered.

4. "Hopscotch" is a practice of starting at the furthest point form the home office and making calls back to the office. A salesman would fly to the outer limits and drive back, for example. The next trip, he goes in the opposite direction in his territory.

Many variables must be considered in designing a routing pattern: (1) size of the area to be covered; (2) distance between accounts and concentration pattern of accounts; (3) priority of calls to be made; (4) transportation facilities available.

No one pattern is best for all territories. The important point is that a pattern should be developed for each territory, considering the variables listed above. Designing routing patterns lends itself to computerized model building that can manipulate the variables to come up with the optimum routing plan.[4]

Preparation for Sales Calls

In considering ways to improve salesman's use of time, attention is usually focused on all those activities surrounding the sales call. Ways are devised to get the salesman to the right customer and to get him on his way to the next account. Actually, a great deal of time is wasted on the call itself. Techniques aimed at reducing the amount of time spent on a call, and to aid in using that call time most effectively, make a great contribution to improved time utilization.

Proper sales call preparation includes identifying decision makers, developing information about the account before the call, and preparing for the call itself.

One of the real problems in using call time efficiently pertains to identifying decision makers. One survey estimated that as much as 64 per cent of industrial sales calls are made on the wrong man.[5] As companies grow in size and complexity, it becomes increasingly difficult to identify "decision makers", "decision influencers" and "decision implementers". Authority is often confused with power. Those in positions of official authority, designated by title, do not always have the power to make purchasing decisions. In many firms, for example, purchasing agents are administrators who make out purchase orders based on requisitions initiated in other areas. In others, they have complete purchasing discretion. Salesmen who call on titles, without investigating the decision structure of the firm, run the risk of calling on the wrong man.

Information developed previously in analyzing the territory is useful in call preparation. A checklist of the information that a salesman needs prior to making a call includes the following:

A. Information about the company:

1. What is the company's business?
2. What does it sell?
3. What and where is its market?
4. Who are its customers?
5. What size is the company—how measured?
6. How are they organized?
7. Who does the buying for your product?
8. Who makes the buying decisions?
9. Who influences the buying decisions?
10. When do they buy your type of product?
11. How often do they buy?

12. In what quantities do they buy?
13. How much do they buy of your product in total?
14. How much business do they do with the competition?
15. Who is the competition?
16. Who are the customer's competitors?
17. What is the financial standing of the customer?
18. What are the customer's plans that will affect the use of your product?
19. What are the needs and problems of the customer?
20. What value does the customer place on different features of your product?

B. Information about the individual to be called on:

1. What are his job responsibilities?
2. What are his business problems that your product can help solve?
3. Where is he the organizational structure?
4. What are some of his personal interests?
5. What is his business background?

Each call, then, will have a specific objective that is derived from the long-range objective of the account and represents one step toward the ultimate goal of getting and holding a stated share of the account's business. In preparing for a specified call, the salesman must develop objectives and strategies specifically for that call.

Control of Salesman's Use of Time

The planning approach to time and territorial management requires that a control mechanism be built in to assure that performance proceeds according to the territorial plan. In its entirety, a control system for territorial management involves the entire concept of sales control and supervision.

Any control and guidance system, from the most basic to the most sophisticated, must contain four distinct elements, or steps:

1. Standards of performance must be established as the starting point. These evolve from the goals to be accomplished and are estimates of the efforts and results expected of the salesman. A comprehensive sales control system attempts to relate efforts to results in order to evaluate the profitability of sales results in terms of the amount of effort expended. These ratios of efforts to results also provide a means for evaluating the productivity of sales efforts. In focusing on time utilization, however, as a *part* of sales control and supervision, the emphasis is on efforts standards.

In setting efforts standards, the areas or activities of the salesman for which standards should be set are first identified. This may be done by analyzing the salesman's job description to determine what activities he must perform. Next, a review of territorial objectives suggests the activities necessary to accomplish the objectives. The Workload Analysis performed in designing the territorial plan also suggests areas for efforts standards.

Having selected the standards to be used, the next step is to quantify them. This is best done by the manager *and* the salesman working together. Standards that are imposed by the manager run the risk of not being accepted by the salesman and are usually not accomplished. Standards set by the salesman alone may be unrealistic. A joint effort offers the best chance of producing standards that are realistic, acceptable, and attainable.

2. Performance data collection is essential to improve time utilization. Before a salesman can improve the effective use of his time, he must analyze how it is presently being used. Basically, data on actual performance must emanate from the salesman himself. The most commonly used tool to record and communicate performance data is the call report.

The call report system is seen as a tool of communications. As such, it should allow for two-way communication. Salesmen experience frustration when they submit detailed call reports and never get a return message regarding the substance of the reports. They question whether or not anyone is reading the reports and the value of the reports. At the very least, a summary recap of activities reported for a period of time should be tabulated from the reports and returned to the salesman. In addition, the ideal is some form of comment and suggestions from the managers to the salesmen concerning the data reported.

Although comprehensive call reporting is more commonly used, reporting systems using the exception principle, where only those activities which require management's attention are reported, is much more profitable. It cuts down the amount of reporting and reading, and results in increased communications since management's attention is flagged to every important report.

Effective reporting systems do not require the salesmen to gather and report information that can be obtained from another source, such as a reports of sales that can be obtained from an analysis of orders written or as a by-product of the invoicing process. Generally, the salesman is the most expensive source of information.

Successful reporting systems look upon the call report as a tool for future planning, rather than simply a historical record. Provisions should be made to allow the salesman to plan the date and objective of future calls on a particular account.

3. *Analysis* of actual performance against predetermined standards reveals strengths and weaknesses in selling performance. Ratios of efforts to results, and efforts to standards, suggest areas demanding managerial attention. When results are below standard, effort analysis usually indicates the probable cause. It tells the manager where to look further for the cause of poor results. In addition effort analysis enables the manager to identify potential weaknesses since poor productivity

follows poor efforts. Identified soon enough, trouble can be avoided since it usually develops over a period of time rather than suddenly exploding.

4. Correction. The type of corrective action required is usually suggested by the analysis of below-standard performance The time and duty analysis discussed above ofter leads to a correction in time allocation. After data on actual time utilization has been collected, the following questions should be asked by the salesman.

(a) What am I doing that doesn't have to be done at all?

(b) What am I doing that can be done better, as well, or sufficiently, by someone else?

(c) How much does this activity contribute to my objectives?

(d) What activities should I be doing that I have neglected?

(e) Have I set the right priority on my activities, that is, do I spend time in relation to the relative contribution each activity makes to my objectives?

Correcting inefficient time utilization is basically a matter of self-discipline. It requires careful analysis and introspection into one's present activities, and a discipline to focus on objectives. One of the real problems in this regard is the problem of dealing with crises. The day-to-day operating emergencies that arise steal time from the important activities that one has scheduled. In most cases where self-discipline is not exerted, immediate attention is given to the emergency. Apparently there is confusion between urgency and importance. One automatically thinks that urgencies are important. In reality, many urgencies are temporary and are not important in the long-run. Yet the executive often drops everything to "put out a fire!" The urgent interruptions must also be evaluated in terms of their relationship to objectives and especially with reference to opportunity costs.

Summary and Conclusions

The underlying concept of this report is that sound territorial planning is the key to effective time utilization. A Model for Time and Territorial Management has been designed which describes the processes of territorial planning, implementation, and control. The elements embodied in each process are identified and emphasis has been placed on techniques to develop these key variables, including account analysis, territorial goals and objectives, workload analysis, salesman's time allocation, selling strategies, call schedules, routing and travel plans, planned sales calls, standards of performance, data collection, and corrective action. *Sound principles of time and territorial management do exist.*

Specifically, this report recommends that

1. The use of a time and duty analysis should be made a regular practice of sales management. It is the first step in a program of improving time utilization. One must know how time is presently being used—or wasted—in order to increase its productivity. The effective executive conducts a time and duty analysis of his own activities periodically since he recognizes the natural tendency to slip into bad habits and waste time doing things that are routine, easy, and ego-building in the short-run rather than things that are different, difficult, and do not provide immediate ego satisfaction.

2. Call frequency patterns, including the number, duration, and interval between calls, should be developed based on account potential. These patterns should be established and adopted as standard operating procedure for the salesman.

3. More attention must be given to assisting the salesman in preparing sales calls. This includes gathering marketing intelligence, identifying decision makers, and planning sales presentations, to enable the salesman to save time on calls and to do a more effective selling job, geared to the *identified needs of the buyers rather than the obvious needs of the seller.*

4. Finally, the focus on sales volume must be shifted to sales profitability. Measurement techniques must be developed to overcome this major obstacle. However, caution must be exercised to assure that this obstacle is not simply a rationalization. Companies *are* applying the concept of profit contribution to the sales force, despite the lack of an absolute measurement theory. Any measurement technique, if applied equally to all units of operation, will yield a *comparison* of results, if not an *absolute measure*. This enables management to compare customer to customer, salesman to salesman, product to product, time period to time period, or any combination of these elements. It is a start into the most important measure of effectiveness—profit.

NOTES

1. Laboratory of Advertising Performance, *Cost of an Industrial Salesman's Call in 1969* (New York: McGraw-Hill Publication Co., 1970).
2. *Ibid.*
3. Laboratory of Advertising Performance, *How a Salesman Selling to Industry Spends His Time* (New York: McGraw-Hill Publication Co., 1964).
4. See, for example, "Computer Routing: Putting Salesmen in Their Place," *Sales Management*, March 15, 1970.
5. "64 per cent of Industrial Calls Are Made on the Wrong Man," *Sales Management*, February 6, 1964.

5

Management of Market Research

Introduction

MARKETING Research involves a study of consumer preferences, habits and attitudes. It also involves an exemption examination of trends, so that its findings indicate the future pattern of the market and assist in shaping a company's forward policies. It helps us to decide how a company's immediate market operations should be directed. All our decisions on the improvement of existing products or the development of new ones, the adoption of new selling methods and the application of new advertising techniques are the more effective for being taken in the full and intimate knowledge of the markets, which continuous research is designed to provide.

To large manufacturers of consumer goods, economies come largely from mass production and mass selling of standardised lines. This standardisation is only successful if the resultant products appeal in properties and performance to the greatest number of people. There are many millions of customers in India. They vary widely in their tastes. They are conditioned by different social, cultural and religious backgrounds. We must have products which are acceptable alike to the rich and the poor, to the educated and the uneducated, to the Punjabi as well as to the Tamilian.

Hindustan Lever Ltd.

To discover what preferences are most general in this variegated pattern of consumers, we choose a representative sample of them and find out what their opinions are by questioning them. The result is intended to reflect the opinion of our universe of potential customers. The size of this sample is determined mathematically once we have postulated the number of categories of people it shall contain to fulfil the particular purpose in view. The combined opinions and attitudes of the individuals composing this sample will be representative of our universe within a calculable margin of error, provided the *questions we put to them are so phrased as to evoke the respondent's* true opinion and not an opinion adapted to please the questioner or to express what the respondent thinks it is respectable to any rathern than what he really thinks.

The framing of questions to ensure that the respondent is no tempted to disguise his true feelings calls for great skill. For example, people who believe that good form requires them to have a bath every day, sometimes sincerely 'think' they have a bath every day, whereas in fact they only have a bath four times a week when the weather is cold. In a foreign country it was once found that if everyone cleaned his teeth as frequently as was claimed, the toothpaste manufacturers would be unable to supply the total demand. Similarly, we find that in Kerala people are inclined to say that they take a bath four times a week, and some may even claim to do so twice a day, whereas in Saurashtra nobody minds confessing to washing himself and his clothes only once a week or even much less frequently. The mental attitude to washing in Kerala is conditioned by an abundant supply of water whereas the habits in Saurashtra have been formed by a geography in which water is scarce and precious. In Northern India, there are still women who will not admit to using vanaspati because it is socially more estimable to use ghee. And in most U.P. households both the wife and the husband will treat the choosing of anything, whether cooking fat or soap, as the prerogative of the male, despite the fact that the investigator may often have an uncomfortable suspicion that, then it comes to the point, the wife makes the husband's choice for him.

These shynesses, reticences, resistances, subconscious blocks or what you wish to call them, run through the whole of MR. Therefore, in addition to the straight forward technique of so phrasing the questions that they are completely neutral, a great many techniques have been devised to set people's subconscious at ease, to get at the facts below their lapses of memory and to allow for their desire to confirm to convention. We may, for instance, ask a group of house-wives in for a cup of tea and get them sufficiently relaxed so that they will talk freely and even admit the prejudices which, in answer to formal questions, they might feel were too ridiculous to mention. These are obvious examples. Beyond them lie the more surprising discoveries thas have been brought out by touching the deeper layers of the mind. Women are, for instance, quite often allergic to advertising that suggests that some new product will save them a lot of time in the kitchen because they feel that it is their capacity as home-makers that gives them their prestige in the family; if making a home is made too easy, what will happen to the respect their husband and children feel for them? We have done some investigations which suggest very strongly that many of the prejudices people have about Dalda do not really have anything to do with Dalda at all but are only a way of venting their resentment against a world which, for many professional class people, is narrower and more difficult. Buying Dalda instead of ghee is a very good way of economising; so they transfer to Dalda the resentment they feel that the world has now became a place where they have to watch every rupee.

Another technique is to try simply to get the housewife to talk freely, with the investigator doing no more than listen sympathetically, prompting only when the flow stops. In that way, we can sometimes discover what the associations are which really matter in people's minds. These are not always either predictable or logical; for instance, it is not necessarily the rich woman who buys Sunlight; it may be the poor women who values its lather and the case with which she can do her washing with it; the rich woman whose washing is done for her by servants quite often feels that they are so wasteful of soap anyway that it is best to buy for them the cheapest brand on the market. We use the results of marketing research in order to influence the decisions we have to make from day to day in the running of our bùsiness; and nowadays there are hardly any decisions on the marketing side which we can make without taking into account the research results.

We begin with a picture of our market. Who is it who buys our products? They are not bought equally all over the country. Dalda, for instance, is bought far more in the hard fat areas of the North than in the oil areas of the South. Sunlight is specially strong in Eastern India. We have to find out exactly what the map is like for each product and whether the reason for its strength or weakness in particular areas is due to the habits of the local people or to something in the product. For ınstance, Dalda sells well both in Maharashtra and in the Punjab, but that in itself gives a guidance on how we should split our advertising between the two. Marketing research shows that we have a much lower percentage of the total hard fat market in the Punjab and that therefore Punjab is much more likely to reward a major advertising effort than Maharashtra. Again, Sunlight sells quite satisfactorily in the Punjab, but marketing research shows that whereas in Eastern India it is used largely as a general laundry soap, in the Punjab it is used mainly for washing particularly good clothes. The Punjab therefore offers an immense opportunity for the expansion of Sunlight's use into general washing.

Until we know the shape of the market, we do not know where to strengthen our distribution or how to split up advertising. We may find sometimes that we have reached saturation point, that may further consumption of our products can be only attained by a quite disproportionate expenditure, and we might then even slacken our advertising or make our distribution less intensive. And of course if marketing research shows that our product is bought only by the professional class because it is suitable only for the educated, we would not spent a lot of money advertising it in publications read only by farmers or industrial workers.

We not only have to find out who buys these products and where. We have also to find out what they think of them. We have a very clear idea of what our products can and cannot be expected to do, and the temptation is always to think that our image of them is so based on technical facts, that the public must think of them in exactly the same way. Sometimes this is not so. It is no consolation that we are right and the public are wrong. The public beliefs are a fact. We do not expect the mountain of public opinion to go to the Mohamed of our knowledge. On the contrary, we are at pains to bring the Mohamed of our knowledge to the mountain of consumer opinion.

With a product we have had on the market for a long time, Marketing Research is only one of several ways of knowledge. We can, for instance cross-check a great deal of what Marketing Research tells us from our sales figures, which tell us quite as clearly as Marketing Research can, whether we sell more in U.P. than in Karnataka or in Malabar Hill than in Parel*; and, though the figures themselves will not tell us why, sometimes we can find that our from what our dealers and shopkeepers and salesmen tell us; or sometimes we can guess what is giving us our sales from the laboratory's reports on the performance and quality of sales from the law does not permit Dalda to have the taste of ghee and are no surprised when we find that Dalda is not used for those purposes where it is the ghee taste which is essential.

Marketing Research is no a panacea. It does not provide an answer to every question. Sometimes people find it so difficult to define what they mean that we are driven back on our own general judgement. For instance, it was discovered a long time ago that when people buy a toilet soap they look at almost anything except its capacity to clean—the luxury of its appearance, the purity of its colour and, above all, the pleasantness of its perfume. The reason is obvious. Every toilet soap will wash the dirt off one's face. Thus far Marketing Research gave a perfectly clear answer, but when we tried

*Malabar Hill and Parel are areas in Bombay city.

to find out which colour or perfume or wrapper people like, we very rapidly got frustrated. One cannot get adequate explanations out of most people as to why they like the perfume or colour they like; their reasons are too intangible, too indefinable, perhaps too deep in the subconscious. The standard way of praising a perfume is to say that it is nice, and since different people call perfumes of almost every note and composition nice that is of very little help. In one presses them they may say 'strong' or 'weak'. But since different people have different definitions of 'strong' and 'weak', one tends to find that the same perfume is being praised for both qualities. Equally, people will talk of the purity of a colour or of its whiteness. ('Pure' is a word of clear meaning when applied to ghee or to morals; but what is a pure as against an impure blue? And white is a colour of infinite shades! One has to use one's judgement as to which shade of colours or perfumes the public would probably like, and then, within the narrow range thus selected, make a final choice by making people their preferences as between, at the most, three or four tablets, the only difference between which is the perfume or colour or whatever the variable is one is testing. Moreover, as people's preferences are usually accurate only between two products at a time, even to test is a pretty elaborate business. To test the whole possible range is simply impossible.

Thus a large part of marketing research effort is *Product Testing*. The company was faced with a problem in marketing Rinso. They had to decide whether to choose for the powder a soap base which would give a superlative lather provided warm water was used, or an alternative base which, though giving a less spectacular lather, would dissolve well in cold water. They prepared experimental powders with the alternative bases and gave trial packets of both to a selected sample of housewives. The majority preferences was in favour of the cold water-soluble product and as a result of this they were able to formulate Rinso to be most suitable for a country where the water is rarely heated for washing. In 1957 this company introduced 9 Lather Shaving Cream—Erasmic. Before launching this product they carried out widespread product tests, and the results measured by Marketing Research to ascertain that the product was of sufficiently high quality.

Social and economic changes have the most important bearing on business. For example, the development of new industrial colonies like Chittaranjan and Sindri where the habits of the villagers living on a subsistence level change quickly when they become industrial workers with regular pay and modern amenities, their standard of living rises suddenly and they begin to consume products which they could not afford before. A study of these new dynamic townships that are not only the company's main products but also their special lines and toilet preparations.

Besides research into current products and people's existing habits and preferences, a growing and important use of research is looking into the future to study possible modifications and changes in products to make sure that the company keeps pace with shifts in consumer requirements and habits. It is as much their responsibility to investigate future demands of consumers as to satisfy present demands. In a free economy, consumers' wishes are never static, and it is important to look ahead and find out what consumers are likely to went in the future. This is particularly important in a country like India where society is changing fast and will change perhaps even faster in the future.

In recent years the company applied marketing research techniques to estinating the size of the groundnut crop. The official figures do not come out until the end of February, and since the heaviest buying season of the year is in December, January and February, they must form their own assessment of the crop to guide them buying policy of groundnut oil and seed. This took a very rough sample of roadside farmers and confined themselves to a few simple questions. The margin of error with such a technique is considerable, but they had found that they get an answer, which was reasonably near the final official answer, and also that they get an idea, which the official figures give only months later, of where the crop had been good and where the crop had been bad, which has a very considerable influence on the relative prices they different factories will have to pay.

When they are satisfied that they are making the right product, a product which will both do a good technical job and will also satisfy the desires or prodes which the public wants it to satisfy, there still remains the question of how to tell the public that this desirable product is there to be bought. The answer is advertising, and all consumer goods manufacturers must spent a lot of money on advertising, particularly in India, where advertising has not only the task of trying to sell a particular brand of product against its competitors, but may often be required to introduce the product-type as one which is a necessary part of a higher standard of living.

The company would naturally like to find out whether its advertising money is being spent to the best effect. That is not easy. When people buy something, they very rarely remember why they first bought it. Very few people ever say that they first bought Sunlight Soap because they read in the "Times of India" on the 15th January, that it washes white and bright. Partly this is because they do not know that is what happened. Advertising comes to them from many angles—Shop displays, cinemas, press, posters—and it is hard to identify just what sparked the final decision to buy. Partly it is because people like to think they make their minds up for themselves and resent the idea that they were moved by the pretty girl in the advertisement. Because of all this, it is not easy to test how effective advertising is in making people buy. What we can test is whether the people have seen the advertisements and whether they remember what the advertisement said. In these respects, the results of the tests of the company had done on their own advertising are generally satisfying. Lifebuoy advertisements, for instance, had been seen and remembered by about half the people they had asked. Cinema-goers seem to be receptive to advertising films and they have normally been well remembered. In one enquiry Rexona soap display material was recalled by a high proportion of respondents.

Though it may be difficult to assess how effective any particular advertising campaign or subject has been in creating a sale, nevertheless, we have constantly to develop our judgement in them. Motivation research attempts to supplement intution with scientific enquiry. It involves investigation of consumer attitudes and behaviour and particularly of the reasons, whether they be conscious or unconscious why people buy and what influences them in their choice, then we will be in a better position both to give them the products they want and also to present and advertise them in a convincing way.

The function of a Company is to try and give the consumer products which he will like and which will do the job he wants them to do. Before we can do that, we must find out what the consumer will like, what is the job he wants them to do, as distinct perhaps from the job we think he ought to want them to do, whether the products the company can make come near enough his ideal—and whether the methods of telling him about them are adequate. ***For all these purposes, there is no tool more valuable than Marketing Research.***

"Sixty-three per cent food shoppers walk into their super markets without a shopping list, and make seven out of ten purchases on impulse" Du Pont's Law. If this is true in the U.S., there exist certain external factors which influence the customer to perchase a certain brand of a commodity. The customers' attitude and behaviour in a competitive economy may be said to influence to large extent the survival and profitability of a business enterprise.

When economic life was less specialised, the manufacturers knew their customers personally. A shoe-maker before starting the work on a pair of shoes had the advantage of having talked directly to his customer to ascertain his requirements. Today, in contrast, due to spread of customers and number of intermediaries, the direct communication between the shoe maker and the purchaser is inevitably meagre and unsatisfactory. The manufacturer of today has to find other means of knowing the type of people buying his products or their reactions towards them. Seven out of ten customers make purchases out of impulse along. This happens because an individual cannot purchase all brands of a commodity but has to select one out of the many which are available in the market. Here, the question arises; does the customer reach for a white and blue package of tooth-paste because the colours represent cleanliness to him? Does the housewife prefer the toilet soap in pink wrapping because it makes her feel feminine? The attitudes, desires and reactions of the customers are of crucial importance for the survival of the manufacturer.

Let us take an instance of relative strength, singularity and combination of causes that lead to the purchase of a given product, say, Coca-Cola for house consumption. The factors could be the customer's previous exposure to Coca-Cola and to other drinks—the price taste, colour, convenience of availability, the handy bottle size in respect of carrying, storing and serving—in comparison to competitive drinks. These variables by no means exhaust the list, but do serve to indicate the complexity of cause and effect relationships. Thus the need to establish and maintain communication from the customer to the manufacturer led to the development of the techniques of Marketing Research.

Marketing Research in its broadest sense includes marketing products and sergices, selling policies, preparation for selling, the selection and training of salesmen, advertising and all other matters which deal with the disposal of products and services produced. Marketing research also involves the study of consumer preferences, habits and attitudes. To avoid confusion in the use of terms like marketing research, market analysis, sales research, consumer research, advertising research and markets research, the American Marketing Association made the following comments in clarifying the relationships between these terms:

"Marketing Research is the inclusive term which embraces all research activities carried on in connection with the management of marketing work. It includes various subsidiary types of research such as Market Analysis, Sales Research which is largely an analysis of sales records of a company. Consumer

Research which is concerned chiefly with the disconvery and analysis of consumer attitudes, reactions and preferences, and Advertising Research which is carried chiefly as an aid to the management of advertising work. The term Market Research is often loosely used as synonymous with Marketing Research."

"Modern business has become so complex and wide that the distance between a manufacturer and his consumer has been increasing day by day. With the help of Marketing Research the manufacturer can keep in touch with the changing trends in needs, preferences and attitudes of the consumers towards design, shape and colour of the products. Emphasising the importance of Marketing Research, Alfred P. Sloan Jr., President of General Motors said, "As a result of large scale operations and world-wide distribution, producer and consumer have become more and more widely separated, so that the matter of keeping a business sensitively in tume with the requirements of the ultimate consumer becomes a matter of increasing importance. Through consumer research, we could bridge this gap."

How it is Used

That marketing research has to be and is being employed by manufacturers to understand the requirements of their customers may be illustrated by the example of Rinso. Before manufacturing 'Rinso', Hindustan Lever considered it necessary to decide whether for making this power soap, a soap base which would give a superlative lather provided warm water was used or an alternative which, though giving a less spectacular lather, would dissolve well in cold water, should be used, Experimental powders with alternate bases were prepared and the trial packets were given to a selected sample of housewives. This survey showed that the majority preferred a cold water soluble product and thus 'Rinso' was produced. If such surveys are made before manufacturing every product, the manufacturers can minimise the risk in producing new things and the consumers will also be happy to buy and use such products which can be used with convenience.

Marketing Research does not merely aim at getting accurate information about the consumers' likes and dislikes but it also provides the executive with an objective approach to making marketing decisions which will best achieve the goals of the business enterprise. Many marketing executives believe that occassional conversation with the retailers for information about the purchase of their product is adequate to understand consumers' needs and reactions. Based on this sample information, they try to generalise for the total population of consumers while making decisions about future marketing policies. But in doing so they cannot determine the degree of remoteness of this generalisation from the actual truth and they are unable to determine the amount of risk involved in taking such policy decisions based on insufficient information. In contrast to this, the techniques of Marketing Research can help to achieve this generalisation with pre-determined degree of remoteness (or risk) from the truth. In the companies the Secony-Vacuum Oil Company decided to change its name to Secony Mobil after conducting a Marketing Survey. Likewise, Western Clock Company, in order to expand their markets, carried out an extensive consumer survey which gave them valuable data on public preferences regarding trends in styles, sizes, etc. When they produced the clocks according to this information, the clocks presented an entirely new appearance. Each clock was smaller, thinner and a fine example of modern design—finished in lustrous black and nickel, with an attractive new dial, clearly legible figures, and graceful perced hands and, increase in sales followed.

Advertising Research

Let us now see how the techniques of Marketing Research can be utilised in ascertaining the impact of communication from the manufacturer to his prospective consumers. Since no manufacturer—despite the quality goods he may produce—can survive if he is unable to market his products, it becomes necessary for him to create a 'brand image' for his goods in the minds of prospective consumers. This is done through advertising.

Given a certain budget for advertising, the technique of Marketing Research can help to know the media, periodicity, design, colours, etc., of advertisement with a view to propogating the 'brand name' or 'message' to the maximum number of potential consumers. An effective advertising campaign is that which will impel the maximum number of consumers to buy the advertised 'brand'. Marketing Research also can help subsequently to evaluate how far this goal has been achieved.

Distribution Research

Another important aspect of Marketing Research is distribution research, which helps in determining effective distribution policies. An analysis of the market and study of consumers' purchasing habits can decide when and where the product should be distributed; whether the product should be distributed on a nation-wide basis or only in selected areas; whether in all shops or only in selected stores; whether it should be in all towns or only in the major ones.

Marketing Research is a management tool. It helps the excutives to do their jobs better and makes their tasks easier by providing information upon which they can base their decisions. Marketing Research helps to raise the level of exective performance by narrowing the area within which the executive must rely upon judgement alone. Marketing Research can also help to isolate the basic causes of marketing inefficiency and enable remedial measures to be taken. Business policies can be formulated on facts revealed by research rather than on hunches, guess work, opinions or casual impressions. Above all a business firm which undertake Marketing Research enjoys the goodwill of its distributors and consumers alike.

Note on How to Assess Market Potential

In the absence of available data for the assessment of markets, manufacturers and marketers are forced to set sales targets on the basis of:

1. Population figures
2. Past Sales

The former method presumes that towns of equal size have purchasing power of equal strength, while the latter ignores changes in the pattern of consumer demand and purchasing ability. The need for a more accurate assessment of the market potential being thus evident, it becomes desirable to determine what factors would provide reliable indicators of market potentials.

More than twenty kinds of basic statistics, in addition to population figures, are collected and analysed, out of which twelve are adopted. It is a more realistic and reliable guide than an index based on a single factor because when several of them are taken into account, weak spots in individual factors tend to average out.

Where the Market Lies

Advertised goods in India are, with rare exceptions, marketed and bought almost entirely in the urban areas. The standard of living in rural areas is generally low, and the well-to-do rural dwellers travel to the nearest town to buy such goods.

Of the 2,892 towns and cities which comprise the urban area, there were over 504 with a population of over 20,000 each. These accounted for 70 per cent of the urban population, and a much higher proportion of the total market for consumer goods and services. However, the consumption potential of each area does not depend upon the number of people therein. The people of each town can be divided roughly into three economic classes: (1) Lower, consisting of unskilled manual workers, petty shoapkeepers, labourers, etc., (2) Middle consisting of skilled workers, clerks, shopkeepers, professional classes, etc., (3) Upper, comprising business executives, successful merchants and professional people and so on. It is the middle and upper classes, those with money to spend and the desire to spend it who are the current and potential consumers of advertised goods. And this potential varies from area to area, having as fixed relation to the total population. Moreover, the number of middle and higher class people is not static in any place; with increasing population, rapid urban growth and rising income, the number grows continuously—underlining the need for continuous and up-to-date market research.

Analysing the Market

To arrive at a true measure of the relative consuming capacity of each area, a total of twelve economic indicators may be used. To assess the value of each of these indicators, and to construct a combined Consumer Index for each town, it was necessary to have a base. Each economic indicator has, therefore, been measured against a common yardstick . . . the score assigned to each statistical item pertaining to Greater Calcutta, which, as the largest market on the basis of the data, was chosen as the base town for the Index. The combined potentiality for Greater Calcutta 100.00 indices for each of the other 503 towns and cities were obtained by adding up the scores of individual items, which were calculated in proportion to the base of Scores.

Significance of the Economic Indicators

1. Population: This is the basic factor of the market, every other factor depending on the equality and quantity of the human factor.

2. Population other than farm and factory labour: Prospects with "discretionary spending power," *i.e.*, money to spent on consumer goods and the desire to spent it, are found mostly among the non-labouring class people.

3. Increase in population (1961-71): The growth of towns is calculated by adding births, subtracting deaths and taking into account figures of migration. There being usually little variation in the birth and death rates of different cities and towns, it is the difference in migration rates which is mainly responsible for variations in

the growth. Faster growth is thus indicative of larger buying opportunities for employment, and of increased buying ability in the area.

4. Number of literates: Literacy and buying power are usually closely linked, and areas with a higher ratio of literates to the total population are generally better markets.

5. Number of domestic radio sets: The possession of a radio set is indicative of buying power and cultural standards, and the ration of radio set owners to the total population provides a good indicator to the potential of a given area.

6. Number of private cars: The owner of a car is obviously a member of the "discretionary buying classes", and the number of private cars in relation to the total population of an area provides a realistic indication of the potential of the area.

7. Number of banks: The growth of banks depends on the existence and growth of demand for banking facilities which are caused, in part, by the development of savings potentials and of the banking habit among the public. The number of banks supported by a city or town is a realistic indication of increase in incomes and in discretionary spending power.

8. Number of doctors: A town which supports a large number of doctors is clearly more prosperous than a town with the same population supporting a smaller number. Apart from the purchasing power of the population, the number of practitioners of modern therapy, as compared with unregistered or unqualified pracittioners, is indicative of a modern outlook, respective to improved goods and services.

9. Number of chemists and druggists: Their number being regulated by the amount of turnover obt inable in the area, a greater number of chemists and druggists in

indicative of greater demand for patent medicines and drugs, of the necessary purchasing power of modern outlook.

10&11. Number of cinemas and number of cinema seats: These provide a measure of the ability and desire of people to spend on entertainment. This being a "luxury", the number of cinemas and cinema seats calculated as ratio to the population of an area indicates spending potential.

12. Domestic consumption of electricity: The use of electricity in the home adds to domestic comfort, contributes to a higher standard of living and is available only to those with initial and continuing purchasing power. Thus a town with a high consumption of electricity domestically has a high percentage of population with "discretionary spending power".

The Consumer Index brings to light differences in the purchasing power of markets which may not be discerned by comparing their population alone. For example, whereas Ajmer and Coimbatore had almost equal population of 1.9 lakhs, the latter had a potential which is 133 per cent greater than the former. Poona, with a population of 5.9 lakhs, had a potential 17 per cent greater than Kanpur, which had a 20 per cent larger population. And Varanasi and Madurai had comparable populations, but the latter was a better consuming unit by 42 per cent. The value of such facts to marketing managers is tremendous.

Note on Method of Estimation of Consumer Index Numbers

Market statistics are obtained mostly from official sources, as most official figures may be accepted as more authentic. Where no official sources of information are available, recourse is made to private sources. These relate to the figures for doctors, chemists and druggists, cinemas and cinema seats. The figures for doctors, chemists and druggists should be cross-checked, by comparing figures from lending pharmaceutical companies. Cinema statistics could be obtained from film distributors. Town-wise figures relating to most of the market factors could be obtained directly from these sources. It is necessary to make town-wise compilations for all towns in the case of domestic radio sets and private cars, and for some towns in respect of domestic consumption of electricity.

Domestic radio sets: District-wise figures may be obtained from all States and 90 per cent of them are distributed amongst the towns in each district, in proportion of population. It is assumed that 10 per cent of the radios would be in smaller towns and villages. This method in no way detracts from the value of the data. If, for instance, District A has more radios than District B, the conclusion is that District A is a better market than District B. This value is preserved in the town-wise estimates. Statistics cover licensed radio sets only. This is considered to show the true position in relative terms. Human nature not varying greatly, if a certain proportion of the population of one town tends to have unlicensed sets, the ratio will tend to the repeated elsewhere.

Private cars: District-wise figures can be obtained from all States. The same method as for radio sets may be followed in the town-wise breaking up of district and regional figures. All cars are likely to be in towns of over 20,000 population and no reservation be made for smaller towns. The state-wise figures may broken up town-wise on the basis of population, the position in neighbouring places being taken into account.

Domestic consumption of electricity: Complete town-by-town data may not be obtainable for all States. The data lacking for a few towns in each of the other States, may be estimated on the basis of figures for neighbouring towns.

Banks: The number of banks in towns of less than 1 lakh population was disproportionately high. This was attributed to the existence of banks doing mainly loan and chit fund transactions, whose value from the viewpoint of savings potential is considerably less than the value of normal banks. These banks were estimated as representing 50 percent of the banks in each towns and were disregarded when computing index numbers.

Cinemas and Cinema Seats: It may be necessary to take both these sets of figures, as there is no correlation between them and, where seating capacity tends to be inflated as, for example, in Tamil Nadu by the fact that ground space is filled to capacity by squatters (lower class), the relative values are distorted. By taking both statistics into consideration, a truer picture can be obtained.

Establishing the Base City

It is not possible, from available statistics, to make a quantitative assessment of the sales potential of each town and city. What is possible is to establish sales potentials in relative terms, *i.e.*, in the form of index numbers. It is important to establish a common measure for one kind of factor in all cities covered; it is also necessary that a greater weight be assigned to data more significant of the discretionary spending power, and data of more recent years. Since Greater Calcutta tops the list in respect of almost all marketing factors, it naturally emerges as the biggest single market in India and each factor relating to Greater Calcutta may be taken as the standard by which to measure the same factor in the other cities and towns surveyed. The scores assigned for all factors in Greater Calcutta, the base city, total 100, which is the Consumer Index Number for that city. The actual measuring against the base city yardstick may be done in two stages; first, indices may be compiled for individual factors in proportion to the base index, then these may be combined to yield the Consumer Index Number for the town in question.

Sources of Market Data

Market data is obtained from different sources.

Item	*Source*
Population	Census publications
Domestic Radio Sets	Postmasters-General of the States
Private Cars	State Transport Commissioners and Regional Transport Authority
Banks	Reserve Bank of India
Doctors, Chemists & Druggists	Leading Pharmaceutical companies
Cinemas and Cinema Seats	Film distributing companies
Domestic Consumption of Electricity	State Electricity Boards and Electricity Undertakings. Central Electricity Authority

Motivation Research

Motivation Research is a recent marketing tool, developed to assist marketing to create, develop and innovate product and measure the influence of advertising on the prospect. Motivation can be defined as well those factors which make people act an move towards certain goals. Research concentrates on the "why" of buying. The method of research is borrowed from social sciences to uncover and evaluate the motives or desires that are behind human behaviour.

Human beings are guided by many motivations, some intrinsic, some extrinsic—coming from within and without. when the motives are rational, action can be explained; the irrational cannot be explained—it is a part of the human psyche. It is like asking: "Are you against sin ?"—you cannot afford to say no. Our thinking is very often conditioned—why are good things on top and bad ones below—why are angels white and devils black ? The condemnation of black is a hangover from the primitive which cannot be explained away simply as superstition. Most often, we are fooled by our senses; we still use them without realising they are a guide to help use make judgements. Knowing how our minds operate should permit us to act more rationally and shift objective reactions from emotional ones.

The two principal schools of motivational theory are derived from:

1. Gestalt Psychology. The Gestalt School was developed by Wertheimer, Kohler, Koffka and Lewin.
2. Psychoanalysis which was developed by Freud, Adler, Jung, Rank, Sullivan, Kardiner and Fromm.

These two distinct approaches have different implications as to the way the consumers will react towards goods or towards the various appeals presented in advertising. Under the Gestalt method of psychoanalysis of perception, the individual will regard the product as "an instrument which takes him nearer to his goal." Under Freud's psychoanalysis the symbolic aspect of goods replaces the symbols of the individual's suppressed desires and makes him more interested in "symbols of mastery than in working tools."

These two distinct approaches remain unbridged and influence the decision of the choice of the method to be used or rather are two distinct approaches to the problem. Motivation Research has been in an experimental and perhaps a time will come when a formula combining the two distinct schools will be evolved. In the present situation, the two schools influence the interpretations and lead to distinct and different conclusions. In practice, it has been found that both the schools have certain relevance to the irrational of the human psyche. Neither offers an infallible conclusion.

"Psychology begins with the precept that all behaviour occurs for a reason—that is all behaviour is the result of motivation. The job of the researcher is to understand the perception—the meaning and singnificance it has for our prospect so that we may know the basis of such motives." "Bridges to the mind are specific human motivations which act as go-betweens from objects to the mental and psychological cogwheels of the human personality."

Different stimuli act under different circumstances. In personal choice of clothing "men are influenced by women"—what women think is important. In a study conducted in America, it was found that "in 98 percent of the cases what is bought depends on what the woman says." On the purchasing habits of men, a clothing storekeeper said:

> "They always come with their wives, with their sweethearts. Inhad a case, like that only yesterday where a young fellow came in—he picked out some shirts. He said he would have a mind of his own. If a man come alone, then you have a chance to sell him unless you don't have the article. When he con.es with a woman, it is hard to sell him."

The motive is indicative of the broadly accepted research on why men dress well. In such instances, motive is "not merely to decorate the body but to impress a particular person"—the chosen person.

People's attributes towards things need to be seen from different perspectives. For instance, the size of the capsule is in inverse relationship to its potency—"the smaller the pill the more effective it is." In another study it was found that an analgesic tablet failed because the manufacturers advertised that this pill could be swallowed without the need of water. People simply did not believe that paid could be relieved by a pill without having to drink water and the product failed miserably.

Appetite is a biological occurrence. In the older psychological textbooks, it is defined as "drive originating in a tissue". Appetite is not a simple need nor is it aroused by a simple stimulus. The state of physical health affects and changes appetites as does the state of mental health, the emotions, perceptions and the imagination. In experiments, psychologists placed a quantity of corn before a clucking flowl and allowed her to eat until full. Then she stopped pecking. Next the corn was replenished and the packing machinery in the hen began to operate again. The Swedish psychologist David Katz has called this the "two-component theory of motivation" a descriptive name for motives and appetites depending both on inner need and outer incentive.

Advertising of food, in some of the American journals illustrates this point admirably. Food is appetising but a new dimension has been added to it—the adventure of eating or trying different foods. The basic motivation for the food may be common but the outside stimulant has changed the type of food which is sought.

Appetite relates to communication in at least two ways:

1. Desire for cross-cultural communication; eating foreign food is a way of establishing communication with a new culture.
2. Desire for more intimate contact—here the appeal to appetite and the response of appetite to the appeal places human relationship on an entirely new level of communication.

One of the classical studies of motivational research has been conducted in the field of prunes. The case was reported in the *New York 'Post'* of June, 1, 1955. Dichter and Vicary were employed independently by separate groups in the prune industry to find the causes for the sluggish market. Dichter found some startling reasons why people disliked prunes. He found that the prune was a dried-out, worn-out symbol of old age—he recommended that prunes be renamed "black diamonds" and surrounded with an aura of preciousness and desirability. Vicary reported that Americans have an "emotional" block about prunes' laxative connotations. And Vicury recommended a blunt solution to exploit the core of the market by advertising the laxative features.

A well known manufacturer submitted an identical set of problems, separately to two leading commercial practitioners of motivation analysis:

1. What is the present status of this corporate personality of ours.

2. What should the role be:

   (a) as a service personality? and,

   (b) as a sales influence?

"A" conducted 200 interviews in various parts of the country. "B" conducted 200 interviews in one city. 1. The findings were diametrically opposite—in answer to the first question, "A" found the corporate-personality warm, understanding, real. "B" found it cool, aloof, abstract.

2. "A": "Cannot afford to tie up specifically with the products and warned that 'the personality would fall down on the job as far as the psychological role is used as a sales service".

"B": "Large number of customers and prospects favourably disposed towards the corporate personality acting as salesman."

The findings were based on the personal opinions of the analysts rather than on reactions and attitudes of the dependable sample of customers and prospects.

Statistical Quantification and Standardised Questioning

There have been a number of studies indicating the usefulness of motivational research to marketing men in two distinct areas of application. When a product begins to decline in sales due to reasons other than those of quality, motivation research can help to plan innovation of the product to give to it a new appearance by changing the package, and colour and readjusting the communicative element of the product with consumer motivation. The second is when the product fails to make progress in the market due to its image as in the case of prunes. Basically it is the 'communication element' which needs to be examired whether it is at the product level or advertising; the important thing is not what the product does, but what it means to the consumer—to discover the motives or desires that are behind human behaviour of the consumer market.

The starting point of motivational research is marketing research. Motivational Research is an additional dimension of market research and therefore we must first know how many people do what. Only when this is known does the next step of knowing why begin. In the competitive markets of the West, where products compete for a share in the discretionary income of the consumer, motivational research has a positive contribution to make. Where the competition is between similar products, in quality and price, and if one brand is selling more than the other, the manufacturers would naturally like to know why the consumer prefers to buy one in preference to the other. What is the basis of brand loyality—the elements that bind a consumer to a particular brand? Research was conducted to examine the strength of 'brand' in the market. People who were Coca Cola enthusiasts did not consider Pepsi Cola to be equal in taste and flavour to Coca Cola. When Pepsi Cola was packed in Coca Cola bottles and Coca Cola in Pepsi Cola Bottles, it was found that the drink in the Coca Cola bottles was considered to be genuine and different from the one bottled in Pepsi Cola bottles. The packaging and the name had built a deep image in the subconscious; the sense of taste was not strong enough, or to put it in the jargon of psychology, the symbolisation of the brand was so deeply impressed on the subconscious that Coca Cola stimulated the behaviour pattern which brought about psychosomatic satisfaction. The brand association was stronger than the stimulus to the physical taste.

Motivation Research as a tool of Marketing

(1) It is being increasingly used to examine the 'motives' behind a brand;

(2) to associate motives which would build such brand loyalties so that the product may have a continuity of market on an ascending scale.

Motivation Research is not a science in the sense that cause and effect follow a pre-determined pattern. In dealing with the human elements, the irrational cannot be overlooked and therefore in the application of Motivation Research, the margin of error will deserve careful consideration. The method is scientific but the interpretation of data obtained, requires experience. Motivation Research has borrowed the 'depth interview' technique from psycho analysis as a clinical application—the approach is individual; in its application to motivation research, it is communal. The individual must be representative of the group to typify the sample so that statistical conclusions may be accurately drawn.

Psycho analysis divides people into types but the typologists are almost as numerous as the analysts.

Jung talks of introverts and extroverts.

Rank groups people into neurotic and creative;

Horney into the compliant, aggressive and detached types;

Frommlists five orientations of personality.

One great difficulty in applying such typologies is that no related classification for families or households is available and they are the purchasing units among whom research must be conducted. Research therefore, relies on broad homogeneous groups and the sample is constructed on a community basis. The universe of the sample, therefore, is the most important part of Motivational Research.

The next most important consideration in the application of Motivation Research is 'the problem'. The problem forms the basis of assumption. It must, therefore, be formulated in clear terms and determined that the assumption relates to motives in the consumer situation. The assumption that may appear on the superficial level may not be relevant to motivation and would need to be tested first. Dr. Ernest Dichter quotes the example of baby food. "The problem was how best to advertise baby foods. The obvious assumption was that the best method was to promise the mother that this baby food contributed to the health of her baby; we did not accept this assumption" states Dr Dichter. "Through 350 interviews which permitted mothers to talk realistically about babies, motherhood, and feeding problems, we discovered that while motherlive was partially operative, a much more tangible and effective motivation at work was the mother's interest in making her feeding chore more convenient and pleasant. Promising her therefore", concluded Dr Dichter, "that this particular brand of baby food would be enjoyed by her child, would be less likely to result in rejection, and would cut down feeding time considerably, proved to be a more effective appeal."

The assumption determines the method that may be used. In dealing with research of motive we are confronted with the problem of semantics can people express clearly and meaningfully the rational and irrational of their deep seated motives? Very often people themselves are not aware of their own motives and even if they wish, they may not be able to express them. In many areas, language is an imperfect tool of communication. This is so when precise conveying of taste and tactile sensations are concerned. In such cases symbolic language, such as pictures or music is often more powerful than a direct statement--such words as "mild", "smooth" cannot be measured. These have no basis to assign value since there are smoother words which lend themselves to comparison in a similar group of word meanings. In such cases, motivational research uses non-verbal tests which enable the researcher to assign mathematical value to the meaning. In studies of various brands of margarine, one of the principal criteria of the housewife's choice is the texture—she wants the margarine to be smooth as butter; at the same time, most housewives find that all margarines are not equally smooth—there are rougher kinds too. When it comes to describing the various gradations of smoothness, they are hard put to express their experience in an adequate manner. Nor is there any possibility of ascertaining that several consumers use the same expression in describing similar texture sensations.

"To overcome this semantic hurdle, a simple test was devised—respondents were shown five abstract pictures representing as many gradations of smoothness, unevenness and roughness. They were given a list of six different brands of margarine and asked to qualify the smoothness of each by identifying it with one of the pictures. The results of the test were illuminating. Over three-fourths of the respondents allocated the same picture to the same brand of margarine."

Yet another method was used to determine the reasons of the drop in the sales of Instant Coffee. Market research had shown that the housewife was not buying Instant Coffee because she did not like the flavour. This was the simple answer to the simple question: "Do you use Instant Coffee? If the answer is no, what do you dislike about it?" "I don't like the flavour." An easy answer to a complex question.

To discover the motives behind this dislike of flavour which resulted in non-purchase of the product, a different method was used. Two shopping lists were prepared. One list contained Maxwell House Coffee and the other Nescafe. Except for this change, all other items on the shopping list remained the same. A representative group of housewives was approached and told to project themselves "until you can characterise the women who bought the groceries; then write a brief description of her personality and character." The results thus obtained were interesting:

1. 48 percent of the people described the women who bought Nescafe as lazy, 4 percent described the women who bought Maxwell Coffee as lazy.
2. 48 percent described women who bought Nescafe as failing to plan household purchases and schedules well. 12 percent described the women who bought Maxwell Coffee as failing to plan household purchases and schedules well.
3. 4 percent described Nescafe—thrifty. 16 percent described Maxwell—thrifty.

4. 16 percent described Nescafe—no good, 4 percent as good. 16 percent described Maxwell as—good.

The typical descriptive comments were:

"This woman appears to be in a hurry—single—she buys Nescafe.

"My assumption on what she bought such as Instant Coffee can be made in a hurry."

"I'd say she was a practical, frugal woman—she bought Too May Potatoes."

We may conclude by quoting Dr Dichter—"our research, our motivational thinking, concentrates more on the techniques of human strategy, which are necessary to bring about the desired goal. The question which we ask ourselves, before undertaking and analysing a motivational problem is "what will I have to know in order to be able to advise the client on the proper advertising, sales programme, propagandistic or educational approach." "From the psychological point of view, the basic conflict we face is one between wanting to hold on to the *status quo*, wanting to return to the womb, to hide, to be fatalistic, or to face the world by accepting the challenge of change."

Motivation Research as a marketing tool is a promise of change; like most technologies this new descipline, too, is in a state of continuous change. Though empirical, we however, experience that it is giving the manufacturers who have the courage to use it, the means to advance their objectives. This, therefore, is a very good reason to give Motivation Research a trial and scope to serve the methodical, progressive marketing men.

Consumer Research

The contribution of behavioural sciences to buying patterns cannot be lifted out and shown in any singular form in as much as the socictal characteristics are dynamic factors revealing undying changes. For a marketing decision, the changes should always be judged in their dynamics and not as mere facts of transformation. The reasons are two-fold; buying motives are largely the reflections of the dynamics that take place on the socio-economic consumer profits, underlining interpretation in terms of what they hold for a marketer. Secondly, the seller-buyer relationship has a close bearing on the kind of marketing interpretation these changes are accorded.

We may extend these arguments further by setting out certain sociological parameters for marketing decisions. All the factors discussed below may not be strictly sociological by definition, but are so broader acceptance.

Media Research

Language is another socio-demographic demarcation at the national level. Besides the 14 languages recognised by the Indian Constitution, at least an equal number of them are in vogue as lingua franca in the country. A knowledge of the use of different languages by different communities, when combined with information on reading habits of people as reflected in the newspaper and other periodical circulation data help the marketer for undertaking media research, leading to effective planning of advertising and other publicity gamuts.

The position occupied today by the *trade press* in terms of information and knowledge transmitted through printing is far from satisfactory. Development of trade press is hampered by low literacy, restrictive growth of general press, lack of press-oriented commercial techniques and so forth.

The newspaper and other periodical *circulation data* alone do not provide the marketer with the necessary tools for media research. Specific probe studies into the reading habits of people are 'essentials' before any meaningful selection of media can be made. The need for undertaking such probe studies is worth examining. Emphasizing the importance of media selection to profitable utilization of advertising, Professor Borden wrote in his "Economic Effects of Advertising":

"Fundamental from a profit standpoint is the selection of media which will reach prospects who can readily be induced to buy, because advertising addressed to poor prospects entails high costs. But even when competing periodicals ostensibly reach the right people for a particular advertiser, there still may be a marked difference in their advertising effectiveness, because of differences in the extent to which subscribers read the periodical and the varying interest aroused for different products by the editorial contents and by the physical setting which advertisements are given."

With the available information and data in India, the advertising agencies in India have not been able to provide information for use in determining to what extent various media reach those whom the advertiser wishes to address and the extent to which consumers see and read those media. The marketer has only to closely watch the relationship that at times exists between linguistic features and buying propensities. Goa and Pondicherry provides striking examples of regions which show isolated qualities of individualities from the States to which they are parts. The writer knows of an instance where a marketing organization of antacids had to follow a different promotional strategy suited to the buying culture of these areas. The antacids were promoted in these areas on the basis of its qualities in dispelling the groggy effects of excessive consumption of liquor.

Caste and Religion

The significant area in which the Indian consumers differ from their western counterparts is the impact religion has on the day-to-day conduct of Indians. Mr. Leon V. Hirsch, an American marketing professor, in the course of his work in India, observed:

"The religious Hindu or Jain who is a practising vegetarian may not be motivated to eat sugar believed to be made with bone char, no matter to what level its price may fall, but the same person will carefully shop around and bargain to get the best value for his money in the purchase of Khandsar."

This is a foreigner's assessment. Perhaps this may not be tenable in today's conditions in villages and towns but this clearly shows the deep inroad religion has made into consumer motivations and behaviour. It has also been the general experience of the marketers of canned beef products that the consumer resistance on grounds of religion has been quite formidable.

Educational Characteristics

The degree of sophistication marketing men can employ in their selling programmes will be determined, by and large, by the level of education that a nation possesses. New vistas of intellectual, emotional and aesthetic sensitivity that will raise the cultural level of the living, imply many things for marketing managers. For example, books, better and sophisticated wants for new things, travel and other cultural activities assume symbols of existence as distinct from ostentation, as a nation's educational level rises. Also a rising level of education presupposes shifts in advertising strategy, many marketers may wish to upgrade their appeals. Many factual data may be desired by more customers to match the benefits of education. The level of literacy along with languages and reading habits has great import for the marketer while selecting the advertising media.

The tend toward increasing amounts of education offers other opportunities. The increasing popularity of technical handbooks on industrial goods and price and product catalogues on consumer goods may be partially credited to the fact that educated persons prefer to know the 'facts' and make their own decisions. Large manufacturers of consumer and durable goods have been able to convince educated people that lower costs of operation have enabled them to operate on lower prices. Some durable goods manufacturers have been able to make business, even at higher prices, by concentrating on quality. The cases in point are electrical appliances, radios and steel furniture.

Households and Families

Consumer behaviour is also influenced by the ways in which individuals group themselves for residential and other purposes. It is necessary to consider households and families, two major sociological determinants of spending and consumption patterns. No serious studies involving socio-economic patterns of households and families have so far been undertaken in India to enable marketing insights for selling organizations in this country. A recent survey on the household patterns of Calcutta's population conducted by a researcher revealed the following characteristics:

> "About a quarter of the population of the city, live a single life without their families, and they form more than half of the households. The vast majority of these people are male, married and migrants. They are educationally backward, containing a higher proportion of illiterate persons. More than 85 percent of these are concentrated in three groups of occupation—unskilled manual work, skilled labour and trading. About 87 per cent earn less than Rs. 100 per month, their average earnings amounting to Rs. 73 per month (The City of Calcutta—A Socio-economic Survey, S.N. Sen, *Economic Weekly*, Bombay, Vol. IX, No. 14.)

The above finding, in isolation may not help a marketer for reaching a base for a marketing programme. But if the presence of similar societal features can be confirmed by empirical research, it will certainly guide the thinking of marketing men towards a scheme of action, oriented to the existing condition.

Social Class Membership

While income has generally been the most widely used behavioural indicator in marketing, social class membership weaves its own pattern on the behaviour of the consumer. Can we take it that the individual's consumption patterns symbolise his class position? In a way, the answer should be yes. It is demonstrated that social class position is a more significant determinant of the consumer buying behaviour than just income. The confluence of income, education and occupation create in combination an awareness of social status with the consumers.

Although the Bata shoes have the quality image before the consumers, they are priced out compared to other private brands in its class. Still the middle-class consumer attaches a meaningful possession to this nationally advertised brand, despite the fact that their prices fall outside the pale of his paying capacity. The same person demonstrates no hesitancy in going to smaller shops for buying unbranded goods of day-to-day convenience. Perhaps this tendency could best be described as a typical attitude of a middle-class consumer in the purchase of personal wares. Taste in personal wares, he considers, so elusive and subtle that he would like to draw support from the store's taste which has more or less social acceptance.

There is thus a social class system operative at least in metropolitan markets which can be isolated and described. The kinds of things a person will or will not buy are strongly related to his class membership, and also whether he is mobile or stable. Likewise, the individual's store loyalties and his spend-save aspirations will in considerable part be class-oriented. It is true that we cannot use fully extend this proposition as a matter of universal application to all our buying situations.

Consumer Disposition

The consumer decision to purchase or not to purphase a given commodity, to acquire or not to acquire a service results from his disposition arising from these factors acting in Unison. True, no factor acts in isolation but the intensity of different factors present themselves in varying degrees in each case. The foreign marketing expertise has demonstrated that these factors can be measured with a reasonable degree of accuracy and brought into broad homogeneous groups, provided the marketer has the personal skill and an effective organization behind him for collecting, shifting, analysing and interpreting the relevant information and data on consumer decision-making units. In today's India, however, the company resources in terms of undertaking extensive consumer studies and market surveys are limited first, by many organizational constraints; secondly, by several external factors, such as inadequacy of governmental and private data collection agencies, poor trade press development and lack of industry data.

Are not then the problems in marketing faced by the Indian businessmen today grave enough to stimulate their thinking in terms of undertaking consumer studies and market research? Although no definitive answer appears possible, the reasons are not far to seek. To any careful student of Indian society, the regional variations are too great to permit generalizations. India's is a complex economy in which the situations of different consumers and business groups vary greatiy. Also perhaps the conditions of sellers' market in which the Indian businessmen have been moving today and the lack of intellect, experience and equipment at the disposal of marketing organizations in India may be cited as deterrents in face of undertaking such tasks.

Even those few non-company agencies specializing in market research and allied services that exist today in India have been somewhat functioning in an apologetic fashion. Again, only very few advertising agencies have within themselves market research cells for fulfilling the research needs of their clientele.

Although progress that has been made so far in the direction of assessing consumer needs and the markets by different marketing organizations is small, there is no denying the fact that at least a beginning is made by a few large companies through the creation of Economic Units and Market Research Cells within their own organizations with a view to evolving sound guidelines for the companies marketing operations.

Other than the social transformations that create market changes, there are segmentations of the market possible for the manufacturer who can discern needs within existing patterns. This type of marketing sophistication can detect a latent interest in diet foods, industrial equipments, electric appliances, or radio and television before the markets are fully developed. Markets created by products devised to meet special needs or desires are no less segmented from a marketer's point of view than those divided by age, sex, income or geography. An evaluation of different product appeals that can be imparted through advertising, sales promotion, package design or new vending methods will often enable the marketer to know consumer behaviour in its different forms and facets.

Sales Forecasting for Small Industry

Sales forecasting means attempting to determine, on a sound basis, the volume of sales which can reasonably be expected at some future date.

Uses of Forecasting

1. For making policy decisions that involve budgeting. If a company needs a certain gross to operate profitably but future sales of products it now makes will not bring in this volume, knowing this situations, steps can be taken to increase sales.

2. For controlling inventories. With better control, management can reduce storage costs and be less likely to get caught with high-priced merchandise in a declining market. In a rising market, sales are not lost because of failure to fill orders.

3. For improving production control through a more accurate picture of the future. Such a programme will help to: (1) improve efficiency in the use of equipment; (2) prevent unnecessary costly overtime; (3) prevent costly storage of finished material; (4) improve employee morale, and (5) reduce expensive starts and stops.

4. For setting up an accurate yardstick for evaluating territories and salesmen. This is possible because a realistic quota can be established for each area. It wiil serve to show which territory is not producing its share of sales. It also helps the morale of the staff to know that the management has made an honest effort to set fair quotas.

5. For planning production realistically. It may be unwise to build an expensive plant to meet a short-term increase in demand. However, it can be an excellent investment to increase long-range facilities when construction costs are low.

6. For allocating wisely the money to be spent on sales promotion and advertising.

7. For eliminating or replacing unprofitable products.

8. For developing effective financial control.

9. For establishing personnel policies more efficiently. If a company knows in advance what the demand will be, it can put into effect a programme to expand or retrench manpower in such a way as to maintain good morale.

A Good Forecast

Check points in judging whether or not it is a good forecast: (1) it should be as accurate as possible, as proved by subsequent events; (2) it should be kept current and up to date by little effort and expense; (3) it should be based on data in which the management continues to have faith; (4) it should be flexible enough to meet the various company needs; (5) its cost should be kept within the company's budget.

Preparing a Sales Forecast

Any small unit can do reasonably accurate job of sales forecasting without hiring a large staff of experts. To do so follow five steps:

Assign responsibility for preparing the forecast to an individual who (1) understands the rudiments of studying figures; (2) is familiar with the particular business; (3) realize that all statistical results must be tempered by judgement and experience; (4) organize all internal figures logically; and (5) make use of the many external statistics available.

Developing a Forecast

(1) ***Preparing the internal figures*****:** The first steps is to prepare **the** Company's internal records. They should be broken down by months. customers, sizes, uses, territories, or by any other characteristics important to the particular business. In developing figures for the first time, go as far back as practicable. About 10 to 15 years is a safe period, since it will include several business "swings" in the national economy. If the business does not have detailed internal figures for any substantial period, make the forecast in light of what is available. But remember, the less the historical data, the greater the chance of error.

Some *project future sales* completely on what they have done in the past. This approach has several weaknesses. For example, an item considered a luxury one day can become a necessity the next day. But market and sales problems for a luxury item are not the same as those for a necessity. Consequently, a change in the marketing policies of the company would be required.

(2) *Determining a Company's share of the market*: The second step is to relate the sales to the total sales of the industry of which the company is a part, and thus establish the share of the market which you can expect. To do this we need some external statistics to which the internal figures can be

compared. These figures can be obtained from sources like the survey reports conducted by the Department of Industry and Commerce, other publications of Government bodies like the Directorate of Commercial Intelligence and Statistics, Chambers of Commerce, etc.

(3) The third step is to *relate the industry's sales to national statistics* which reflect the influence of the national economy on the future sales of the industry. Suppose the product is a component used in Radio sets. A logical starting point would be to analyze future consumer plans for purchasing radio sets. How are these plans tied to disposable income (money left to spend after taxes)? What will the effect of the national economy be on disposable income? In this way the forecast is not tied just to history, but also to basic causes that are changing the day-to-day economy. An industrial unit can also study the figures regarding GNP, Production Index, Employment etc.

Be Kept Up-to-date and Readily Available: Some figures may generally be more accurate, but not available frequently enough to be useful.

Be Broken down into a Useful Form: Some statistics require a great deal of work before they are in a usable form.

Be Collected by a Reliable, Non-biased Source: The accuracy of the figures in necessary in order to base confident action on them.

Be Collected by a Stable Source: Chances should be good that these statistics will continue to be collected and published in the future. Having to convert to a new source can cause a great deal of extra work and uncertainty.

The figures that best fit the above standards are the statistics issued by the Government. Next to them are the ones issued by trade organizations, trade papers and magazines, the financial houses.

Company sales should be plotted against the industry sales. When sales depart from the pattern formed by the last 3 to 5 years' operations. try to determine what caused your company to get a larger or smaller share of the total market. We might check up on sales promotlon, advertising campaigns, and the like to get an idea what to expect from the future efforts and those of competitors.

Sometimes it is impossible to get accurate statistics on a particular industry's sales. If this is true in a particular case, the following techniques may be used to get a good approximation:

(1) study consumer surveys made by newspapers and trade magazines showing relative positions held by various brands or firms in a particular area;

(2) run a sample survey to establish the firm's position in the industry;

(3) canvass salesmen and main accounts as to the total sales of the kind of product;

(4) determine the total from studies showing the consumption per capita and extend this to cover the entire market.

(4) *Interpreting the figures*: The fourth step is interpreting the figures that have been compiled. The work done up to this point can lead to unsound decisions if proper weight is not given to the following facts:

1. Prices may change; therefore, a prediction of increased rupee volume could mean an actual decrease in number of units sold. Of course, the opposit holds true for a prediction of a decrease in rupee sales. Some calculation must be made of what prices will be.
2. Demand may change; for example, a news release pointed out that an automobile market had recently been sent an order that buggy whips. This company, at the beginning of the century, had to take heed of the

change in demand for horse-drawn equipment and change its product.

3. Judgement may be faulty; therefore, the soundness of the forecast should be tested against opinions of salesmen, major accounts, and articles in trade paper and business publications, etc.
4. Conditions may change; therefore, the forecaster must continually keep up-to-date on what is happening to the economic health of the nation.

Examples of how some companies are using the above procedure for forecasting.

A clock company which manufactures expensive speciality clocks—used both in homes and ships—makes a forecast for the coming year's sales based on the average figured from the previous year's sales compared with commercial and consumer disposable income. That figure is then tempered by the judgement of the sales department as to trends in home furnishings.

A small soap company ties its sales forecasts to the number of families, size of families, and disposable income. This company has found from Government and trade studies that the amount of soap used per family depends on the number of young children and the amount of money the family has to spend. These figures are obtained from Government publications and from surveys made by the Government or by trade papers.

Using Available Statistics Below are listed some of the types of data that may be available at little or no cost, and a brief suggestion as to how they might be bsed in forecasting.

A. Types of Data Useful in Predicting the General Economic Situation

1. Gross National Product—This is a weighted index of all types of economic activity based on all phases of the national economy.

2. Manufacturer's Sales, Inventories, and Orders—These figures trend to show the balance between supply and demand. For example, an inventory build-up tends to show that supply is getting ahead of demand.
3. Industrial Production Index—This presents a picture of actual business activity. The index is based on the physical output of factories and mines.
4. Bank Debits—Since most business transactions are made by cheque, this figure shows with reasonable accuracy the upturns and downturns of business.
5. Employment—Growth of the labour force generally anticipates a growth in demand. A decline in employment foretells a decline in production.

B. Types of Data Useful in Forecasting the Purchasing Power of the Consumer

1. Disposable Income—This shows the actual amount of money the consumer has available to spend (personal income after taxes).
2. Hours and Earnings—This indicates the average wage of the industrial employee. It is an indication of the power of the consumer to absorb manufactured goods.
3. Retail Sales—This shows the rate at which the final user is purchasing goods. It reflects changes in buying habits.
4. Wholesale Trade—This is also a measure of flow of goods to the consumer. It points up inventory buildup and structural changes in retail purchases.
5. Consumer Buying Plans—Field surveys are used to determine what the consumer intends to buy (in certain durable and nondurable fields) the methods of financing, and the price class of the planned purchases.

The Department of Commercial Intelligence & Statistics in India publishes figures on industry and trade. A forecaster should study his specific problem and then study several approaches to make sure which of those mentioned fit his particular needs best.

6

Sales Force Response to Financial Incentives

RENE Y. DARMON

Problem Setting

How do salesmen react to financial incentives? Marketing theorists and managers have generally answered this question with assumptions more than with hard facts. John Farley's normative model for setting commission rates is based on the assumption that salesmen strive to maximize their financial gains;[1] incentive and commission plans which are increasingly used by managers for compensating salesmen[2] rely on similar assumptions. This article reports a case study where different behaviorol hypotheses were tested on their ability to explain salesmen's reactions to financial incentives and especially to a change of compensation scheme.

The salesmen compensation scheme can fulfill at least three major functions: (1) remunerating salesman for their work

Editors' Note: Previously unpublished article which is largely based on an article by the same author in *Journal of Marketing Research*, November 1974, pp. 418-426, published by the American Marketing Association.

(compensating); (2) inducing salesmen to devote the largest possible amount of effort to their task—in quantity and quality (motivating); and (3) channeling salesmen's effort toward various activities according to the objectives and priorities of the firm (directing).[3] This study is not concerned with salesman remuneration, but rather with the other functions of motivating and directing the sales force, aimed at influencing salesmen's activities —and consequently sales and salesmen's earnings—in such a way as to contribute to management's objectives. Once his objectives are defined (and they will probably include some desired level of sales and profits), a sales manager cannot properly determine the tactical aspects of the compensation scheme unless he under stands the effects of certain tactics and tools on sales and profits. This raises two important questions:

1. How will a new compensation plan affect sales and gross profit (overall, as well as by product line)?
2. How will a new compensation plan affect salesmen's earnings (selling costs) and net profits ?

These questions can only be answered if the sales manager is able to assess his salesmen's reactions to a variation of the compensation scheme. Therefore, the answers the sales manager is likely to give to these questions depend heavily upon the assumptions he makes about his salesmen's behaviour and the way he expects them to respond to his stimuli. Consequently, one can expect the manager's objectives to be met as long as his assumptions about his salesmen's behaviour are correct.

Identifying salesmen's behavioral patterns concerning money incentives also has managerial implications for recruiting and training the salesmen. The sales manager faced with the task of recruiting would like to select among potential candidates on the basis of behavioral patterns. For example, he may prefer to hire salesmen who will try to maximize their income—and therefore, who will be easy to motivate and direct with money incentives—than salesmen who would try to minimize their effort to get some desirable level of income. Training the salesmen to increase their performance requires different training objectives and methods depending on the behaviour patterns they display, *i.e.* changing undesirable behavior patterns and reinforcing desirable ones.

Surprisingly enough, in spite of these important implications, there is little positive knowledge of how salesmen behave, and managers must rely more on their own beliefs and intuitions than on hard facts.[4] Research in organizational behaviour has shown that money is a potential motivator of human behaviour which is effective under a wide range of circumstances.[5] However, there is great variation of opinion and empirical evidence as to how much motivation it can provide.[6] Very few theories deal with this problem, and when they do, their scope and predictive power are limited.[7] Moreover, the salesmen motivation problem has so many unique characteristics that is some question as to whether the findings and theories from other fields can be readily applied, These distinctive characteristics include a higher independence in the organization of their work, the possible existence of distinctive personality traits[8] and/or socio-economic characteristics; they also include the directing aspects of the compensation plan which is specifically a sales management problem. In spite of these differences, little attention has been given in marketing to an understanding of the behavioral processes which could explain salesmen's responses to financial incentives and the asumptions made on salesmen response to money incentives are often implicit and vague.[9] In an attempt to deal at least in part with this problem, the study reported here outlines a possible methodology and reports an empirical application.

The Hypotheses

Five sets of possible assumptions about salesman behaviour were tested. These assumptions have been selected because each is supported in at least some field of knowledge. These hypothetical behaviour patterns are briefly described below.

The salesman follows habit patterns or opposes changes. In this case the prospects of earning more or less money does not motivate the salesman. He will behave the same as before, even after a change in remuneration. This is the assumption implicitly made by the (naive) statistical analyst who projects past sales trends into the future and ignores possible changes in the compensation scheme.

The salesman is interested in sales achievement. Although maximizing sales has a direct effect on his commissions, the assumption is that the salesman is interested only in securing the highest possible sales volume, irrespective of his earnings. This is subjeet to the constraint that the salesman has a limited amount of time for selling activities. These assumptions are consistent with the views of industrial psychologists who see the salesman as striving for the gratification of higher-level needs (in terms of Maslow's hierarchy)[10] or as striving for quota achievement.[11]

The salesman works to reach some acceptable level of income (or sales). This set of assumptions describes a hedonistic salesman who works as little as possible to reach some income level that he deems sufficient, or to get a sufficient sales volume in order to get along with his supervisors and keep his job. These assumptions are similar to those made in McGregor's Theory X in which working men are described as passive, indolent, and working as little as possible.[12]

The saleman is interested in increasing his expected monetary gains. In this case the salesmen tries to earn as much money as he can, subject to the constraint that he can only dispose of a limited amount of time for selling purposes. This view is consistent with that of the orthodox economist who sees the salesman an independent entrepreneur trying to maximize profits. These are also the assumptions about salesman behaviour made by Farley.[13]

The salesman tries to increase his satisfaction. Here it is assumed that the salesman tries to find the most satisfying allocation of his time (his scarce resource) between work (a time-consuming and income-generating activity) and "leisure" (income-and/or time-consuming activities). This set of assumptions probably meets the approval of economists who would consider the salesman as a supplier (and a consumer) of his time who tries to maximize his utility function.[14]

Model

A model which simulates salesmen's response to financial incentives (in terms of sales and salesmen's earnings) is used. For each of the hypothetical behaviour patterns just discussed, this model simulates how a salesman should (1) allocate his selling time between the different product lines, and (2) change his work intensity level when his level of remuneration is altered. Therefore, given a specific set of behavioral assumptions, the model can relate the variations in the remuneration level and the commission rates to a salesman's activities, and consequently to his sales and earnings. This model focuses on the variables over which the salesman has direct control and which are affected by financial gains.

The sales territory, characterized by such elements as its potential, size, and so on, displays sales response functions to a salesman's effort. These response functions are influenced by marketing variables (such as the marketing mix), environmental variables (such as competition. economic trends, and seasonal cycles), and by the level of competence of the salesman in charge of the territory. Given these response functions, the salesman performs at a certain level of activity in his territory. This results in a certain amount of sales for the company (and of earnings for the salesman). The salesman's activities include both level of activity and the allocation of time and effort between the different product lines.

In this model four major determinants of salesman's activities are considered:

1. The behaviour assumptions designed to explain how the salesman reacts to financial incentives.

2. The salesman's motivation which is directly related to the compensation scheme used by the firm (as well as to nonfinancial incentives).

3. The salesman's perceptions of the sales response functions in his territory to his selling time which are continuously revised as the salesman gets results from his territory and interacts with it. There seem to be rational arguments to support both the presence and the absence of a time lag between the moment some results are known to the salesman and the moment when his perceptions are changed. Since the salesman is constantly interacting with his territory, he may be sensitive to economic trends and may therefore adjust his behaviour to the new situation rapidly. Alternatively, it may be argued that he may have a tendency to rely on his past experience and to take changes as unusual and temporary until they have lasted or sufficient length of time. Therefore, this model takes into account the perceptions of the salesman's sales response functions both without and with a time lag of one period of time (to be defined by the model user.)

4. The salesman's expectations concerning his earnings and the way each product line should contribute to his earnings. These expectations are directly influenced by the particular features of the compensation scheme used by the company and by the salesman's sales expectations. According to motivational psychologists,[15] it seems reasonable to expect that the goals a salesman strives to achieve (level of aspiration) are closely related to his level of performance and to his expectations. The salesman's level of aspiration is in turn positively related to motivation and to results history; it is also influenced by the gap between sales expectations and actual sales results.[16]

The variables and relationships which are not explicitly considered in this model are implicitly included in the model parameters and are assumed to remain constant over the period of time to which the model applies.[17]

Application

In this empirical study the model parameters were estimated in a first stage on a test group of salesmen. In a second stage the models with estimated parameters were used for predicting sales for another group of salesmen (validation sample) assuming different behaviour patterns. These forecasts were made over a period of nearly four years, two years before (1969-70) and two years after (1971-72) a major change in the compensation scheme was introduced. Moreover, sales predictions for each model were compared with actual sales as well as with sales predictions for each model were compared with actual sales as well as with sales predictions generated by a "naive" statistical model (double exponential smoothing) which assumes no effect of financial incentives on salesmen's activities. Nine models were tested on both groups:

Model "N": "naive" statistical model

Model 1: the salesman maximizes sales (subject to his selling time constraint)

Model 2: the salesman minimizes his work to reach an acceptable income level.

Model 3: the salesman maximizes his expected gains (subject to his selling time constraint)

Model 4: the salesman maximizes his "satisfaction" (subject to a time constraint)

Models L1, L2, L3, L4: these models are the same as Models 1,2,3, and 4, but with the assumption of a lagged reaction to changes in economic conditions included.

The input data required by the model are the monthly sales results obtained by each salesman in each product line, the time available to each salesman for selling activities, the commission plan features, and the sales trends and seasonal patterns. The data used for these tests were from a few branches of a division of the International Harvester Company in the Philadelphia area. The test group consisted of twelve salesmen and the validation group of eleven salesmen. In this company's division, the salesmen had to allocate their time between selling three major product lines. Two types of salesmen were involved: account salesmen selling to a few large accounts, and retail salesmen selling to smaller accounts in a sales territory. Before 1971 retail salesmen were compensated with a salary plus commissions on sales (same commission rate for the three product lines). Account salesmen were compensated with a salary plus a bonus which was a complex function of sales and expenses. At the beginning of 1971 both plans were replaced by a unique plan for both types of salesmen. It included salary, commissions on sales and profits (different rates for each product line), and a bonus based on salesman's sales and profits. The selling time available to each salesman was estimated from company records; seasonal and economic activity indices were directly derived from industry sales.

Results for the Year Following the Change

The analysis made on the test group of salesmen led to the identification of two groups of salesmen. The first group could be characterized as having a low income elasticity of leisure. For this group variations in sales and in income were both positively related to expected variations in income. An increase in the remuneration level seemed to motivate these salesmen to work harder. Thus, assume, for instance, that a salesman in this group could have expected a 20 percent increase in his income with the new compensation scheme (if he had sold the same amount as the year before). Then. he would have taken this opportunity to work harder than before and to increase his sales by about 85 percent and his own income by 66 percent.

The second group of salesmen could be characterized as having a high income elasticity of leisure. For this group expected variations in income were positively related to actual variations in income, and negatively related to variations in sales. These salesmen chose to work less than before (and therefore sold less), but still realized an increase in income. In the same instance as before, if a salesman in this group could have expected a 20 percent income increase after the new compensation scheme was introduced, he would have chosen to decrease his sales by about 12 percent but still managing to increase his income by about 5 percent. Conversely, these salesmen reacted to a decrease in their expected income by increasing sales, but not enough to catch up with their previous income level. Both groups of salesmen could then be characterized as "satisfaction maximizers."

Results for Other Years

It was found that the nine models applied on any period of time had statistically different performances. The model where the salesman is assumed to minimize his effort to reach some acceptable level of income (Model 2) gave the best results before the compensation plan change for the overall period after the change (except for the year following immediately after the change of compensation plan) and for the whole period under consideration. This is why two new models (Model 5 and L5) were introduced in the analysis at this point. Models 5 and L5 are a mixture of Modeles 2 and L2 for the year 1969, 1970 and 1972 where no change in compensation plan occurred, and of Model 4 and L4 for the year 1971 where the change in compensation plan took place. From a behavioral point of view, such models have the following implications: generally, each salesman has in mind (consciously or not) a certain income level he wants to reach, given a specific remuneration scheme which is offered to him. Then he *adjusts his level of activity* to reach this income. When the remuneration structure is altered, the salesman reconsiders the amount he wants to earn and consequently readjusts his effort (so as to reach his highest possible level of "satisfaction").

When the analysis was repeated on the eleven models, as could be expected, Model 5 fitted the data better than all other models for the whole period under consideration.

Results Obtained from the Validation Sample

The eleven models were tested on the validation sample data according to the same procedure which was used on the test sample. However, this time, the relevant parameter values estimated from the *test* sample were used. The results obtained from the validation sample have shown significant consistency with the results obtained from the test sample. More importantly, Model 5 performed better than all other models before and after the change in compensation plan and for the overall fit. The fact that Model 5 performed better than Models 2 and 4 shows that the same behavioral patterns found in the test sample could also be found in the validation sample. Moreover, the two groups of salesmen with different income elasticities of leisure were also identified in the validation sample.

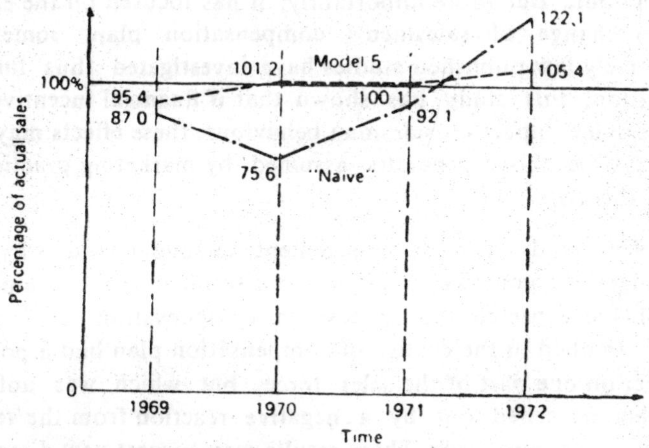

Figure 1. Total sales forecasts with Model 5 and with the "naive" statistical model (as percentages of actual sales)

Finally, Model 5 was used to forecast total sales, knowing the proportion of salesmen falling in each group (45 percent

in group 1 and 55 percent in group 9). Figure 1 gives the total sales forecasts expressed as a percentage of actual sales generated by Model 5 and by the "naive" statistical model for the period 1969-1972. It can be seen that Model 5 always gave better predictions.

Conclusions

These results show that Model 5 has a higher predictive value than the simple "naive" statistical model. Taking into account the different variable included in the model certainly improves the forecasts. Furthermore, the previous analysis suggests that the model gives at least a partial explanation of how the salesmen have reacted to the changes in financial incentives in this particular case study.

This study has provided additional evidence to support the proposition that financial incentives have some effect on human behaviour. But more importantly, it has focused on the effects of a change of salesmen's compensation plan, something relatively few published studies have investigated thus far. In addition, this study has shown that if financial incentives do have some impact on salesman behaviour: these effects may not always be those generally assumed by marketing practioners and theorists.

This study helped management to understand why the changes in compensation plans failed to increase the company's profits as expected: the increase in compensation level which was implied in the change of compensation plan had a positive effect on one part of the sales force, but which was unfortunately cancelled out by a negative reaction from the second part of the sales force. These results may suggest new directions for recruiting salesmen displaying desirable patterns.

In addition to the obvious restrictions imposed by this special case, some additional limitations should be pointed out: the study has shown that in the case of one specific sales force, salesmen reacted to change in compensation plan *as if* they had followed a specific behavior pattern. Since behaviour patterns have been inferred rather than observed, no definite conclusion can be drawn as to what the behaviour pattern actually *are*. Relating such results to salesmen's attitudes toward money incentives is another possible direction for further research.

NOTES

1. John U. Farley, "Optimal Plan for Salesmen's Compensation," *Journal of Marketing Research*, (May 1964), pp. 39-43.
2. Richard C. Smyth, "Financial Incentives for Salesmen," *Harvard Business Review*, 46 (Jan.-Feb. 1968), pp. 109-17.
3. Rene Y. Darmon, "Salesman Behaviour and Compensation Structure," in Ronald Curhan (ed.), *Combined Proceedings* (Chicago: American Marketing Association, 1974), pp. 503-8.
4. Charles S. Goodman, *Management of the Personal Selling Function* (New York: Holt, Kinehart and Winston, 1971), pp. 383.
5. Robert L. Opsahl and Marvin D. Dunnette, "The Role of Financial Compensation in Industrial Motivation," *Psychological Bulletin*, 66 July 1966), pp. 96-118.
6. W.F. Whyte, *Money and Motivation* (New York: Harper, 1955), p. 1.
7. J.S. Adams, "Toward an Understanding of Inequity," *Journal of Abnormal and Social Psychology*, 67 (November 1963), p. 422-36.
8. Davin Mayer and Herbert M. Greenberg, "What Makes a Good Salesman," *Harvard Lusiness Review*, (July-August 1969), pp. 119-125.
9. See for instance Leon Winer, "The Effect of Product Sales Quotas on Sales Force Productivity," *Journal of Marketing Research*, 10 (May 1973), pp. 180-3.
10. David C. McClelland, "Money as a Motivator: Some Research Insight," *The McKinsey Quarterly*, (Fall 1967), pp. 10-21.
11. Same as footnote 9.
12. Douglas McGregor, *The Human Side of Enterprise* (New York: McGraw-Hill, 1960).
13. Same as footnote 9.
14. Kelvin Lancaster, *Introduction to Modern Microeconomics* (Chicago: Rand McNally, 19[illegible]9).

15. See for instance E.A. Locke and J. F. Bryan, "Grade Goals as Determinants of Academic Achievement," *Journal of General Psychology*, 79 (October 1968), pp. 219-28.

16. See for instance Kurt Lewin, *A Dynamic Theory of Personality: Selected Papers* (New York: McGraw-Hill, 1935).

17. A more detailed analytical formulation of this model as well as a more complete account of the following application can be found in Rene Y. Darmon, "Salesmen's Response to Financial Incentives: An Empirical Study," *Journal of Marketing Research*, 11 (November 1974), pp. 418-26.

7

Retraining the Experienced Salesperson

JOHN J. WITHEY

Introduction

Salesmen never receive enough training. Regardless of amount of selling experience, updated training is always necessary. As the selling process, indeed, as the entire marketing process, becomes more dynamic, the need for continuous training of salespeople will accelerate.

Modern sales organizations realize the importance of continuous training. Retraining activities are viewed as a vital contributor to profit increases. As a result, a growing number of sophisticated and effective programes for retraining the experienced salesperson are being developed.

A large portion of the expanding interest in retraining efforts can be traced to a rapidly changing sales environment. New and dramatic developments characterize virtually every

Editor's Note: Previously unpublished material prepared especially for this collection.

major industry in the world. New and more technically oriented products are appearing in both the industrial and consumer goods sectors; new methods of collecting and using sales related information appear almost continually; new types of selling tools and selling situations are common-place. These and other developments demand continuous re-education on the part of salespeople.

Training programmes aimed only at the newly hired salesperson are unable to prepare that person for sales environments and circumstances that have not yet evolved. As recently as 1969, Cundiff and Still reported survey results of 500 purchasing agents of which sixty percent felt that majority of salesmen calling on them either had never learned or had forgotten how to sell![1]

The importance of retraining activities is directly proportional to the degree of change occurring in the marketing environment. A current example of this relationship is taking place in the food-distribution industry. Retail food outlets are consolidating, forming larger, multiunit chain operations. These chain outlets, including both supermarkets and restaurants, are changing traditional purchasing procedures. Centralized buying, concentrating purchases on a few multiproduct suppliers, simultaneous product line planning for an entire group of retail outlets, standardizing mark-ups at a fixed percent above supplier costs—these are but a few changes, all being administered by increasingly better educated and highly professional purchasing agents doing business from plush offices in downtown highrises located in large metropolitan cities. This is quite a switch from the kitchen-door order-taking done by numerous small vendors and even more numerous mom-and-pop food service operator owners. Clearly an up-to-date set of selling skills are prerequisite for sales success in the food-distribution industry.

In most industries change is a constant phenomenon and retraining really means continuous training. Gardener-Denver Corporation was perhaps a pioneer in putting this philosophy into practice. In 1966 this heavy equipment manufacturer initiated a continuous training programme in which salesforce members were brought in from the field for one-week intensive training sessions. At that time, a complete cycle covering the entire force took about three years.[2]

National Cash Register Corporation also has a training programme that involves rotating salesmen between field assignments and classroom training.[3] The list of companies whose sales personnel participate in refresher courses in salesmanship is growing. Good sales managers and ambitious salespeople both recognize the need for the benefits from ongoing retraining programmes.

Attraction to sales training activities might best be measured by the amount of money committed to it. Unfortunately, published data on sales-training expenses do not separate retraining monies from training expenses for newly hired salespeople. Therefore, the amount spent solely for retraining can only be roughly estimated. *Sales Management's 1975 Survey of Selling Costs* reports the average cost of training an industrial products salesman to be $15,700.[4] For consumer products the figure is $2,350 and for the service industry $10,200.[5] If only ten percent of these amounts were earmarked for sales force retraining, the total amount committed would still be in the millions of dollars.

Selecting Salespeople for Retraining

Retraining programmes are expensive. Out-of-pocket costs for instructors' fees, supplies, accommodation for travel, food and lodging run in the thousands of dollars. In addition, the indirect costs of pulling the trainee in from the field and away from selling are significant. To help control the high costs of retraining, sales force members must be selected for whom the retraining programme will be most beneficial.

Selection of participants must not be done capriciously. Organizations engaged in designing retraining programmes should, in the early planning stages, develop a systematic procedurefor choosing members for retraining classes. Basic to any selection procedure is the criterion that all sales force members will eventually be included. Whatever scheme used should be rotational. Each man or woman will get his or her turn at being retrained. Beyond this basic criterion, there are several alternatives for picking members for retraining.

Alternative 1: Selection serves as a reward for superior performance. Company's retraining programme is offered as an incentive for individual or entire sales departments or divisions who meet and/or exceed some specified performance goal. Logic for this method seems to be that competition among sales force members for scarce positions in retraining classes is desirable. Proponents of this system also argue that dollars for retraining are spent where they will do the most good, *i.e.*, the above average performer. Retraining will make the better man better and not be wasted on the marginal members of the sales group.

Arguments in favour of using retraining programmes as performance motivators are examples of circuitous reasoning. The superior salesman may have the least need for retraining and benefit very little from efforts to retrain him. On the other hand, the below average salesman may gain a great deal from a retraining venture. By systematically excluding poorer salesmen from retraining activities, the gap between good and bad performers can only widen. It makes much more sense to structure a retraining session around a mix of participants characterized by differing levels of past sales performance.

Alternative 2: Selection serves as a punishment for below-average salesmen. This method assumes salesmen don't like retraining programmes, andthat such programmes are a necessary evil. Managers who practice this selection process usually view retraining activities as a means of last resort for a disappointing salesman. As might be expected, programmes set up under these assumptions are almost always under-budgeted, poorly administered and doomed to failure.

Alternative 3: Selection serves the convenience of the parties involved. Individual selections are made so as not to conflict with vacation or holiday periods or, more importantly, not to conflict with periods of above normal sales activity. The idea is to call the salesperson in for retraining when he is least pressured by other activities. Retailers, for example, avoid the last quarter of the year for retraining because sales force members are typically overburdened with pre-Christmas sales preparations. Many businesses avoid retraining during the summer months due to vacation schedules that create extra demands on non-vacationing salesmen. In large companies there are usually sufficient differences among sales territories in terms of seasonal demand levels so that recruits for continuous sales retraining classes can be attracted without placing undue stress on any one department or territory.

There is nothing inherently wrong with filling salesmen retraining classes in a manner most convenient to the people involved as long as the basic rules are followed. The procedure must be systematically applied from month to month or year to year and all salespeople should be included. Sometimes these constraints limit the amount of convenience a selection procedure can effectively have.

Alternative 4: Selection on the basis of seniority. Under this arrangement participation in sales training refresher courses is automatic at certain predetermined points in the salesman's career, After a given number of months or years of service, the salesman is regularly retrained and updated. Companies serious about the need for continued retraining regularly adopt this from of selection process. It is probably the most popular of any of the four alternative selection choices.

Testing the Seniority Myth

One of the underlying assumptions behind the seniority basis of choosing salesmen for participation in retraining courses is that more experienced salespersons absorb more in such courses. Theoretically, the more on-the-job experience a person has acquired, the more able that person is to comprehend new solutions and suggestions for dealing with sales problems. The theory goes on to conclude that a relatively new person, one with lesser amounts of selling experience, will retain less in a retraining course. Such an individual will have fewer sales experiences with which to relate and, consequently, will be less "tuned-in" to the messages of the instructor.

Recently the author set out to test the relationship between sales experience and performance in retraining programmes.[6] Fifty salesmen who were part of an ongoing sales training programme were studied. Men selected for study had similar job responsibilities, but with experience that ranged from six months to six years. Participants were given a series of special examinations at the conclusion of each training unit. The programme consisted of five separate units, each covering different subject matter.

The impact of sales experience on training effectiveness was measured by correlating examination scores with amounts of selling experience. Measures of correlation between performance in the training sessions and amount of selling experience were made for each of the five topics. Results of the correlation analysis appear in Table 1.

In this study, measures of correlation reveal the degree of difference in training session examination scores that is explained by differences in time engaged in field sales work. As shown in Table 1, results of the correlation analysis are similar across all five areas of salesmanship training. For every session topic approximately thirty percent of the differences found in test scores appear to be related to differences in selling experience. Squared correlation coefficients vary by only three percentage points from the highest to the lowest. Again, this means that sales experience or seniority was only able to explain about one-third of differences in ability to absorb material presented in retraining programmes. Overall, this is not a very strong relationship; varying amounts of sales experience do not seem to go very far in explaining differences in the success of retraining classes. Approximately seventy percent of test score differences were not found to be related to amount of selling experience.

Table 1. Training effectiveness and selling experience: correlation analysis

Session topic	*Correlation coefficient* r	*Coefficient of determination* r^2
Creative Selling	—.557	.31
Buying Techniques	—.529	.28
Territory Management	—.548	.30
Preplanning	—.548	.30
Overcoming Objections	—.548	.30
Overall Measure of Correlation	R=—.539	R^2=.29

F test of significance performed on the overall measure of correlation producted a value of 6.63391 at the .02 level.

Also significant in this study was the nature of the relationship uncovered between learning effectiveness and amount of past sales experience. It appears that there is an inverse or negative association between performance in sales retraining classes and selling experience. To the extent that a relationship does exist, the data imply that as time on the job increases, ability and/or willingness to respond effectively in refrèsher type trainning classes decreases. Such a conclusion is supportive of the frequently heard argument that training should be completed before habits are formed that are difficult to break.

In summary, (a) There does not appear to be a strong degree of association between the amount of time spent in a sales related position and the ability to perform in sales retraining classes; (b) The limited amounted of influence selling experience does have on learning effectiveness in sales retraining activities appears to be destructive. As sales tenure increases, learning effectiveness decreases.

Results of the correlation analysis suggest that selecting sales training participants on the basis of seniority (alternative 4) will not contribute a great deal to the overall success of the training programme. Sales training programme designers are advised to choose members for their programmes on some other basis than strictly time served the organization.

What to Teach Experienced Salespeople

Sales retraining programme content must be specific to the company. Effective retraining sessions are custom made and tailored to the individual firm and sales personnel involved. Programme content must be carefully constructed with the individual needs of the participants serving as the primary basis for subject areas included.

The case for customized sales training programmes has been made elsewhere. Conomikes has argued for "audience oriented" prorramme content.[7] He would have salespeople and even customers provide the appropriate subject areas for inclusion in retraining activities. Cundiff and Still outline a content-selecting procedure defined as difficulty analysis." Their idea is for the sales manager to "discover what difficulties his sales people are encountering in the field so that he can devise the proper training to help them overcome those problems.[8] Implementing an audience-oriented approach to developing sales retraining materials could include the following.

(*a*) *Survey of Purchasing Agents.* **Ask purchasing agents to evaluate the quality of salesmanship exhibited by salespeople who call on them. Be sure to include both large and small accounts.**

(*b*) *Survey of Salespeople.* **Determine aspects of selling that are causing sales force members difficulty. Questioning should not be done by management personnel, but instead by an outside consultant or researcher. To insure honesty and objectivity, respondents should be anonymous. Salespeople surveyed should include those with the best and poorest records.[9] One way to collect data about sales problems is simply to have the intended trainer travel with a representative group of sales people prior to the start of the training programme and observe for himself the problem areas.**

(c) *Analysis of Job Descriptions and Performance records.* Often salesman register weak performance in one or more dimensions of salesmanship merely because they are unclear about the precise nature of their job responsibilities. For example, a national food wholesaler found its accounts receivables turning over at a slower than average rate. Investigation revealed that credit and collection policies had never been formally established or enforced with the salespeople. The company's credit department did some of the collection work while salesmen were expected to assist with the rest. Salespersons were untrained for collection work, resented having to do it, were not directly rewarded or penalized for collection performance and, consequently, were not effective in their collection efforts.

In addition to job description analysis, salesman productivity analysis can also reveal necessary areas of training. Problems with call patterns, expense control, territory coverage, etc., may be identified through careful study of an appropriate set of records.

The important point is to develop content for training programmes that directly benefits the participants of the specific group to be trained. Realism and timelines are the necessary ingredients for topics included in successful retraining programmes. Content development techniques that are audience oriented result in timely and realistic subject areas.

Subject Areas

Keeping in mind the goal of company-specific programme content, it is possible to identify subject areas that in most cases cut across any well designed salesman retraining programme.

(a) *Updating of Company Sales Procedures and Policies.* As a firm or industry mature, it often becomes neccessary to change the selling approach, customer mix, territory alignments or salesman compensation package. Major changes such as these require reeducation as well as explanation. Normal sales meetings cannot accomplish this dual task. Usually required are multiple-session training seminars.

(*b*) *Usual Salesmanship Topics.* Accent or emphasize those that have been identified as particularly troublesome to programme participants. Planning or pre-approach work, making product demonstrations, how to ask and respond to questions, overcoming objections, closing the sale. etc,; any or all of these topics might be appropriate for retraining sessions.

(*c*) *Product Knowledge.* Product knowledge is certainly deserving of a prominent place in the over-all training effort of any sales organization. This dimension of training should, however, be separate from other facets training programme components. Separation of product knowledge training from other areas of training protects the entire programme from degenerating into a forum for vendors and suppliers to promote their own wares.

(*d*) *Definition and Significance of the Concept of Integrated-Marketing.*[10] Experienced sales personnel often lack a perspective the interaction between functions in the organization that together contribute to the total sales task. Special emphasis should be given to the idea of total marketing systems and the role selling activities play in their success or failure.

(*e*) *Order Processing Systems.* Crucial to retraining salespeople is to familiarize them with the order processing system operating in their organization. Salesmen need to know reasons for time delays in receiving information pertinent to order status, credit position, shipping data, etc. Salesmen should also be educated to the possible sources of error in information transmission. Most business firms are not organized so that sales personnel have any direct responsibility over order-processing activities; nevertheless, salespersons should understand the flow of an incoming order as it moves through the organization. This can best be taught simply by having each salesperson follow an incoming order through the organization from point of sale to customer's receiving dock.

(*f*) *Acquqinting Salesmen with the Logic of the Company's Inventory Policies.* Why are inventories carried at certain levels?

Why do inventory levels vary? Why are there differences in product movement rates? Why are there changes in total number of items stocked? The list of questions will only be complete when expanded by members of the training class. Such questions, largely beyond the control of class participants, deserve answers. Salespeople can only fully appreciate their role in the company when the rationale for inventory decisions is understood.

(*g*) *Interface with Traffic and Distribution Operations.* In conducting training sessions, this writer is continually surprised at the number of sales problems that are directly related to transportation or physical distribution considerations. Salesmen, especially experienced salesmen, should be taught such things as how truck routings are assigned and how loading procedures followed at the company's shipping dock effect unloading convenience at the customer's receiving location. Salesmen should know the problems of traffic management and the impact of those problems upon the job of salesman. To assist with the instruction of this area of sales retraining, traffic supervisors, warehouse managers and dispatchers might be invited guests to training sessions.

(*h*) *Expected Changes in Marketing Activities.* A final area of instruction recommended for any programme aimed at retraining experienced salesmen is simply forecasting the future. Training participants should be encouraged to speculate on such things as growth patterns in their industry, changing demands of customer groups, significant changes in product mix, changes in order processing methods and technology, etc. Each prediction is then analyzed and discussed in relation to its expected impact on sales procedures. The goal is for experienced salesmen to become aware of their changing responsibilities as the company's marketing task changes.

The above eight areas of instruction tend to be universal in well-designed salesman retraining programmes. As already specified, however, the actual curriculum will be unique to the firm and the personalities engaged in the training.

Improving Retraining Sessions

Training sessions should be conducted at a site separate from, but near, the sales office itself. A conference room in a nearby office area is a good spot to hold the sessions. Such a practice allows for the avoidance of undesirable interruptions but ermits demonstrations of problems and their possible solutions right at the point of their accurrence, if necessary. A popular procedure is to conduct training sessions near the work site, but at nonwork times, that is, evenings or Saturdays.

The best sessions are usually the seminar/discussion type but with one significant difference: seminar leaders are the participants themselves instead ot the official director or instructor. Session content becomes dependent upon the problems, actual and perceived, of the trainees. Also, as already mentioned, classroom type seminars can turn into on-the-job demonstrations if necessary. The group merely leaves the classroom and proceeds on into the sales office (as might be necessary when explaining the order processing system). This may be a planned feature of a particular session or simply occur on the spur of the moment.

The optimum number of training sessions is somewhat dependent upon the necessary content of the entire programme which will vary from company to company. Usually, however, a complete programme can be accomplished in eight sessions, each roughly three hours in length. If possible, time between sessions should be limited to no more than seven days. If more than a week elapses between training meetings, continuity is sometimes lost and effectiveness reduced. Work schedules of the participants and availability of instructional facilities will no doubt influence the time sequence of the sessions, but whatever schedule is ultimately developed, it should reflect the desire for intensity in the overall programme. Material presented-in a prior session should be retained and carried forward into the next meeting.

Group size should be limited to ten. Larger groups reduce the quality of individual interaction, a vital ingredient in this method of instruction. In a small group no member can avoid being drawn into the discussions. Participation and learning are guaranteed for every person in the class.

Standardized teaching aids are not very useful in this type of training. Conventional textbooks and standard problems arenot recommended for use in sales retraining programmes. In most instances whatever teaching materials are needed must be created by the instructor. Materiales used must be designed to fit the particular needs of the company doing the training and to fit the skill levels of the members in the training group. Important to remember is the fact that good training meetings for most salesmen do not resemble a college or even a high school classroom. The goal is to help working salespeople better cope with situations *currently* being encountered in their own work environment. Training sessions must stress the practical and solve problems that the individual participants are presently experiencing. Teaching aids, to be effective, should be developed almost on the spot to highlight particular issues.

The above comments are not meant to downplay the importance of teaching aids in sales retraining sessions. Indeed, good, well designed, to-the-point classroom aids are almost mandatory for meaningful teacher/student communication. Lectures won't work. Long case problems won't work. Films, slides and other visual tools are useful as attention getters, but unfortunately, they are usually prohibitively expensive to specifically tailor to the needs of a particular firm. Most effective is the brief "caselet or incident," addressed particular problems faced by the group. Of course, this means developing a new set of teaching aids for each firm and, in some cases, for each group within the same firm. Customized teaching aids are not overly burdensome to prepare. An instructor skilled in perceiving the unique problems and personalities of a group can easily develop appropriate teaching materials.

Experienced in conducting training sessions has revealed that an effective layout for the classroom is two long worktables separated, but facing one another. The instructor's table (not podium) is located between the work tables at either end.

Major benefits of this layout lie in the mobility afforded the instructor. Distance between instructor and individuals is minimized. Recommended instruction technique includes plenty of walking between the tables with face-to-face conversation between instructor and trainee. It should be remembered that most participants in sales force retraining groups have had little or no formal college level education. For the most part trainees are uncomfortable in classroom environments. For learning to take place, uncomfortableness must be replaced with confidence. A relatively unstructured classroom layout can assist in achieving this objective.

Effectiveness of Retraining Efforts

The relationship between sales performance and sales training is a tenuous one. Attributing changes in salesman productivity to participation in retraining programmes is largely a subjective process. In short, it is very difficult to accurately measure the contribution salesmen retraining programmes make to improvements in sales performance. Difficulties in objectively evaluating retraining activities are due to the multitude of other activities that directly or indirectly influence selling performance. Advertising expenditures, actions of competitors, economic conditions, etc., all play a role in determining the results of salesmen's efforts. The variables that influence company sales are so numerous and complex that it is impossible to isolate the solitary role enjoyed by retraining programmes.

Despite difficulties, however, management should continue to search for reliable methods of evaluating retraining effectiveness. Investments in retraining can be substantial, making it imperative that some procedure for assessing the ruturn on that investment be provided. Recommended procedures include:

(a) Experimental designs that attempt to control as many intervening variables as possible to isolate the "before and after" performance results of retrained salespeople.

(b) Oral and/or written examinations administered at varying intervals following completion of the programme. Examinations of this type typically measure retention rates of content presented in the training sessions.

(c) Rating scales that permit trainees to rank themselves and each other on attitudes toward various dimensions of selling. Ratings collected periodically measure attitude changes, degree of assimilation and acceptance of new ideas, as well as changes in feeling and biases toward one another.

Sources and Costs of Instruction

It is almost impossible to generalize about instructional sources and cost. Basically the programme developer has three instructional sources from which to choose: a specialist hired from outside the company on a consulting arrangement only; some member(s) of the firm's sales management staff; or an in-house specialist hired on a full-time basis to develop and instruct sales training programmes.

In all but the very largest organizations, the outside specialist is the best choice. The sales training consultant should assist with the programmes' planning and development as well as in its administration. Members of sales management, while closer to company sales problems and more familiar with company policy, usually don't have the skill or the time to participate in salesmen retraining programmes. The in-house training specialist can serve best as a coordinator among the numerous parties involved in a total sales retraining programme but his usefulness as a classroom instructor is limited.

Cost of instruction varies but the adage "you get what you pay for" is appropriate. Company-specific, customized programmes are more expensive than "canned" programmes. Fifty dollars a classroom hour is perhaps a reasonable rule of thumb to apply when considering an outside specialist to instruct an individualized retraining session. *Sales Management's 1975 Survey of Selling Costs* reported sales training cost increases of 9.8 percent to 13.3 percent during 1974.[11] Costs of instructional staff alone were reported as $1,000 per man in the industrial products industries and $400 per man in the consumer goods field.[12]

Summary

Key decisions in the development of sales retraining programmes are selecting participants for the programme, building appropriate programme curricula, designing programme format and evaluating programme results.

Participant selection should follow a carefully constructed plan. Crucial to whatever plan is followed is that all sales force members be included, and that some systematic, rotational pattern be employed in their selection. Choosing participants solely on the basis of seniority does not appear to significantly improve programme success.

Effective retraining programmes usually require customized subject content. While such subjects as product knowledge and salesmanship principles may be common to most retraining efforts, actual topics should be a function of the participants involved and their unique difficulties. Identification of these unique difficulties is a significant part of the planning that precedes the training sessions.

Programme format should consist of small training groups, specially developed teaching aids and much student-instructor interaction. In most cases, the best source of instruction is an outside specialist or training consultant.

Finally, attempts must continually be made to accurately measure retraining programme results. Possible procedures include before-and-after performance comparisons, periodic oral or written examinations, and rating scale techniques that measure attitude change in salespersons.

Salespeople play a vital role in any successful marketing strategy. Especially important is the experienced salesperson. His retraining must not be neglected or shortchanged. Training activities for experienced members of a sales force are deserving of upper-management attention. Marketing managers are accountable for recognizing the continuing need of their sales force to be updated through formalized retraining programmes. Marketing and selling situations are never static. Successful salespeople are those who adapt to constantly changing circumstances. Retraing programmes serve as a catalyst in this adaption process.

NOTES

1. Richard R. Still and Edward W. Cundiff, *Sales Management: Decisions, Politics and Cases*, 2nd ed. (Englewood Cliffs, New Jersey: Prentice-Hall, 1969), p. 238.
2. Leslie Rich, "The Ins and Outs of Sales Training," "*Dun's Review and Modern Industry*, 88 (August 1966), p. 35.
3. *Sales Management*, 108 (April 3, 1972), p. 3.
4. "1975 Survey of Selling Costs," *Sales Management* (January 6, 1975), p. 54.
5. *Ibid.*
6. Results of the author's study appear in *Sales Management* (August 4, 1975), p. 93.
7. George Conomikes, "What Kills Sales Training in the Field?," *Sales Management*, 97 (July 15, 1966), pp. 115-119.
8. Still and Cundiff, *Sales Management: Decisions, Policies and Cases*, p. 297.
9. Conomikes, "What Kills Sales Training in the Field?," p. 116.
10. For a description of integrated marketing, see: Philip Kotler, *Marketing Management: Analysis, Planning and Control*, 3rd ed. (Englewood Cliffs, New Jersey: Prentice-Hall, 1976), pp-14-16.
11. "1975 Survey of Selling Costs," p. 54.
12. *Ibid.*, p. 55.

8

Products and Market Controls

MARKETING as a separate corporate function was reorganised much later than the other functions. In the initial stages of industrial development of a country, the manufacturing or production function was considered most important. At the manufacturer had to keep account of his money transactions, the importance of the accounting function was recognised. As his production increased, he had to employ more and more labour and he soon discovered that to deal with labour and to motivate them, special skills were called for and thus was developed techniques of labour management and human relations. Purchasing became an important function as the cost of new materials and components had a direct bearing on the selling price and it was only with careful control of the costs of raw materials and components could competition be met.

As industrial production in the modern economies started pouring out goods and as competition among manufacturers of similar products increased, the business executive realised that consumption was not automatic and consequently selling of marketing assumed great importance, When goods were not being sold and finished goods inventories started piling up, the manufacturer complained of "overproduction" and started to cut back on production. This so-called overproduction existed

Report of Seminar on Marketing Policy and Research, APO, Tokyo.

even when the large majority of the population did not enjoy even the very necessities of living. The manufacturer did not realise that it was not "overproduction" of goods that was the problem but "underproduction" of markets. It was not realised that *just as raw materials*, labour and capital can be moulded to produce products for sale, people, their needs and wants and purchasing power can be moulded to create markets to absorb the so called "overproduced" goods.

We can attribute to Henry Ford the credit of being the first businessman to conceive the idea of creating markets when he set the minimum salary of a Ford employee as $ 5.00 a day to enable every worker to purchase a car for his own use. He thus combined a sound wage policy with enabling every worker to be a consumer. In other words, he created his own markets.

The creation of markets and the concept of marketing as a separate corporate function thus assumed importance first in America soon after World War II and later in Europe and during the last few years in Japan. The creation of the European Common Market is a good example where markets are created by free interchange of capital and skills with the simultaneous breakdown of artificial trade barriers so that employment and markets are at peak levels.

There is one overriding consideration which focuses on the importance of marketing. While all the functional areas can be considered as within management discretion, the market is one area where management has no veto power. Markets consist of people who have free discretionary spending income and they buy the product or service which is offered at the right place and at the right price, and at the right time. Since markets are the life blood of one's business, it follows that the company must serve this area of market opportunity and that the strategy and tactics of the firm must be market oriented.

In the early stages of industrial development, a company fixed its production facilities first and adjusts all the other functional activities around it. Marketing, or sales which was the original term for it, was considered as something taking place after the product was manufactured and sent to the warehouse. Sales was considered as the transfer of a product which the user wanted for which he was willing to pay in money. But with rapid industrial development and the user being faced with the choice of a variety of products, the stress was no longer only on manufacturing. Marketing dominates the scene and all the functional activities are concentrated on the company getting a lion's share of the market.

The 'functional' mix is adjusted for maximisation of the market opportunities. For instance, and personal policy of the company would have a bearing on motivating the sales staff to give their best. In recruiting salesman and compensating them, due regard must be had to the fact they will be out on the field and separated from their families for a considerable period each month. For the efficient conduct of the marketing activities through a budgetary control system, the full cooperation of the accounting department is necessary. The purchasing function as well as production targets are directly related to the sales forecast made by the marketing department. All this clearly demonstrates the close inter-relationship of the various functional activities and the determination of a proper mix of them for operation at a high level of efficiency.

Just as a proper "functional mix" is needed for maximising the output of the company, a proper "marketing operation. Let us now examine what constitutes this marketing mix and how the mix is to be adjusted.

The marketing operation comprises of (a) Marketing elements and (b) Marketing activities or functions. The marketing elements are:

1. The product:

    (a) Consumer goods

    (b) Industrial goods

    (c) Utilities

    (d) Services

2. The package
3. The price

The various activities or functions in the marketing department are centered around these elements, and they can be classified as follows:

1. Selling
2. Distribution
3. Advertising
4. Merchandising
5. Promotion
6. Servicing

Besides these, there are two important functions which are necessary for an efficient marketing system. They are:

(a) Effective Communication

(b) Marketing Research

Without effective communication to and fro, the marketing system would break down quickly and confusion would set in. Marketing research provides an effective tool to management to locate areas of trouble and to take effective measures to counter it. These two functions help to keep marketing work smoothly and healthily. What every marketing man must realise, and this is of very great importance, is that all the elements and functions are present in every marketing situation. The most elementary form of marketing is vending or hawking. For example, we see people hawking cigarettes on the streets. They sell a few packets of cigarettes per day their selling is limited both *in space and time*. But marketing encompasses all the elements and functions mentioned above and these are to be found in every marketing situation and extend both the space and time.

Whenever a marketing problem arises, the marketing manager must clearly understand the problem and be able to isolate the problem from the apparent ones. Having understood the problem he them examines which of the elements and functions of marketing are concerned with the problem and adjust the "mix" of these suitably to arrive at a solution which would attain the objectives of the marketing division. He might have to have a little more of some and less of an other to arrive at the proper mix. This concept is known nowadays as the "Total Marketing Concept" and the "Marketing Mix." The context could be well understood if we refer to an actual case.

Steuben Glass Company

Steuben Glass Company were manufacturers of high quality glassware for decoration, presentation and as pieces of art. They were usually heavy pieces of glassware consisting of vases, bowls, and plates with intricate etchings on them, the motifs being chosen from world renowned works of art. The prices of the glassware ranged from a minimum of about Rs. 500 to about Rs. 25,000. In the early 1950's, Steuben Glass were being sold in America through about 3,000 outlets including department stores, jewelery shops, gift shops and others. They were advertised on all national media including newspapers, magazines, radio and TV. The sales of Steuben Glass, however. started to decline. The President of the company got worried and decided to get rid of the Director of Marketing and engage a new Director. The new Director after taking over, studied the problem and reduced it to the following simple analysis:

1. The product is a high-priced quality product bought as a status symbol and suitable for gifts and as a presentation item.
2. The average American family was not a buyer of these products.
3. By selling through all possible outlets, the product was getting a "cheap" brand name.

4. Advertising it through all possible media also created a "cheap" brand image.

The new Director of Marketing reduced the number of outlets from 3,000 to 500, chose only one good store in every town, and restricted the advertising to a few selected media aimed at the richer class. After these changes, there was a distinct improvement in sales and it started to go up. In this case, the marketing "mix" chosen was advertising and distribution. By "mixing" them in the right proportion the objective was achieved.

In other problems, more of the mix may have to be used; sometimes a product change may be called for, or a price alteration. Merchandising methods may have to be changed, special promotions arranged or new packaging adopted. As marketing is a dynamic situation, the marketing manager must be constantly on his alert and have a "Total Marketing Concept". The direction that Marketing should take therefore to see that the firm is engaged in integrated production (creation of utility) to serve most profitably an are of market opportunity, in other words, the objective of the whole system of action is maximum impact at the point of ultimate sale to precipitate purchase action within the boundary of optimum cost and revenue relationships.

Control

To maximise the results, it would be necessary to establish controls so that all activities are so directed to achieving the objectives. There are many definitions of control and one of the best definition is by Henry Fayol the French industralist who lived over 50 years ago. His definition was: "The control of an undertaking consists of seeing that everything is being carried out in accordance with the plan which has been adopted the orders which have been given, and the principles which have been laid down. Its object is to point out mistakes in order that they may be rectified and prevented from occuring again." The mistake he refers to means an error in action, opinion or judgement; a misconception or misapprehension.

So control, like the other elements of management, deals exclusively with people. It does not deal with inanimate objects. When we talk of control, we are talking of reviewing and analysing the performance of people.

Control is closely related to delegation. Responsibility has to be delegated as the tasks of marketing today are very complex and have to be performed by a large number of people both on the line and staff side. Control can take two forms. The first type of control that you find in a large number of companies especially the small and medium ones is the activity control. The activity of the salesman for instance, the number of calls he makes per day, week or month, the number of orders be books, number of days he is on the road are all controlled by the daily, weekly and monthly reports he turns in. The sales manager studies these reports and if the salesman falls behind in his activities he is asked to explain. This form of control is easy to operate and follows.

But while this may give a qualitative picture of the salesman, his character, habits and performance, yet it does not give a quantitative measure of whether the salesman is helping towards the objectives of the sales department which is to achieve (a) a large sales volume (b) a high net profit and (c) continued growth. The salesman can make a number of calls on prospects without resulting in sales or he may make a few cells, which can bring in a large sales volume. The activity type of control therefore does not give any indication of whether the company's objectives are being related.

The second form of control which is a better measure of performance and which is increasingly being adopted by a large number of companies is the budgetary form of control. The budgetary control if properly planned and administered, can give a realistic picture of the company's day by day position in relation to its objectives.

The sales budget starts with a realistic sales forecast. The marketing department, after a thorough study of its past years' performance and general economic and business conditions makes an estimate of its next year's sales. This estimate is broken down into quantity and value and assigned areawise, productwise and sales personnel wise. The targets are set for reasonable periods in terms of sales volume. The expenses to be incurred to achieve these target are also set forth so that the budget in effect consists of credit and debit side. A proforma is made up for the sales department and a close watch is kept on the budget and at regular intervals the performance is compared with the target and variances are noted. The variance is the indicator for the need for corrective action.

While the budgetary form of control is in closer relationship to the objectives of the marketing department than activity control, it lays very little stress on the activities of the salesman as long as he meets his targets. Yet there are certain activities in the marketing department which is not measurable in the budgetary system. Missionary selling, sales promotion, new cells, service calls, etc., are very necessary for the continued growth of the company even though they do not result directly in sales volume and profits. These activities can only be controlled by the activity control method. Hence a judicious mixture of both activity and budgetary control is necessary for the efficient operation of the marketing function.

We might thus say that for maximising the output of a company, a proper "functional mix" is necessary and for attaining the objectives of the marketing department which is (a) large sales volume (b) high net profit and (c) continued growth, a proper marketing mix is needed operating under a Total Marketing Concept and the control measures to be adopted to attain the objectives is a proper blending of activity and budgetary forms of controls.

Pricing Policy

Price may be considered a vehicle for moving the product. Therefore, the price of the product must be shaped according to the realities of the market, the competitive nature of the area in which we are working and the demand level of the group we are trying to sell. Convenience in use, modern and scientific packaging, design and application features, quality refinements, availability. etc., all these have a strong influence on the pricing policy.

A pricing policy in general is based on 3 simple objectives:

(a) To market the goods

(b) To recover the cost

(c) To generate reasonable return on investment.

Pricing policy is one of the complex problems of marketing. Many factors are to be considered before a decision is made about the price. Let us approach this problem from the product angle.

1. Identical Products

Considering first the identical competitive products which permit little in the way of differentiation between one product and another, a careful study of the various important factors is very essential to determine the the price *viz*:

(a) A distribution channel in the market concerned: Whether conventional distribution channels to be passed or circumvented. If so, to what extent.

(b) Price of the identical competitive products in the market and their availability in that particular area.

(c) The supply/demand situation of the new brand of product in terms of the entire market.

2. A Unique Specsalized Product

Products that offer highly specialized services, like transistor, multi-mixer, etc., tend to become common amongst the particular class of society that can afford to possess them. Soon at one stage or the other, the demand will tend to diminish, unless there is an exclusive improvement in the commodity. All these commodities would have been made at a great cost in production and this would have to be recovered. Therefore, by and large, in situations like this, an initial high price policy is followed. However, this high price policy and the period of maintaining the high price are to be decided after taking into consideration other important aspects, *viz*:

(a) Lead time, anticipate before completion places a similar product on the market.

(b) Projected volume in terms of units at various price levels and the effect of these volume price relationship or total profit.

(c) Financial position of the company *i.e.* its ability to finance the marketing and manufacturing of the new product on the basis of future earnings.

3. Highly Stylized Products

Pricing policy for highly stylized new products is a cautions and careful decision. These products have a high prestige or snob value and have to be catered to a particular section of higher society only as otherwise their prestige value will be lost. In such cases a high price policy is followed so that these products are only within the reach of the higher strata of society. There is yet another facet. that when these types of commodities become common very soon, they have to be added with new attractions, like new gadgets, new features, etc. Therefore, 'low price' is not an advantageous strategy here as it would be with other commodities. The 'high price' will continue as long as the 'intensive advertising effect' holds on. Therefore, without intensive advertising, the demand cannot be sustained and accordingly the 'high price' also will not be able to continue for long,

Other Considerations

Another aspect of 'pricing' is when and how to change the price. While announcing the price changes, however, the following points have to be considered carefully;

(a) Has the announcement been properly timed to synchronise with 'peak demand period.'

or

(b) Has it been made in the face of a still completion.

(c) Has the change been made to coincide with festivals and seasonal changes.

A careful consideration of the timing of the 'price change' will help to explain the reasons to the trade and the consumers.

A change in price becomes effective only after an interval of time. It also depends whether the change has been for a higher price or a lower price, and it also depends, as has earlier been stated, on the type of the product. Normally it takes a longer time for a lower price change to become effective as in the case of food products and highly stylised products, because the doubt about standard of quality plays on the consumers' minds for some time till they are convinced that the price has been lowered due to increased sales, or as an incentive or whatever effective explanation is provided for to the consumer. By and large, much depends on how convincingly the announcements are made, and what reasons are offered as an explanation for the price change, be it lower or higher.

Other considerations for price change are trade discounts, cash discounts, and maintenance of prices at the stockists/wholesalers/retailers' levels. Also credit facilities influence the price structure and the price will usually be higher in such a case.

9

Role Clarity and the Salesman

JAMES H. DONNELLY, JR. AND JOHN M. IVANCEVICH

One of the major causes of job tension is a lack of *role clarity*; that is, either the non-existence of information needed to do his job effectively, or the lack of adequate information, leaves the worker with an ambiguous perception of his role.[1] It has been shown that a lack of role clarity increases the probability that a person will be dissatisfied with his job, will experience psychological stress (job tension), will seek opportunities for improving clarity and satisfaction, will be less innovative, and will generally show a lack of job interest.[2] While different groups within the same organization may experience different amounts of role clarity, there appear to be several factors associated with the sales position that make it more susceptible to a lack of role clarity than other positions in the firm.

First, the salesman must often perform with *inadequate* or *non-existent* information. This can occur in his relationships with customers as well as with his company. In many instances he lacks clear-cut knowledge of his customers' needs or has little indication of whether or not they are interested in his

Editors' Note: Reprinted from *Journal of Marketing*, January 1975, pp. 71-74 published by the American Marketing Association.

proposals, whether their potential business is worth his time and effort, or what the probability of making a sale is. Within the company, the salesman often is not provided with adequate information concerning his performance. This lack of performance feedback has long been a bone of contention between salesmen and their managers.[3]

Second, most salesmen occupy a *boundary position*—one that requires much crossing of boundaries between departments within organizations. Such positions are very likely to exhibit a lack of role clarity.[4] The salesman's boundary position in relation to his customers is obvious. However, he is also frequently required to coordinate his activities with other departments within his own firm (*e.g.*, production). Often information necessary to achieve this coordination is not provided, and conflict results between different functional areas of the firm.[5]

Finally, the salesman's occupation might be called *semi-innovative.* Most salesman are required to develop new business, and much of their workday is relatively unstructured. Innovative roles are very susceptible to a lack of role clarity. This is because innovative personnel are often expected to seek a change in the status quo which other elements of the firm are attempting to maintain, and the information to perform this role effectively is usually nonexistent.[6]

Despite the fact that the selling role is highly conducive to a lack of role clarity in most firms, the sales occupation has seldom been the subject of research that focused on role clarity and emotional reactions to it. In the study reported here, the authors sought to empirically test the question of role clarity as perceived by sales force members, both in terms of its effect on several job-related factors and its importance for salesmen as compared with another group in the organization. The results reveal that greater role clarity may lead to better job performance.

The Study

The present study examined perceived role clarity among a group of salesmen and related it to five specific job-related factors. Previous research conducted on role clarity in various organizational settings provided the working hypotheses that were tested in the present study.[7] These hypotheses were as follows.

Greater role clarity among salesmen is associated with:

1. More job interest
2. More opportunity for job innovation
3. More job satisfaction (specifically, more autonomy, esteem, and self-actualization satisfaction)
4. Less job tension
5. Less propensity to leave the organization

The data in the study were obtained in a medium-size manufacturing firm with two plant locations. The salesmen were required to possess detailed knowledge about the product. and they operated with little or no direct supervision. Each salesmen had a great deal of opportunity for innovation since he, in effect, served as a consultant to prospective customers.

For comparison purposes another occupational group (first-line production supervisors) in the same firm was also studied Both of the groups were at the same level in the organization. A total of 86 salesmen and 48 production supervisors provided the data presented here.

Definitions

The six key variables in the study were defined as follows:

(*a*) *Role clarity*—the extent to which required information is communicated and understood.

(*b*) *General job interest*—the overall interest a person has in his work.

(*c*) *Opportunity for job innovation*—the opportunity a person has in performing his job to try out his own ideas.

(*d*) *Job satisfication*—viewed as a multidimensional phenomenon. In this study it was defined as the individual's satisfaction with three distinct job satisfaction facets: autonomy, esteem, and self-actualization.

(*e*) *Job tension*—the frequency of being psychologically bothered by work-related matters.

(*f*) *Propensity to leave*—the inclination or disposition to leave the job.

Six indexes were developed for each participant based on his responses to questionnaire items designed to measure each variable. In developing each index, the authors borrowed from previous research.[8] Samples of the questions used to measure each variable and develop the indexes are provided in Table 1.

Table 1. Samples of questionnaire items used to develop indexes for role clarity and five job-related factors

---

I. *Role Clarity Index*—determined from five questions composed of five alternative responses that were scored on a 1 to 5 scale as follows:

(Not clear at all) 1 2 3 4 5 (Perfectly clear)

1. How clear are you about the limits of your authority in your present job?

2. Do you feel you are always as clear as you would like to be about what you have to do on your job?

3. Do you feel you are always as clear as you would like to be about how you are supposed to do things on your job?

II. *General Job Interest Index*—determined from three questions with five alternative responses that were scored on a 1 to 5 scale as follows:

(Contd.)

1. **On most days on your job, how often does time seem to drag for you?**
   (About half the day or more) 1 2 3 4 5 (Time never seems to drag)
2. **Some people are completely involved in their job—they are absorbed in it night and day. For other people, their job is simply one of several interests. How involved do you feel in your job?**
   (Very little involved) 1 2 3 4 5 (Very strongly involved)

III. *Opportunity for Job Innovation Index*—determined from four questions with five alternative responses that were scored on a 1 to 5 scale as follows:

1. **How often do you try out, on your own, a better or faster way of doing something on the job?**
   (Rarely or never) 1 2 3 4 5 (Once a week or more)
2. **How often do you get chances to try out own ideas on the job, either before or after checking with your supervisor?**
   (Less than once a month) 1 2 3 4 5 (Several times a week or more)

VI. *Job Satisfaction Indexes*—the three job satisfaction facets were measured by a total of nine questions with six alternative responses that were scored on a 1 to 6 scale as follows:

(Strongly disagree) 1 2 3 4 5 6 (Strongly agree)

Autonomy

1. **My job allows me to set goals and objectives.**
2. **My job is very challenging.**

Esteem

1. **My job is important to the success of the company.**
2. **My job is viewed as important by employees working in other parts of the company.**

Self-Actualization

1. **My job provides me with the opportunity to grow and utilize a wide range of my skills.**

(Contd.)

2. My job provides me with the opportunity to prepare myself for future advancement in the company.

V. *Job Tension Index*—determined from nine questions with five alternative responses that were scored on a 1 to 5 scale as follows:

(Never) 1 2 3 4 5 (Nearly all the time)

How often do you feel bothered by:

1. Being unclear on just what the scope and responsibilities of your job are?
2. Not knowing what opportunities for advancement or promotion exist for you?
3. Not knowing what your immediate supervisor thinks of you, how he evaluates your performance?

VI. *Propensity to Leave Index*—determined by scoring the alternative responses to the following question:

If you were completely free to choose, would you prefer to continue working in this company, or would you prefer not to? Check one.

Prefer to work in this company	Undecided	Prefer not to work in this company

Note: The coefficient alpha measure of reliability was determined for Indexes I-V. The coefficients ranged from .76 to .93, which indicates acceptable levels of reliability for research of this type. See J.C. Nunnally, *Psychometric Theory* (New York: McGraw-Hill Book Co. 1967), Chap. 6.

These questions have been provided for illustrative purposes only. Editorial convenience required some abbreviation. Interested readers may contact the authors for a copy of the complete questionnaire.

Results

Table 2 presents the tests of the various hypotheses and indicates support for each one. It shows that, for the salesmen, the correlations for all indexes and role clarity are statistically significant. This means that the greater the role clarity present, the greater the job interest, the opportunity for innovation and job satisfaction, and the less job tension and propensity to leave. The most substantial association is between role clarity and autonomy satisfaction. Note that only the salesmen showed significant associations between role clarity and opportunity for job innovation and the three job satisfaction facets.

Table 2 also indicates that the associations between role clarity and job interest, opportunity for innovation, and the three job satisfaction facets are significantly more positive for the salesmen than for the supervisors. Thus, the data suggest that while role clarity was extremely important for the salesmen, it was also far more important for them than for the first-line production supervisors.

Table 2. Correlations of role clarity index with selected variables for salesmen and production supervisors

Index	*Salesmen* $n=86$	*Supervisors* $n=48$
General job interest	.39[b]	.28[a]
Opportunity for job innovation	.44[b]	.10
Job satisfaction facets		
Autonomy	.61	.10
Esteem	.54[b]	−.03
Self-actualization	.38[a]	.18
Job tension	−.36[b]	−.39[b]
Propensity to leave	−.31[a]	−.29[a]

[a]$p<.05$ [b]$p<.01$.

Note: A significance test of the correlations between the salesman and supervisors was made using Fisher's z-transformation. An underlined coefficient indicates that the salesmen's coefficient is significantly different at the .05 level from the supervisors' coefficient for that factor.

Managerial Implications

The results of this study indicate that sales managers in the company studied can increase a salesman's job interest, opportunity for innovation, and job satisfaction—while decreasing his job tension and desire to leave—by increasing the amount of relevant information he perceives as necessary to do his job effectively. Considering the importance of these job performance influences to both sales managers and salesmen, the findings clearly illustrate that failure to consider role clarity can be a crucial mistake in sales force management.

The findings indicate that salesmen need a clear understanding of the requirements of their job, what is expected of them, and the specific criteria used to evaluate them. Performance, however, is not the only area within the firm where salesmen often receive inadequate or incomplete information. Other areas frequently cited include product prices, credit policies, discount policies, delivery dates, timing of advertising and sales promotion campaigns, and competitor practices and policies.[9] It appears that providing more relevant information in all of these areas would have a significant positive impact on sales force motivation and satisfaction. Certainly, it is doubtful that a sales force characterized by how job interest, little perceived opportunity for innovation, low job satisfaction, and high job tension will be very productive

Finally, the results also suggest that salesmen are indeed different, at least with regard to role clarity, from production supervisors. The differences are evident in Table 2 and indicate that clear organizational roles are far more important for the motivation and satisfaction of salesmen.

Conclusion

There are several research studies in the organizational behaviour literature that deal with the motivational and leadership problems of such occupational groups as business managers, operating employees, hospital administrators, nurses, and government employees. However, little attention has been given

to similar problems in sales management. This study of one organization found that salesmen differed in several specific areas from first-line production supervisors in their perceptions of the importance of role clarity. Also, it appears that greater role clarity may play an important role in maximizing a salesman's job performance. Certainly, the results point to the need and potential value of more behavioural research using marketing personnel as subjects.

NOTES

1. Robert L. Kahn, Donald M. Wolfe, Robert P. Quinn, J. Diedrick Snoek, and R.A. Rosenthal, *Organizational Stress: Studies in Role Conflict and Ambiguity* (New York: John Wiley & Sons, 1964), pp. 23-25, 74.

2. A.F. Cohen, E. Stotland, and D.M. Wolfe, "An Experimental Investigation of Need for Cognition." *Journal of Abnormal and Social Psychology*, Vol. 51 (1955), pp. 291-294; Robert J. House and John Rizzo. "Role Conflict and Ambiguity as Critical Variables in a Model of Organizational Behaviour," *Organizational Behaviour and Humau Performance*, Vol. 7 (June 1972), pp. 467-505; John M. Ivancevich and Herbert L. Lyon, *Organizational Climate. Job Satisfaction, Role Clarity, and Selected Emotional Reaction Variables in a Hospital Milieu* (Office of Business Development and Government Services Monograph Series, University of Kentucky, April 1972); Kahn et. al., same reference as footnote 1; Thomas F. Lyons, "Role Clarity, Need for Clarity, Satisfaction, Tension, and Withdrawal," *Organizational Behaviour and Human Performance*, Vol. 6 (January 1971), pp. 99-110; and John Rizzo, Robert J. House, and Sidney I. Lirtzman, "Role Conflict and Ambiguity in Complex Organizations," *Administrative Science Quarterly*, Vol. 15 (June 1970), pp. 150-163.

3. William C. Dorr, "Tell a Salesman Where He Stands," *Sales Management*, May 17, 1963, p. 90.

4. Kahn et. al., some reference as footnote 1, pp. 102-103, 115.

5. Bernard M. Bass, *Organizational Psychology* (Boston: Allyn & Bacon, 1965), pp. 338-339.

6. Kahn et. al., same reference as footnote 1, pp. 126-127.

7. Same references as footnote 2.

8. Kahn et. al., same reference as footnote 1; Lyons, same reference as footnote 2; and Martin Patchen, *Participation, Achievement. and Involvement on the Job* (Englewood Cliffs, N.J.: Prentice-Hall, 1970).

9. See Richard T. Hise, "Conflict in the Salesman's Role," in *Sales Management: Contemporary Perspectives*. J. Allison Barnhill, ed. (Glenview, Ill.: Scott, Foresman & Co., 1970), pp. 48-62.

10

The Computer, Personal Selling, and Sales Management

James M. Comer

Several years ago an article entitled "The Salesman Isn't Dead, He's Different" was published.[1] It is now the sales manager's turn—he is not expendable, but he must become more sophisticated. He must learn to participate not only in the development, but also in the application, of new technology. The aggressive, knowledgeable sales manager must prepare *now* for what he soon will be required to do. One important aspect of that preparation must be a through knowledge of, and familiarity with, computer technology and the integration of the computer into his regular activities.

The purpose of this article is to review published reports of the integration of the computer into sales management planning, organizing, and control activities. This is done: (1) to demonstrate the logical, but not necessarily inevitable, progression of a firm from simple computer-based data collection and manipulation into model building; and (2) to point out

Editors' Note: Reprinted from *Journal of Marketing*, July 1975, pp. 27-33, published by the American Marketing Association.

when and under what circumstances a particular system is useful to a sales manager. This latter objective is especially important since complex computer-based systems are frequently touted as the "answer" to the sales manager's problems. Often these computer-based systems are not necessary and a less complex system will suffice, or a simple system must be instituted operated successfully *before* a more complex system can be installed.

To facilitate the review, a categorization method is suggested that divides the literature on computer applications in sales management into two general areas: (1) sales reporting and analysis systems, and (2) planning-oriented systems.

Sales Reporting and Analysis Systems

Firms have had sales reporting and analysis systems for decades. Reporting has been as informal as casual verbal exchanges or as stringent as daily written reports. Sales managers, in most cases, conducted analysis by reading call reports and comparing them with actual sales. They were then expected to draw vital conclusion about such things as salesmen abilities and performance and customer response to programmes. They were also required to make rational decisions about sales territory design, sales force size, and so on. Given these kinds of responsibilities and the expansion of sales forces over wider geographic areas, it is not surprising that published accounts in the 1960s about the innovative introduction of the computer into sales management were glowing.[2]

The enthusiasm of the 1960s waxed over the computer's ability to digest, consolidate, and reorganize data into meaningful reports. The first applications were on the analysis of sales by product, by account, and by salesman or territory.[3] They were designed to facilitate sales management *ex post facto* product, market, and territory analysis. With this capacity, the mechanical aspects of sales analysis were performed routinely for sales management.

However, routinized computer sales analysis proved inadequate in many cases. This led to the development of the next stage—a system that would produce data not only on account sales but also on salesmen call allocations. The immediate objective of such a system was to relieve sales managers of their data-matching responsibility and give them more time for certain planning activities. Such a system was SOAR (Store Objectives and Accomplishments Report).

SOAR was a computer-based salesman reporting and analysis system developed at Pillsbury Company. It covered over 500 salesmen selling some 100 types, sizes, and flavours of products in 25 regions and five zones to over 40,000 retail stores plus direct accounts.[4] The impetus for the development of SOAR arose out of such problems as salesman control and the determination of which retail stores should be called upon, and how frequently, by the sales force. In system operation, the computer prints from a master customer list a SOAR form for each account. The form contains such information as region, store name and address, dollar volume, advertising group, and the like. Each salesman receives a batch of these preprinted forms which corresponds to the accounts in his territory, with one form printed for each call the salesman is to make during a given retail selling period. The salesman then sets both dollar and quantity sales objectives, preferably by store, for the subsequent two or three-month selling period. When the salesman makes his store call, he reports day and time in hours and minutes, presentations scanned, and the results compared with the salesman's projections. The system periodically condenses these results and sends them out to the individual salesman and his immediate supervisor.

At Pillsbury, SOAR was replaced in late 1974 by REACH (Retail Achievement Report).[5] Among other things, REACH puts more emphasis on other salesman activities (such as setting up displays) and on quarterly, rather than monthly, volume goals. An interesting aspect of these modifications is that the sales department did the redesign work. Here is a case where the user, once a system had proved its worth, took over the system, adapted it, and made it his own.

SOAR, REACH, and similar systems are not the ultimate in system development. Weiss has described a direct salesman-computer communication link-up in which salesmen carry a small mobile device that instantaneously records and transmits information to a central electronic facility.[6] The picture that Weiss paints is yet to be completed, and there are many technological and human problems to be solved before it is. In the interim, sales management must clearly define its needs and role in the development of firm-wide information systems. Dodge has made a start in this direction with his enumeration of three general rules for sales management to observe in developing information systems:

1. The marketing information system should be fitted to the existing organizational structure of sales management.
2. The marketing information system should reflect the operational philosophy established for field sales. Accountability at a given organization level specifies the data parameters of output.
3. The marketing information system should be thoroughly understood and accepted by all personnel in sales.[7]

Several additional lessons have been learned in this area. For example, whenever an information system of any kind is designed and installed it must be recognized that the salesman's primary resposibility is to sell, not to collect data. Furthermore, any sales system must be useful and relevant to the people most concerned, the salesman and sales manager. Without their support and participation, the system will be useless.

Management Use of Computerized Sales Reporting and Analysis Systems

It is likely that most firms have some type of computerized sales analysis system. The question of whether the more advanced, SOAR-type system, should be adopted depends on the firm's resources and the conditions it faces in its market. This step should be taken if: (1) the firm has the technical and monetary resources to do so, (2) the market is complex and geographically extensive, (3) major decisions on sales force allocation and size are made frequently, (4) the redistribution system is complex, (5) the sales force is large and organizationlly "distant" from management, (6) the product line is broad, and (7) the probability is high that some of these conditions will exist in the next five years. Two characteristics of these conditions are important: (a) they are independent of the nature of a firm's business, and (b) it is not necessary that all conditions exist in order for a firm to install such a system.

A computer-based system, if correctly designed, serves several purposes. First, it relieves both sales managers and the sales force of many of the onerous, repetitive reporting and summarization responsibilities. Second, it permits a fuller application of management by exception. since highly specific limits on sales performance can be established and monitored. Last, the routinization of control functions permits sales management and salespeople to allocate more time to planning and sales effort.

Planning-Oriented Systems

Some of the first analytical attempts at solving such sales management problems as call allocation relied on operations research (OR) techniques.[8] These early attempts were static, limited in scope, and designed solely to solve the specific problem at hand.[9] It was soon apparent that, in the dynamic environment of sales management, OR solutions might be outmoded as soon as they were discovered. The development of flexible planning systems that had the capacity to incorporate market dynamism was a solution to the static limitations inherent in OR-type approaches. However, useful planning systems are not instantaneously developed and made operational. A variety of preceding systems, perhaps analogous to SOAR, make them feasible. For example, a fully developed salesman reporting-management analysis system fuctions as: a data source for the construction and operation of diverse aspects of the planning system, a monitoring or control device to insure salesmen observation of planning dictums, and a measurement of the validity and reliability of the underlying planning models.

To organize discussion of the various computer applications in this area, a two-way categorization has been devised: data base systems and model base systems. These two systems represent a progression in sophistication rather than a distinction; thus, this categorization is more an organizational device than an attempt to identify unique entities.

Data Base Systems

These systems rely on an aggregated or disaggregated data base for making certain sales management decisions. Normally, these data bases are but an aspect of the firm's computerized marketing information system. Sales management usually must devise its own data extraction and manipulation routines to solve its peculiar problems.[10]

In constructing a data base, the firm will use many sources both inside and outside the firm. The internal sources normally provide microdata such as customer billing records, salesmen call activities, consumer attitudes, and the like, as well as well as information on potential customers and competitive activities, and the like, as well as information on potential customers and competitive activities. Outside sources, for the most part, provide macrodata on industry performance and broad-based changes in the economy, and disaggregated microdata. The composition and construction of these data are beyond the scope of this article. What is of concern is how sales managment uses a data base system. Several examples demonstrate this use:

Prospect Identification. One firm identifies prospects for its salesmen by collating facts about sales territories from existing data, SIC information, and various product characteristics. These various data sets are combined into a matrix so that top prospects in a territory can be identified.[11]

Customer Profiles. A firm profiles each customer in its data bank. This profile includes customer features and reasons for using a competitive product. It is the feeling in this company that not only is the salesman better prepared for his calls with this kind of information, but sales forecasting and product design problems are also more easily solved when customer needs are more clearly defined.[12]

An NICB report detailed a number of specific sales management applications of a computerized data base. Some examples are: J.T. Ryerson and Son, Inc., redesigned its sales territory structure based upon marginal profit figures; Girdwood Publishing Company reorganized its sales force in both the line and staff functions; and Diamond Crystal Salt Corporation has a wide spectrum of applications, ranging from developing salesmen call policy through analyzing individual account profitability.[13]

The foregoing are some of the applications of computer technology. These applications do not relieve either sales management or field sales personnel of many deci ion-making responsibilities; rather, they organize data in such a way as to facilitate decision making. On the other hand, a model base system does, insense, substitute computerized "decisions" for personal ones.

Model Base Systems

These systems have at their heart a model or series of models for data manipulation and output generation. Often these models are designed to solve one specific class of problems or assist in making a particular type of recurring decision. Whatever the situation may be, it is the independent verified model, which manipulates data and prescribes courses of action, that distinguishes this type of system.

Work done in this area can be divided into three groups: (1) call allocation determination, (2) sales territory design, and (3) salesmen routing.

Call Allocation. Lodish, in a pioneering study, developed CALLPLAN: "an interactive computer system designed to aid salesmen or sales management in allocating sales call time."[14] The salesman or sales manager provides information for a territory on: the number of clients, prospects, and geographical subdivisions in the territory; the call length in hours; the sales response period; the effort period in months; and, for each effort period, the total number of half hours available for selling plus travel time, and the maximum number of calls to make on any account. Additional date on historical call patterns per client are used, as well as estimates of client sales response if alternative call allocations are made. Output from CALLPLAN is a series of optimal call allocations to clients and prospects by geographic area, and a comparison of estimated sales from the optimal policy with those of the present policy. Lodish reported fourteen preliminary applications of CALLPLAN. In 1974, Lodish cited additional applications of his model as part of a larger procedure for allocating sales force effort.[15]

Armstrong has also developed an interactive system (SCHEDULE) for determining optimal call policy. Like Lodish's CALLPLAN, it has the indvidual salesman or sales manager provide certain values. These values are transformed via a mathematical programming model into a suggested call allocation policy by account along with expected return for the call allocation. Armstrong cited one application of SCHEDULE with a small sales force. He did not present any statistical evidence that SCHEDULE had improved the sales force call policy, but he did interview the salesmen after they used SCHEDULE. They "agreed that SCHEDULE-prepared call allocation plan. . .were significantly better than the plans they were currently using."[16]

The present author has developed and tested a system entitled ALLOCATE, which assigns effort to subsets of customers and prospects based on their progress toward the saturation state of their response curve.[17] It is a batch-processed system designed to be used by upper-level sales management either as an input device for sales management decisions, such as sales-territory-size, or as a vehicle for determining the effect of alternative call allocation strategies on territorial revenue over multiple time periods. The author tested ALLOCATE on the sales territories of a consumer products firm that was selling through a combination of wholesalers and direct retail accounts. In the test, ALLOCATE not only surccessfully replicated salesman behaviour in selected sales territories, but also demonstrated its capacity to generate the effect of alternative call allocation strategies on revenue over time in those territories.

Sales Territory Design. Xerox Corporation developed a salesman allocation model employing a market grid approach.[18] A grid of intersecting horizontal and vertical lines is laid over a sales area, thus generating a set of cells which contain customers. Each cell must contain data on the expected number of customers, the expected revenue from each customer, and the expected number of calls per day per salesman. The model then allocates calls sequentially to the customer with the highest revenue per call value until all accounts in a cell are called on and all potential realized. Additional cells are combined until the salesman's maximum time limit is reached. This set of cells then constitutes the salesman's territory.

Hess and Samuels have developed a sales-districting model, GEOLINE, which they derived from research and application of a successful computer technique for legislative districting.[19] The model assumes an established territorial set and constructs a predetermined number of compact sales territories using an integer formulation of a linear transportation programme. The solution is not optimal, because the objective of GEOLINE is to design sales territories such that the sales activity measure among the territories is approximately equal. The sales activity measure may be territory potential, salesman workload, or some other relevant criterion. However, GEOLINE output is a set of sales territories realigned quickly, efficiently, and more accurately than by noncomputer methods. Hess and Samuels cited successful field applications by CIBA Pharmaceutical Company and the IBM World Trade Corporation. Since 1970, the system has also been put into operation in a number of pharmaceutical and oil companies.

One output of Lodish's CALLPLAN programme was an estimate of the marginal profit of an additional hour of allocated salesman effort in a territory. Lodish has used CALLPLAN and its output as a basis for the development of a sales districting model.[20] It is a mathematical programming model that is heuristically solved so that the marginal profit figures for each salesman are approximately equal. Output defines: (1) which salesmen are to be assigned to which area, (2) the number of trips to be made by the salesman to each area, and (3) the amount of time to be spent in each area. Lodish notes that five companies realigned territories using his procedure, and they felt the computer procedure made a positive contribution to the improved results.

Salesmen Routing. Truck routing and salesmen routing are part of the operations research touring problem. Several attempts have been made to develop computerized routing models for salesmen and sales management.

Lazer *et. al*. developed a simple computerized model, using Bayesian decision methodology, in which a "routining ratio" is constructed for each account on the basis of the expected value of sales from the account divided by the total time (travel, waiting, and sales) required for that account.[21] The model selects the route that maximizes the total expected value of a "trip" covering all selected accounts, subject to a time constraint. They tested their model by routing the salesmen for a wholesale liquor distributor. In the example provided, a salesman's route was improved from his selected route of $1.98 expected value per minute of selling time to an "optimum" value of $2.03.

A more complete routing system, TOURPLAN, has been developed by Cloonan.[22] TOURPLAN is a heuristic programming approach to the salesman tour problem. The TOURPLAN model employs two heuristics to arrive at an initial solution for the accounts under consideration.[23] An optimal solution is then determined using a combinatorial search routine. The system was first tested in two environments: first, in artificial territories with known and unknown optimal routings; and second, in real territories where salesman solutions were known but optimums were not. In the artificial territories, the system achieved efficiencies (ratio to optimum) of 99 percent to 100 per cent. In real territories, a 90 percent+ efficiency rate was obtained where the corresponding field salesmen were operating at about 85 percent efficiency.

Shanker *et. al.* have developed a computer-based procedure solve simultaneously the sales territory design problem and the salesman call frequency problem.[24] It combines and extends the Hess and Lodish methodologies in several aspects. Input consists primarily of management estimates of various problem dimensions combined with an integer-programming-set-partitioning algorithm. It is an optimizing programme whose solution specifies which customers should be called on by which salesman and prescribes the call frequency. A hypothetical situation was used to illustrate the effectiveness of the procedure.

Two other computer-based systems have been developed that may be adaptable for use by sales management. DETAILER, developed by Montgomery *et. al.* was designed to allocate salesman time to product promotions on a sales call.[25] However, Montgomery describes DETAILER as being used by a product manager and not sales management. Winer's system is presented as a procedure for developing optimal compensation plans.[26] However, it was degigned to determine the best salary career path for salesmen, not to optimize sales or profit generated for the firm.

Planning Systems and Sales Management

The traditions of the sales fraternity maintain that the personal selling function is strictly a person-to-person relationship and that rigorous analysis should be suspect as unrealistic and academic. Although this view is far from accurate, it is a barrier to those farsighted corporate and sates managers who have, or intend to develop, a computer-based planning system for their firms. The fears and prejudices of more traditional sales managers and salesmen must be assuaged, because an intricate system forcibly superimposed on a complex sales force can lead to permanent damage. The problem for the manager is to get the support and cooperation of the sales force and managers for system development.

Several suggestions are made:

1. It is a tenet of human relations theory that involving people in the formulation/design of a project tends to invoke commitment. So, in the system design stage, solicit salesmen sales manager participation wherever possible.
2. The development and installation of any new system, especially one such as this, is bound to cause anxiety about job loss or fears of inadequacy in dealing with the "monster". Although there is no perfect solution, familiarity can help reduce fears and anxieties. Therefore, introduce the system slowly and carefully, and hold frequent training sessions to educate your personnel in system use.
3. In tests, Lodish and Armstrong had salesmen use the systems on their own territories. Both reported salesmen conclusions that the programme allocated calls better than they could. The implication is that the salesmen developed favourable attitudes toward the system because they could, on their own initiative, construct better call routines. The message to management is clear: to maintain salesman morale when you are instituting changes using a system, whenever possible have the salesman see for himself the beneficial effects for his territory.

Planning Systems and Control

Once a firm has computerized planning systems in operation, two questions arise: "How do we know that the planned change is operating effectively?" and "How do we know when to rerun the model(s)?" Both questions reflect the necessary development of control routines to complement the planning models. The first question may be answered in two parts. First, hard criteria for performance evaluation should be established before the change is made. Examples of criteria are average sales or cost per call and aggregate territory sales or cost. Second, after the planned changes are implemented, these changes must be monitored to ensure performance. The second question may be answered either by establishing a policy of rerunning the models at regular intervals or, in the mode of management by exception, rerunning only when behaviour or events exceed certain predetermined tolerances. If management finds it is faced with consistent violations of standards, model validity may be questionable or the sales force may be playing the model instead of doing its job.

Implementing Systems

A large-scale operating system takes years to develop. Therefore, if management wishes to have a useful system available in the future, it must start *now* to develop one. Three stages in the process can be identified: appraisal, design, and implementation.

Appraisal

Most firms who use personal selling have some type of reporting and analysis system. As there is a great diversity among firms, so too is there a broad range of complexity in system design. Each firm must weigh the pros and cons and decide which course of action it should select. Some factors to consider are: (1) the present state of sophistication of the firm's planning system, (2) current and projected product and market complexity, (3) the firm's technical and monetary resources, and (4) current and predicted competitor activities. If the firm decides to extend its present system, a gradual, carefully prepared implementation programme is strongly recommended.

Design

A useful first step in system design is to identify the existing needs of your sales personnel. This can be accomplished through consultation with knowledgeable sales managers and salesmen. Succeeding steps should include an in-depth examination of the models discussed in this article to see if one or more of them is relevant, and the development of estimates of the costs and benefits of designing an original programme peculiarly suited to the present and future needs of the firm.

Before full-scale implementation can occur, designed systems must be field tested for validity and reliability. In fact, part of system design should include the establishment of routine control procedures for insuring the maintenance of validity.

Implementation

In implementing a new system, the firm should proceed carefully in step-wise fashion, adding capability only after such factors as data bases are established and users are trained, Gradual implementation may be technical in nature, progessing from the less complex to the more sophisticated: or it may progress on a geographic basis, from territory to district, region, and ultimately to the national level. Obviously, a schedule that combines geographic and technical implementation is also possible. System implementation should include procedures for involving sales managers and salesmen in the process. Formal feedback systems on problems with system operation perform two necessary functions. First, the firm can check users to be certain they are utilizing the system efficiently. Often opportunities for new applications are identified here. Second, users may not feel as threatened by the system and, in fact, may make valuable contributions if they have a question and suggestion pipeline to designers and corporate management.

Conclusions

This article reviewed published accounts of the integration of the computer into reporting, analysis, and decision making in personal selling and sales management. It was shown that, contrary to tradition, the computer has applications in this area of marketing, but so far only a few problems have been attacked beyond the routine computer-based sales reporting and analysis systems. For a firm to take that additional step requires patient development geared to the capabilities and requirements of the user. Only when the user, be it sales representative or sales manager, accepts system as relevant to his needs and integrates it into his routine can it be truly labelled a success.

NOTES

1. Carl Reiser, "The Salesman Isn't Dead, He's Different," *Fortune*, November 1962.
2. William T. Cullen, "Sales Reporting Systems," and John Lincoln, "Using the Computer for More Effective Sales Force Management," in "Marketing Harnesses the Computer," *American Management Association Bulletin*, No. 92, 1966, pp. 14-18 and 19-25. See also, Phyllis Daignault, "Marketing Management and the Computer," "*Sales Management*, August 20, 1965, pp. 49-60.
3. Cullen, same reference as footnote 2, p. 17.
4. Lloyd M. DeBoer and William H. Ward, 'Integration of the Computer Into Salesman Reporting," *Journal of Marketing*, Vol. 35 (January 1971), pp. 41-47.
5. From a conversation with Mr. William H. Ward at Pillsbury Company, Minneapolis, January 1975.
6. E. P. Weiss, "The Salesman Gets Hooked Into Information System," *Advertising Age*, June 14, 1965, pp. 84-87.
7. H. R. Dodge, *Field Sales Management* (Dallas: Business Publications, 1973), p. 28.
8. Arthur. A Brown, Frank T. Hulswit, and John D. Kettelle, "A Study of Sales Operations,"*Operations Research*, Vol. 4 (June 1956), pp. 296-308; and Clark Ward, Donald F. Clark, and Russell Ackoff,

"Allocation of Sales Effort in the Lamp Division of the General Electric Company," *Operations Research*, Vol. 14 (December 1956), pp. 629-647.

9. For a discussion of operations research and personal selling, see David Montogomery and Frederick E. Webster. Jr., "Applications of Operations of Operations Research to Personal Selling Strategy," *Journal of Marketing*, Vol. 32 (January 1968), pp. 50-57.

10. Two examples of methodologies that rely heavily on large data bases are: Walter J. Semlow "How Many Salesman Do You Need, *Harvard Business Review*, Vol. 27 (May-June 1959), pp. 126-132; and Walter J. Talley, Jr., "How to Design Sales Territories," *Journal of Marketing*, Vol. 25 (January 1961), pp. 7-12.

11. For these examples and others, the reader is referred to Thayer C. Taylor, ed., "The Computer in Marketing—Part II: Sales Force Management," *Sales Management*, March 15, 1969, pp. 71-78.

12. Same reference as footnote 11.

13. National Industrial Conference Board, "Allocating Field Sales Resources," *Experience in Marketing Management*, Vol. 23, 1970, pp. 20-34.

14. Leonard M. Lodish, "CALLPLAN: An Interactive Salesman's Call Planning System," *Management Science*, Vol. 18 (December 1971), p. 25.

15. Leonard M. Lodish, "A 'Vaguely Right' Approach to Sales Force Allocations," *Harvard Business Review*, Vol 52 (January-February 1974), pp. 119-124.

16. Gary M. Armstrong. "SCHEDULE: An Interactive Computer Programme for Determination of the Optimal Allocation of Personal Selling Effort" (Working paper, University of Illinois at Chicago Circle, 1973).

17. James M. Comer, "ALLOCATE: A Computer Model for Sales Territory Planning," *Decision Sciences*, Vol. 3 (July 1974), pp. 323-339.

18. Peter J. Gray, "Computers and Models in the Marketing Decision Process." in *Computer Innovations in Marketing*, Evelyn Konrad, ed. (New York: American Management Assn.. 1970), pp. 158-167.

19. Sidney W. Hess and Stuart A. Samuels, "Experiences with a Sales Districting Model: Criteria and Implementation," *Management Science*, Vol. 18 (December 1971), pp. 41.54.

20. Leonard M. Lodish, "Sales Territory Alignment to Maximize Profit," *Journal of Marketing Research*, Vol. 12 (February 1975), pp. 30-36.

21. William Lazer, Richard T. Hise. and Jay A Smith, "Computer Routing: Putting Salesmen in Their Place," *Sales Management*, March 15, 1970, pp. 29-35. See also James H. Donnelly and John M. Ivancevich, *Analysis for Marketing Decisions* (Homewood, Ill.: Richard D. Irwin, 1970), pp. 252-262.

22. James B. Cloonan, "TOURPLAN: A Sells Calls Routine and Scheduling Programme" (Working Paper 9-73, DePaul University, Chicago, 1973).

23. The first heuristic is developed in James B. Cloonan, "A Heuristic Approach to Some Sales Territory Problems," in *Proceedings of the Fourth International Conference on Operations Research*, D.B. Hertz and J. Malese, eds. (New York: John Wiley & Sons, 1966), pp. 284-292.

24. Roy J. Shanker, Ronald E. Turner, and Andres A. Zoltners, "Sales Territory Design: An Integrated Approach," *Management Science*, forthcoming.

25. David B. Montgomery, Alvin J. Silk, and Carlos E. Zaragoza, "Multiple-Product Sales Force Allocation Model," *Management Science*, Vol. 21 (December 1974), pp. 3-24.

26. Leon Winer and Leon Schiffman, "Developing Optimum Sales Compensation Plans with the Aid of a Simulation Model," in *1974 Combined Proceedings*, Ronald Curhan, ed. (Chicago: American Marketing Assn., 1975), pp. 509-514.

11

Functions and Facts of Advertising

S. GHOSAL

IN 1962 advertising in India was facing pressure of newspaper space. Advertising men called the year 1962 as the year of the *space squeeze.* Import restrictions on newsprint were not a new phenomenon that occurred in 1962. It had been there since 1955 but it seemed to be no more than a threat that was being magnified into a problem by unduly anxious publishing people. Actually, between 1955 and 1962, although the total quantity of newsprint imported into the country increased by nearly 50 per cent, individual publications were allowed progressively smaller quotas compared with their rising circulations. Yet during this period and particularly between 1959 and 1962, the aggregate advertising content in its ratio to editorial content rose in almost all publications and most certainly in the country's four top English ones. Without question, the year 1962 saw a deterioration in the space situation. Against the growing demand for newsprint, the ability to import diminished every day. At the same time, indigenous production of newsprint makes woeful progress, having registered less than 5 per cent increase in the four years prior to 1962 and accounting for only about 25 per cent of total consumption.

The newsprint shortage created a problem only with regard to *availability of advertising space* in just four out of about 531 newspapers and in two magazines out of nearly 7,500! All the big six are published in English, There was no shortage of space outside these six publications; there was no shortage of space in the other newspapers, weeklies, fortnightlies, Even within the press, there existed considerable room for more critical apparaisal and creative planning. But the space-squeeze in 1962 appeared to harden the feeling that *advertising must find new ways, new means, new vehicles through which to reach the consumer*. New ways, new means, new vehicles need not be found by advertising. What must happen and what had become imperative was that media which already existed has to be developed and exploited more effectively by advertising. And this not merely because it was not going to be as simple as in the past to spend the advertiser's rupee in the press but also because of the emergence of markets which the press cannot give access to. For instance, regardless of the process of urbanisation, the potential off-take by rural population in certain areas had assumed proportions that were already interesting and promised to be vast. How were we going to reach them was the question that in 1962 was asked seriously and for the first time was expecting to be answered. And for the first time such media as *billboards* with multi-sheet posters started being experimented with, on an extensive, planned and controlled basis.

A further impetus towards the *development of non-traditional media* was provided by Government restrictions on raw stock for *films*. We had to make rapidly more intelligent and efficient use of a wider range of vehicles of communication—sometimes through the printed word, may be on occasions through the original communicator. the human voice. Nevertheless, we had the media. We had billboards, we had propaganda vans. We had the booth at the mela and the itinerant squad of sandwich boys or men on stilts We had the posters and the leaflets. We had the mud-wall of a village hut. We had all these which put together in a judicious media-mix added up to a mammoth effort. *Advertising needs to find or create new media*. They exist but advertising did not need to use them because the selling need did not warrant their use. 1962 supplied the need.

Export Advertising

The need for efficient, competent advertising was nowhere more felt in 1962 than in the area of export promotion. And in this direction, advertising men continued to suffer frustration because of their inability to make any substantial or even recognisable contribution towards the promotion of Indian exports. Business groups, by and large, shared this frustration and, often tended to be overcritical of Government's tardiness, Both Government and Industry had to learn a lot in a short time. The formation of the Board of Trade was an important step toward, although the absence of a professional advertising man on it was unfortunate. Perhaps the advertising profession could have formed a non-partisan body to formulate concrete prosposals to Government on this subject of paramount in urgency.

In export promotion, the beginning that the advertising community made in the ISA (Indian Society of Advertisers) sponsored conference in New Delhi in 1961 was negatived through want of a follow-up on an industry wide basis. It has this kind of waiting for the signals that limited the image of advertising to the confines of the little league in business circles and make of it a suspect sometimes almost subversive activity in the minds of some:

The opportunity to prove the bonafides, to make arts really useful to the Government and the nation came in 1962 in a manner that none expected. Advertising men reacted to the national emergency in the same way. The results in the form of advertising that was issued bore the marks of hasty reflex action. Certainly, we have seen clearly thought-out advertising directed towards specific objectives. As the Nation as a whole recovered its balance, it was easier for advertising professionals to make more rational, effective contributions through their work. Advertising was in need of concerted, professional action in many direction, particularly in an economy like India's in which its functionst end to get obscured At almost every discussion, meeting or seminar that one attends, the question asked more than any other was '*What is the role of advertising in a controlled economy*?'

Inherent in this question is the assumption that in a protected economy, advertising undergoes a change from its functions and applications in a and fully competitive economy. At this point, it is important to remind ourselves that in all economies of the so-called free world, Government controls exist and indeed tend to expand because of the universally accepted need to relate the efforts of industry and business with national objectives and general welfare. In India, control on economic activities is more extensive and far-reaching because of the need to harness and guide available resources towards the fulfilment of our Five-Year Plans, and the establishment of a socialist society. It was inevitable, therefore, that advertising which everyone thinks of as a tool in the capitalistic manufacturing and marketing complex, should be believed to have little or no place in an economy developing under controlled conditions. Actually, the *functions of advertising remain fundamentally unchanged in a p rotected economy* so long as the economy is based on the one hand on accomplishing production by machines and in the mass and, on the other, getting the goods consumed through mass distributibution to national markets.

Let us examine the nature of protection and controls operating in the Indian economy. Firstly, industry is protected against foreign competition. Import restrictions had virtually shut out foreign goods, and competition is restricted to local producing units. Secondly, in order to make sure that industrial development is balanced and logically phased, Government is largely instrumental in allocating resources of production and vigilant control is being exercised on their utilisation. And finally, there is control of the production capacities of existing units which are not allowed to expand as a matter of course. But the most important thing from the point of view of advertising and its validity in a controlled economy is the fact that there is no attempt to curb feedom of choice in consumption. In no way has the consumer been told except in the matter of alcohol—that you will consume this and not that and certainly the consumer in India has almost in every category of consumption an expanding field of choice. Competition, too, is very much alive and is stimulated as new units of production were established and existing units are disallowed from expanding their share of market through restrictions on capacity.

But production was not running at near capacity; a look at the monthly statistics published by the Ministry of Industry revealed how many industries were working below capacity. During 1961, for instance, *soap* production by the organised sector was only 57 percent of installed capacity, while *vanaspati* production was approximately 40 per cent below capacity. *Biscuits and footwear* also could not produce to capacity. Obviously in every case, this under-utilisation of production facility was not due only to insufficient demand but it was probable that insufficient demand was a factor in certain industries, perhaps the most important one. In this context, how could it be argued that advertising is not required to create and maintain markets? How is advertising's *basic function altered because of controls on production*? Indeed it would appear that advertising must be employed to help ensure more economic employment of capital invested in productive capacity, which one would like to believe is licensed by Government on purely objective calculation.

The creation of an awareness of new wants and satisfaction is something that cannot be totally ignored in the economy; a rise in people's living standards is both economically and psychologically desirable. In simple terms, if the common man and his family are unable to live better, eat better, be better-clothed, indulge in some consumption that is not directly related to survival—does it not then constitute a total negation of our planning and all our aspirations? And here, we must remember the experience of the more advanced nations where despite a higher level of educatian, living standards tend to lag behind rising incomes. And with rising incomes, greater discretionary expenditures are a reality. The Indian Institute of Public Opinion in its 25th Quarterly Report estimated a rise in annual discretionary expenditure in the decade 1961 to 1971 from Rs. 2,974 crores to Rs. 4,826 crores. Where was this additional expenditure to be directed? Guaranteed freedom of choice, but without advertising, would it not tend to be dissipated on traditional purchase or get buried in traditional savings—neither of which could help accelerate the process of a developing economy.

More than in the past but perhaps less than for some time in the future, critics of advertising continued to question its need as an economic activity. More than in the past but one trust less than in the future, advertising men responded with confidence to these critics,

In the early 1960s in India, advertising began to receive a passport to *social respectibility*. We had seen the rather pathetic spectacle of the advertising boys loyally defending the social usefulness of their profession. The advertising profession was willingly acknowledged by Government as a necessary partner to propagate certain national ideas in 1963. It was a pity that an invasion (the Chinese attack) was needed to bring this about! Nonetheless, it was a significant advance in social 'acceptance' that was recorded by advertising. But something more concrete than 'Status' was achieved. The discussion on emergency publicity threw up the suggestion that Government publicity material on national themes should be distributed through commercial firms with large distribution network and one such firm way to be requested to distribute Government publicity material through their own channels and the Central Citizens' Council invited private firms to produce documentaries on a national theme to be distributed through the country-wide circuit of the Government Films Division. A beginning was also made to harness publicity resources in the private sector for a national campaign on Family Planning. All these demonstrated that there was a frank acknowledgement that the resources and 'know-how' of the advertising profession are useful and necessary for furthering national development,

For India, 1963 was an Emergency year. Many commercial firms responded wholeheartedly to the appeal to publicise national themes. The problem was how to sustain and give expression to this enthusiasm. Perhaps the solution was to blend the commercial interests of the advertiser with national objectives.

The emergency had accentuated the rice shortage. The question was whether vanaspati manufacturers could launch a campaign to popularise *wheat-based diet* in areas where rice was scarce? We saw the example of container and foil manufacturers issuing advertisements that helped to rouse public alertness against the danger of food and drug adulteration.

As a result of the 1963 Budget, personal taxes went up and higher levies were imposed on a whole range of products. Individual had less money to spend at his discretion and there were signs of consumer resistance. The Chairman of the ITC Ltd., referred to the increase in selling prices which restrict consumption of cigarettes. Similarly, at the annual meeting of another consumer goods manufacturer, Bengal Potteries, it was stated that the new duties had adversely affected the sales pattern of crockery. The radio market offered another case in point. Experience showed that more effort was needed for each unit of sale. At the beginning of 1963, there was some apprehension that the new taxes and other conditions of emergency would result in cuts in advertising budgets. Actual experience had proved that the cuts were of a marginal nature and advertising did not appear to have been adversely affected during the year.

Industrial Advertising in India

A more significant impact in terms of its implications for advertising lay in the shifts of emphasis and priority in economic planning. This was expressed in the considerably faster growth of producer goods industries. The mid-term appraisal of the Third Plan told us that the rate of growth of consumer goods industries had been comparatively less. On the other hand, there have been spectacular rise in the production of basic metals, fertilizers, heavy chemicals, transport equipment, etc.

This was reflected in advertising in the national press. If we look through the *times of India*, for example, there was evidence of a definite swift growth in industrial advertising. Some statistical verification in regard to the Stateman is interesting. If we compare three months of 1963 with the corresponding period for 1962, we find that the space taken by industrial display advertisements had gone up by 10 per cent while that taken by consumer advertisements has gone down by about 11 per cent. This did not include prospectuses. As for prospectus announcements which appeared in this paper in 1963, only 10 out of 63 such were for consumer products. These examples indicate, the comparatively faster growth of industrial advertising during the earaly sixties compared to consumer advertising. As a matter of fact, consumer advertising had been noticeably affected for certain products hit by the new priorities and cuts in foreign exchange. *Cars and airconditioners* are eloquent examples. In addition, several other consumer industries were working below capacity or below the 1962 level. To name a few: Vanaspati, biscuits, cigarettes, rubber footwear, typewriters, water coolers, electric fans.

This period also witnessed a more intensified drive for import substitution which meant that industries producing intermediates components and equipments were going to accelerate much faster than others. Thus, the value of *automobile components* (excluding tyres, batteries, etc.) went up from Rs. 2 crores in 1956 to well over Rs. 20 crores in 1963. The production of *machine tools* was up by 50 per cent in one year alone in 1963 over 1962. Inevitably, those developments were to push foward industrial advertising was to demand a 're-tooling', of advertising service.

The pattern of *industrial buying* is a subject on which much study still remains to be done. Experience varies from a large enterprise to a small one and from one kind of industry to another. It is interesting do know which levels of technical personnel enter into a buying decision. Sometimes a non-English knowing foreman has an important say in the purchase of certain types of equipment. And that raised the problem of rendering technical terms into readily intelligible words in several regional languages.

As Industrial products were sold in the conditions of a sellers' market, *hard-sell advertising* was not perhaps the requirement. Service Advertising—advertising which helps the users to make optimum utilisation of scarce materials and get the best results from newly manufactured machinery or equipment was an important aspect of industrial advertising. The large volume of industrial advertisements in the dailies an index of the inadequate development of the technical press. In a survey sponsored by the Calcutta Advertising Club it was found that of the 150 journals circulated among senior personnel at the Tata Steel Works, only 20 were Indian publications. Another independent survey of reading habits among senior personnel in the engineering industry in Calcutta and Jamshedpur, showed that most of them habitually read techical journals but very few of these were of Indian origin. However, a base had been created for producing serious and effective technical journals in India. The drive for import substitution and the need to improvise on the basis of materials available in this country, had created the impetus for tackling many new design and operational problems. That in Indian firms of consulting engineers was entrusted with the steel plant at Bokaro, was a matter of enormous significance and not the least of its effects was a considerable fillip to fresh and original technological writing in Indian journals. Some technical journals had already created a certain standing for themselves—notably journals on mining. The question and how to locate those journals which had in fact acquired the respect of practical engineers. Perhaps, the Indian Society of Advertisers should sponsor a readership serveys which could tell us more about Indian technical publications. The Press Institute of India had shown its awareness of the importance of industrial writing and in 1963 sponsored a seminar on industrial reporting. Perhaps the Institute should be able to give expert assistance to raise the editorial standards of our technical and trade publications.

Consumer industries were also growing and had set high targets. There had been some scaling down of those targets from the original figures in view of the emergency but the increase planned was substantial. Thus, in the next two years, production of *motor cycles and scooters* was to go up by about 50 per cent and of *radios* by over 60 per cent. The output of *sewing machines* would rise by 50 per cent while *soap* production was to be more than treble. The production of time pieces was increase by 4 times and of watches. Consumer advertising was, therefore, to grow substantially but, perhaps at a slower rate than before. The import substitution industries on which so much emphasis had been laid were not large advertisers. Even though industrial advertising was to grow faster, its volume was not so large that it conld off set the slower growth of consumer advertising. The rate of growth of advertising expenditure was to be slower than it had been over the past three to four years. The total volume of advertising expenditure was to increase but the rate of growth was to be allowed down.

Let us take a look at the people to whom advertisements were addressed. It could be said that we had fresh evidence of the changing tastes of the consumer.

Advertisers selling mass consumption products were aware of these changes taking place over a period of time. This had been reflected in their marketing methods and in their selection of media but it was interesting to study fresh evidence and find new indications of these changing habits. One such interesting index was the growth of *hire-purchase advertising* in the press. If one looked at the articles offered on hire-purchase terms not by the manufacturers but by hire-purchase agencies one find not only the costly *consumer durables* but even some relatively *inexpensive items*—pressure cookers, for example, which their cost Rs. 75/- each, we are being offered on hire-purchase and office clerks were going to these hire-purchase agencies in order to buy pressure cookers. In other words, what we might describe as the *more sophisticated* durables were finding popularity with lower income groups. A survey in 1963 had shown the rather interesting fact that industrial workers in Calcutta were taking to *cigarettes* on a large scale. The phenomenon was not new but its extent gave it a new importance. Another survey in Greater Bombay had given some further insight into the *buying habits of the lower income groups*. This survey showed that a little less than half of the lower income households in Greater Bombay used *talcum powder* and what was surprising, about one fourth of them were also buying face powder. It was found during the month when the survey was conducted that for every 10 higher income households buying nylon sarees, 150 lower income huuseholds did so. But the most astonishing evidence of changing consumer attitudes was in the LIC's break-through of the *rural barrier*. For the period ending March 1963, two-fifths of all new LIC policies were sold in the countryside. This was remarkable and advertising ingenuity of a high order was needed. *Kerosene operated film projectors* were used by the LIC to exhibit film strips in villages without power supply. It seemed that if the rural consumer was ready for life insurance, conservative living habits would rapidly change and that the desire for branded products in the villages was likely to grow at a quite surprising rate.

Not only were new tastes entering the countryside but a great deal of purchasing power too. Price trends between March 1962 and March 1963 showed a clear advantage for the countryside. Whereas the cost of manufactured articles had gone up by only 3 percent, prices of raw jute were up nearly twice as much. The townsfolk were paying more for what they bought from the villagers while the villagers, by comparison, paid less for urban products. Thus, *there was a substantial inflow of money to the villages*. But who particularly had benefited from this? An attempt was made to define this section and as Prof. Gadgil noted, they were the top 10 percent, in some cases the top 25 percent, of the rural community. More precisely, they were the farmers connected with wholesaling and processing men who had closer contact with urban centres and, therefore, were more susceptible to advertising and urban influences. Such deep going changes inside our society also pushed forward the tempo of mass communication, companies brought us to the threshold of high developments in mass communications in India.

1964 was a year of unprecedented crises; the main problem was hyper-inflation resulting in run-away prices. Whereas the increase in wholesale prices (with the index base in 1952-53 as 100) was only 8 percent between April 1961 and December 1963, the increase during the December 1963/November 1964 period was 15 percent. Against a provision of 30 percent increase in agricultural production during the Third Five Year Plan, the actual rise during the first three years of the Plan had been less than 1 percent. This resulted in the reduction of per capita availability of food grains by 1 percent. In industry, the average annual rate of growth of production in the first four years of the Third Plan had been in the neighbourhood of only 8 percent as against the planned average increase of 11 per annum. This shortfall in industrial achievement was partly due to the agricultural performance, and partly due to the power and raw material shortages since the beginning of the Plan. India's exports increased by 10 per cent, and imports were less by 6 percent. In effect, all these factors depressed the quantum of supplies available in the country for consumption.

On the other hand, the money supply in the economy rose by Rs. 884 crores in the first three years of the IIIrd Plan, of which Rs. 442 crores, 50 percent were contributed in 1963-64. Most of this money was spent either in non-productive defence projects or in Plan projects involving long-term investment. A good part of the money spent in the process in wages and salaries returned to the economy pressing on demand for food, clothing and other necessaries of life. Besides, there was the industrial activity producing largely goods of capital, basic and intermediate nature bringing in its train increase in income and employment which also pressed on the limited supplies available for consumption.

The growth in population of the order of 8 percent in the last three years and the growth in urbanisation also contributed to the swelling of the aggregate demand for goods and sesvices. In effect, too much money was chasing too few goods and the situation was aggravated by a large amount of unaccounted (black) money in the economy. Both the Central and States government budgets were oriented to curb civil consumption; there were the additional surcharge on personal incomes and the Annuity Deposit. There were also additional customs and excise duties together with increased freight and parcel rates, all of which were to raise the prices through increased cost of production and, thereby, to act as a brake on consumption.

In 1964, India had a production-oriented economy, in a period of national emergency, geared to a low level of consumption at high and increasing prices. How did advertising fare in such a situation?

For a standard measure of *trends in advertising*, let us study the columns of "The Hindu." Statistically, the proportion of advertising space to news in "The Hindu," "Times of India" and "The Statesman" was the same, and the physical volume of space sold for advertising was about equal.

Advertising was Service-Oriented

Of the total volume of space devoted to advertising, 52 percent had been taken up by *classified releases, entertainment, service institutions, government organisations and commercial announcements and notifications.* The classified advertising increased by 26 percent, Government release by 43 percent and commercial banks' advertising by 10 percent, over the five-year period, 1959-64. Commensurate with the increase in commercial banks' advertising, savings deposits during the same period moved up from Rs. 229 crores to Rs. 547 crores, an increase of 140 percent.

Advertising Promoted Production

The space taken up by advertising on *intermediate products, capital goods and consumer durables* was 31 percent of the total volume. Space devoted to intermediate products increased by 100 percent, and that on capital goods rose by 71 percent, but the volume on consumer durables increased by only 47 percent over the five-year period, 1959-64.

The manufacturers of intermediate and capital goods had a two-fold problem. On the one hand, they have to locate their buyers among the manufacturers who need their specialised wares, and on the other, they have to find out the scope that exist for their products in many new versions of machinery, products and models that was produced for the first time in India. For example, we discover new uses for *ERW steel tubes*. We advertised an *addressing machine* before large-scale production was organised for it, only to find out the scope that existed for such a machine. A large number of enquiries in reply to the very first advertisement encouraged the manufacturer to finalise his manufacturing programme. Enquiries in response to advertisements which related to the offer of *fractional horse power motors* was also significant, as the replies indicated that the manufacturers had only a limited range but were anxious to find out the purpose for which the motors were needed and were willing to undertake supplies specially adapted to needs.

In a developing economy, it is difficult to estimate the likely demand for these classes of goods. New manufacturers and new technicians arise; existing manufacturers try new ideas. As our economy grow, people tend to get specialised. In 1933, the Sapru Committee on unemployment reported that we had among the people only 40 vocational classifications. According to the census of 1961, the population was classified into over 1300 vocations. Since industrially advanced nations had achieved much greater division of labour, to have as many as 40,000 vocational groupings, and because Indian industries were shaping in emulation of their technical know-how, our vocational divisions too should grow enormously. The manufacturers of intermediate and capital goods had, therefore, to keep in touch with the growing generation of new vocational classes so that they might be kept informed of the industrial raw materials and tools that were being progressively improved and increased in the country. While the technical journals served to some extent in reaching the entrepreneurs and technicians, the daily press was to remain an important medium for this kind of advertising.

As to consumer durables, advertising had to keep pace with the steadily increasing production in this group of products. The main function that advertising must serve was to keep on cultivating new customers because the frequency of repeat purchase in durable consumer articles was limited. For example, a *radio or a bicycle* bought by a family or an individual, do not attract repeat purchase from the same source for a considerable length of time. It was, therefore, safe to asset that all the advertising devoted to this group of products had greatly helped to maintain and promote production.

Advertising Underplayed Consumption

The popular view that "advertising is essentially a thing to induce consumption, to make people buy things they do not want" seem to have been negatived by the trends observed in recent years. On a number of goods and services, the volume of advertising done in 1964 nad been less than what occurred in 1959.

Cosmetics and toiletries	—23 percent
Soaps	—27 percent
Hair preparations	— 6 percent
Pharmaceuticals drugs and medicines	— 2 percent
Baby food	—21 percent
Bicycles	—16 percent
Jewellery	—63 percent

Photographic materials	—51 percent
Fountain pens	—44 percent
Footwear	— 2 percent
Sewing machines	—49 percent
Air Services	—10 percent
Cigarettes	— No increase

The total advertising space taken up by consumer advertising (soft goods, as they are called) was only 17 percent. Among 850 large-size advertisements, each occupying 100 col. centimeters or more, that appeared in 1964, advertisements relating to consumer goods were confined to 120 in number, or a mere 14 percent. It was, possible that the advertising of some of these products had been shifted to magazines or less expensive newspapers. But the fact remained that most manufacturers in the consumer field did not need to promote sales in 1964. Invariably, in all cases, production had increased, and yet they could not keep pace with demand because of limited capacity, restricted maintenance imports, inadequate supplies of indigenous raw materials and restrictive government policies.

Advertising Purvey New

1964 witnessed, in its advertising columns, the entry into the market of nearly *200 new products and services*, and releases of 67 prospectuses. These releases represented one-third of the large-size advertisements that appeared in the whole year. Out of 3200 advertisers as many as 2750, or 90 per cent of the advertisers, had taken less than 100 columns inches or 250 columns centimetres in the whole year for their commercial display advertising. This showed that *most of the advertisers consisted of smallbusinessmen of small-scale industrialists*, and they were coming into the newspaper columns casually only to serve the immediate business or sales problems.

Advertising Supports Healthy Competition

Even in a planned economy, competition has its place. Principally the oil companies and the manufactures of *automobile tyres*, *tea and textiles* were sensitive to competition, and their advertising showed a pronounced increase. Although the total volume of cloth produced by the mills could not, by regulation, increase, the output of superfine qualities were stepped up to satisfy the growing consumer demand for refined varieties. More and more mills offered a variety of products in combination with "Terylene", wool, rayong and cotton both for men and women. This calculated manipulation to put to best use the available imported and indigenous raw materials required to be promoted on a modest scale. The entry of Tata Finlay in the *packaged tea field* made it necessary for the competitors to resort to intensive advertising to safeguard their interests. Similarly, with a number of new units in production manufacturing products of international fame, an increasing volume of advertising became necessary for *automobile tyres* to bring about a balance in consumer demand to the benefit of all concerned. The oil companies had to hold their own in the face of competition from the government-owned Indian Oil Corporation. They, engaged the attention of their customers with one merchandising plan or another. Noteworthy among them was the traffic Burmah-Shell to highlight and contain the traffic hazards.

In an otherwise fluid economy, hire-purchase facilities were still offered and encouraged. *Tooth pastes* were promoted coupled with *tooth brushes*, and "Surf" was offered with a large cake of "Lux" to provide consumer incentives to enlarge a growing market. Allwyn offered refrigerators adapted to the special needs of pharmacies and restaurants. Thus in those fields where it was necessary, advertising supported healthy competition in the larger interests of consumers.

Image Builders

The number of advertisers who used more than 100 columns inches or 250 columns for their advertising in 1959 and 1964 were only 389 and 454 respectively. They represented 11 percent of the total advertisers in those years. Of the 454 advertisers in 1964, only 189 advertisers were advertising in 1959 also; 265 were new. Out of a total of 3200 advertisers, only 189 or 6 percent were regular advertisers desirous of promoting a favourable image about their products and services in the public mind. The rest, though large in number were neither regular nor consistent and therefore, had little chance of impressing on the public mind in the long run.

Government Advertising

A major development of far-reaching consequence to the future of advertising and publicity was the appointment of the Vidyalankar Committee on the Government of India's Plan Publicity. The fundamental aim of Government publicity is to motivate group and individual actions for the realisation of the 'good life' that the Government sought to provide for the people. "The concept of democratic planning implied that the citizens and local communities should be enabled to make their own decision for the realisation of the national aims and that all sections of the population should be closely involved in the work of economic and social development. It is only through such intensive exploitation of national human resources and ingenuity that we could hope to attain the kind of society we desire." In the fulfilment of this objective, the Committee felt the Plan publicity so far had failed. It was its considered opinion that the impact the existing programmes had created on the public mind had been "tenuous, weak and diffused." Aiming primarily on the dissemination of information, plan publicity failed to touch any section of the population. It was then recognised that there must be a two-way traffic of news, views, opinions and comments. Apart from furnishing news to the public to keep them informed of economic and social policies, there must function an intelligence service to obtain, study and analyse publice comment, opinion and reaction. Such a study was to serve as a guideline for evolving proper methods for dissemination of information.

Secondly, the resulting publicity was to be so directed and produced as to persuade and inspire people into accepting the social and material changes, and thus lead to local initiative for decisions. Thirdly, the individual and the group as much as the State, needed the understanding and cooperation of the general community for an integrated development. This could only be done by a total mobilisation of all opinion-moulding cadres of leadership in the community. Fourthly, the root of all ills that beset Plan publicity was the absence of experience to plan the strategy and tractics of publicity campaigns and to ensure the most profitable utilisation of mass media. Finally, the financial allocations for publicity should be regarded a productive investment in the development of human resources which, in the last analysis, is the social and to be reached through the process of economic development.

In an era of hyper-inflation, advertising could do no more than be a complementary agent to service selling. But on the larger purpose of moulding public opinion and social behavious conducive to the acceptance of a new way of life, publicity failed by an inadequate approach to it. If the pronouncements of leaders were any guide, we could look forward to better performance in agriculture and industry in the years ahead and there would be plentiful supplies of consumer goods in the next Five Year Plan Periods. Even so, in a planned economy, it was to be expected that supply and demand should remain well matched, and the scope for advertising, therefore, to promote consumption was limited. But, there is so much to be gained in cultivating the people even under conditions of shortages, demonstrating to them an awareness on the part of business and the Government of their needs and the attempts made to serve them. This was nacessary because in an era of shortages of most basic goods and services necessary for life on the one hand, and the high taxation engendered by the Plan and national emergency on the other, the public mind was agitated over the treatment it got from Government and business. The Business Relations Conference that year was devoted to the '*Social Responsible of Business*' and got together eminent men from Government, business and the community to focus attention on the subject. The deliberations at this conference revealed that *our social leadership had passed from teachers, priests, landlords and princes of the old to the modern businessmen and politicians.* It was in the moral and ethical conduct of these two classes of leaders that the future well-being of our people rests.

It was generally agreed that most people in business, Government and society were good, and all that was needed to do was to reform the minority of black sheep among them. It was felt that an organised and informed public opinion could correct the evils in society that corrupted business, Government and the people.

Businessmen should forge a moral code among themselves so as to strictly watch out and weed out the wrong-doers through their professional clubs and trade associations.

Since the Government had matured from a law and order organisation to a welfare state, it must ensure special representation in its legislatures for the class of people who purvey those means of social welfare, namely, the means of production, distribution and consumption.

Consideration of the social responsibilities of business was not isolated to this one conference. The time had come them for businessmen in India to use advertising in a big way to cultivate public goodwill and help the Government in its drive for a socio-economic revolution conceived in its Plans.

Evidence of such advertising was present in 1964 with at least 75 business houses highlighting research, export, quality-oriented production and the philosophy of service. But this was inadequate, considering that we have as many as 6000 public limited companies and 19,000 private limited companies, and the fact that *hardly 3000 of them enter our advertising columns at all and less than 200 do a continuous, consistent job.* The time had come for our businessmen to look closely into the socio-economic problems and see how they could help to create a elimate for fruitful cooperation between the Government, business and the community.

There are manufacturers depending on agriculture for the use of their products such as *tractors and fertilisers,* and there are many industries which depend on agricultural raw materials, namely, *textiles, sugar, jute and tea*. The country was literally in a state of crisis in agricultural production, Many of our undertakings depending on agriculture for their prosperity could give a helping hand in orienting public attitude to the fields of production in which they were interested and thereby help agricultural production as a whole. Similarly, a large number of capital and intermediate goods manufacturers had a sake in reorienting public attitude towards shortages and shortcomings under which the daily administration of our business labours.

The adverising of Gabriel India was an example worthy of emulation. *It is the long haul that pays*: Some years ago, at the Westinghouse laboratories in New York, a great bar of steel, eight feet long and weighting half a ton was suspended vertically from a chain. Parallel to it by a stout thread hung a cork from an ordinary bottle. The cork weighed perhaps half an ounce. The man in charge of the experiment said, "Now start swinging the cork gently against the steel bar and we'll see if, in the long run, it can make the bar move over." Again and again, the small cork swung against the steel bar but for a long time the pendant bar seemed to hang motionless as if it did not feel the slight impact of the tiny cork. After ten minutes, however, when the frail cork had tapped gently against that heavy bar of steel hundreds of times, a sort of nervous chill seemed suddenly to go through that great bar of steel. Another two minutes, and the chill turned into plainly visible vibrations like those of a sick man with fever shaking in his bed. These vibrations increased in rapidity and in strength, until after twenty-five minutes, that great steel bar began to swing like the huge pendulum of a grandfather's clock."

Every little effort we-make in our approach to cultivating public goodwill in its on interest can bring us large dividends in the years ahead.

Summary

"The Hindu", "Times of India" and "The Statesman" are the three daily newspapers in India which received the maximum volumes of advertising and they all carried most of the national advertising released from Bombay, Calcutta, Delhi, Madras and other metropolitan centres. A study of the columns of "The Hindu" was, therefore, made to get a broad idea of how its advertising columns were used in 1959 and 1964, the former a developing paceful year and the latter a year of crises.

The study showed that more than half the volume of space-52 per cent—had been devoted to classified releases, entertainment, Government organisations, service institutions and commercial announcements and notifications. The remaining 48 per cent of the space was shared by the manufacturers of intermediate, capital and consumer durable goods to the extent of 31 per cent, and 17 per cent by the manufacturers of consumer goods (soft goods).

As to Government advertising, the Vidyalankar Committee which reported on what Plan Publicity was and what it should be stated that the Government's publicity efforct had completely failed in the fulfilment of its objectives. The committee recognised the need for research, and on the basis of it to deliver the message to the public persuasively to inspire them to accept a new way of life. The Committee also laid down that *publicity expenditure should be considered a productive investment in the development of human resources rather than think of it as an inevitable expenditure to provide information.*

1964 was a year of unprecedented crises. The main problem was hyper-inflation resulting in run-away prices. We had a production-oriented economy in a period of national emergency, geared to a low level of consumption at high and increasing prices. In such a climate for business, advertising, far from promoting consumption or cultivating a desire for "unnecessary" goods or services", merely served as a set of techniques and facilities to help its user as a complementary agent to service selling.

On balance, both commercial advertising and Government advertising tended to be "tenuous, weak and diffused," It played very little part in orienting public attitude to strive for the good and progressive life sought to be achieved both by the Government and private enterprise. As a result, public discontent over the behaviour of private business and the many acts of commission and ommission on the part of the Government was manifest in many public forums that focused attention on the social responsibilities of business and governments.

The need, therefore, was for every business house to look closely at the social problems as they affected the present and future interests of the business and the community, and to use its resources in advertising to serve society in the best way possible to ensure more production, better distributions and equitable consumption.

Issues in Advertising-Case

Western India Chemicals Company

The Western India chemicals Company was established in 1933 to manufacture soap. With the setting up of a Company involving the expenses of maintaining a modern factory using the finest raw materials and dedicated to produce the highest quality soap plus a regular distribution system backed by advertising, it was obvious that the quality of their product and service would result in their washing soaps being more expensive. How much more expensive was a question of fine judgement since overheads had to be paid for, yet the Company could not afford to be priced out of the market.

With their lack of machinery and modern manufacturing techniques, however, 'desi' manufacturers could not produce a true milled toilet soap. Consequently, it was obviously to the Company's advantage to stimulate the growth of the milled toilet soap market since they could ask the consumer for a higher retail price and make a reasonable profit margin. The Company's aim was to use its manufacturing skill to produce soap that could be offered at the lowest retail price, consistent with a fair return to the Company. There was, a vast potential for milled toilet soaps in India since the population was large and growing, and the market had not been exploited.

Advertising Aims

In the context of the Indian soap market, the general advertising aims of the Company were three-fold:

(a) To persuade people who did not use soap to use it;

(b) To persuade people using soap for working with both clothes and body to use a separate soap for each purpose;

(c) To persuade people using a separate soap for body washing to use a true milled toilet soap.

To promote the use of a separate soap for toilet purposes for all classes but particularly the middle and lower classes where the vast potential lay, it was felt that an unsophisticated inexpensive soap clearly suitable for body washing was needed.

In the U.K. the Lifebuoy Soap was introduced for two reasons:

(a) To widen the Company's range of washing soaps.

(b) To use residual oils technically loss suitable for Sunlight and thereby to improve factory efficiency.

The product was given a red colour to make it quite distinct from Sunlight and existing competitive brands. The use of cresylic in the soap was a novel idea at that time, stemming from the use of cresylic as a disinfectant in hospital cleaning. The early resistance to this unconventional health soap was overcome by heavy advertising and promotional activity and by a growing public consciousness of the value of hygiene. It was first introduced as a soap for scrubbing floors and paint-work and general household cleaning. It was sold as a health soap for washing away germs in dirt. However, although it was an unmilled washing soap, advertised for general household cleaning, it began to be used by poorer people as a toilet soap since they were attracted by its quality, health appeal and inexpensive unit price.

In India Lifebuoy was first imported from U.K. in 189s. In those days, it was sold through agencies with little or no concerted advertising effort to support it. At the outset, Lifebuoy must have suffered from a grave disability. The use of cresylic as a disinfectant was a Western concept (one of the by-products of industrialisation) and therefore Lifebuoy was likely to have appealed as a health soap only to westerners living in India and perhaps to wealthy people in large towns with a modern hospital, where, perhaps cresylic was used as a disinfectant. With the setting up of the Indian company, Lifebuoy was manufactured in India and the product began to have a concerted advertising effort for the first time.

Company Advertising

The Company felt that an unsophisticated, inexpensive soap clearly suitable for body washing was needed to persuade consumers to use a separate soap. Experience in the U.K. seemed to suggest that Lifebuoy might be the right product to stimulate this change in consumer habits. To this end, therefore, from 1933 to 1947, the advertising for Lifebuoy was designed to put over the Western concept of a cresylic soap giving protection against disease and generally safeguarding health. This health appeal was very generalised, that the advertising was fairly effective might be judged from the fact that, between 1933 and 1947, the cresylic section of the toilet soap market was expanding 2½ times as fast as the milled toilet soaps section.

By 1947, the Company was running an advertising campaign designed to establish the historical appeal of Lifebuoy. This campaign "*Mr. Kapur remembers*" illustrated a character of middle age. In the copy he remembered how in his youth, too, Lifebuoy had played an important part in guarding his health against disease. Since even his mother had used and recommended Lifebuoy, the inference was that Lifebuoy had been guarding health since time immemorial.

At this time, the Company began to feel, as a result of observations, in the market, that although the Lifebuoy market was very wide, it was not regular. A market research for Lifebuoy was instituted the results were as follows:

Market Research—1947

The average expenditure of 400 consumers on soap was 6 annas per month and of this:

8.6 per cent was spent on premium priced toilet soaps

37.1 per cent was spent on popular priced toilet soaps

54.3 per cent was spent on cresylic soaps

Lifebuoy Users and Non-Users

Of Lifebuoy users, 55 per cent were regular and 45 per cent occasional.

Regular Users	*Occasional Users*
95 per cent used it for toilet purposes	65 percent used it for toilet purposes
5 percent used it only for antiseptic purposes	36 percent used it for antiseptic purposes when necessary

Non-users did not use the product because:

(a) They did not like the cresylic perfume although they associated it with an antiseptic/disinfectant soap.

(b) They never had skin trouble, had therefore, did not need an antiseptic soap.

The Company's reading of this market information was that Lifebuoy with its cresylic odour and definitely established itself as a health soap. As a product, it was buoyant but 45 per cent of its users were only occasional users and this required further investigation. The fact that 36 per cent of the occasional users used the soap, when they bought it, for antiseptic purposes *when necessary*, coupled with the fact that many non-users said they did not use it since they never had skin trouble confirmed previous observations of the Company that the health image of Lifebuoy was specifically related to skin diseased.

The Hands Campaign

The advertising problem, therefore, was to;

1. Change consumer thinking that Lifebuoy had a specialised use for clearing up skin disorders. For a really mass appeal, Lifebuoy needed a more general health image;
2. Persuade consumers to use the soap regularly;
3. Keep the appeal of the soap well away from the appeal of the true milled soaps since, because of the Company's long-term aims, the growth of the milled toilet soap market should not be interfered with.

To achieve this, a simple yet compelling campaign was needed to put over a more general health appeal so as to persuade consumers to use the soap every day. At the same time, the appeal had to be distinctive and quite removed from regular toilet soap advertising.

This problem was solved with the 'hands campaign'. Each advertisement had an illustration of hands touching every day objects which contained dirt and germs. One illustration would be hands touching things like greasy bicycle machine parts and so on. Another would be hands touching less obviously dirty things like money or string. In the copy, Lifebuoy promised to wash away obvious and hidden dirt and with it the germs it contained to preserve health away from disease which these germs would otherwise bring.

The Advertising Problem

At the end of 3 years, Lifebuoy progress and its advertising was reviewed thoroughly. From the sales point of view, Lifebuoy had in the five years prior to the hands campaign, risen 13 per cent and during the three years of the campaign, had risen 81 per cent. On the other hand, the company's true milled toilet soaps like Lux and Rexona had risen 100 per cent although this was on a somewhat smaller base.

The following information was elicited from Marketing Research.

1. On average the 500 contacts spent 7 annas per month on soap. On this, the split-up was as follows:

Popular Priced			*Cresylic*		*Premuim*	
Total	*Lux*	*Rexona*	*Hamam*	*Total*	*Lifebuoy*	*Total*
37.2%	16.3%	14.0%	4.6%	53.5%	53%	9.3%

2. 95 percent of Lifebuoy users were using the soap regularly.
3. The wealthy class wore using Lifebuoy only for washing their hands.
4. The middle class were using Lifebuoy mainly for washing hands, but for complete body washing in the north, where the climate was hotter.
5. The working class were on the whole using Lifebuoy for complete body washing.
6. Toilet soaps were generally considered to be expensive whilst cresylic soaps were regarded as economical and had curative/preventive qualities.

7. Usership of Lifebuoy was spread throughout the social groups although the heaviest quantity was bought by the middle and lower classes.

8. Its non-users and even some of its users disliked its cresylic smell. *What change was required either in the product or its advertising*?

12

Profitability Analysis by Market Segments

LELAND L. BEIK AND STEPHEN L. BUZBY

By tracing sales revenues to market segments and relating these revenues to marketing costs, the marketing manager can improve and control his decision making respect to the firm's profit objective.

First expressed by Smith in 1956, the concept of market segmentation has since been elaborated in many different ways.[1] It has recently been defined by Kotler as "... the subdividing of a market into homogeneous subsets of customers, where any subset may conceivably be selected as a market target to be reached with a distinct marketing mix."[2] The underlying logic is based on the assumption that:

> ...the market for a product is made up of customers who differ either in their own characteristics or in the nature of their environment in such a way that some aspect of their demand for the product in question also differs. The strategy

Editors Note: Reprinted from *Journal of Marketing*, July 1973, pp. 48-53 published by the American Marketing Association.

of market segmentation involves the tailoring of the firm's product and/or marketing programme to these differences, By modifying either of these, the firm is attempting to increase profits by converting a market with heterogeneous demand characteristics into a set of markets that although they differ from one another, are internally more homogeneous than before.[3]

The concept of market segmentation may be used for strategic alignment of the firm's productive capacities with its existing and potential markets. By analyzing market needs and the firm's ability to serve those needs, the basic long-run policies of the firm can be developed. Through choice of target segments, competition may be minimized; through selective cultivation, the firm's competitive posture may be greatly improved.

For both strategic and tactical decisions, marketing managers may profit by knowing the impact of the marketing mix upon the target segments at which marketing efforts are aimed. If the programmes are to be responsive to environmental change, a monitoring system is needed to locate problems and guide adjustments in marketing decisions. Tracing the profitability of segments permits improved pricing. selling, advertising, channel, and product management decision. The success of marketing policies and programmes may be appraised by a dollar and cents measure of profitability by segment.

Managerial accounting techniques have dealt with the profitability of products, territories, and some customer classest but a literature search has revealed not one serious attempt to assess the relative profitability of market segments.[4] Although the term "segment" has a history of use in accounting, this use implies a segment of the business rather than a special partitioning of consumers or industrial users for marketing analysis. Even when classifying customers, accounting classes are formed by frequency and size of order, location, credit rating, and other factors, most of which are related to controlling internal costs or to assessing financial profit.[5]

After indicating the value for marketing decision making, this article will delineate a framework for cost accounting by market segments. An industrial product example is constructed to demonstrate the process and to spell out the features of the contribution approach to cost accounting as applied to accounting for segment profitability. Further discussion extends the concept to a consumer situation and specifies difficulties that may attend full-scale application of the technique. The expectation is that the technique will better control marketing costs and improve marketing decisions.

Market Segmentation and its Utility

To have value for managerial judgements, Bell notes that market segments should: (1) be readily identified and measured, (2) contain adequate potential, (3) demonstrate effective demand, (4) be economically accessible, and (5) react uniquely to marketing effort.[6] For present purposes, the key criterion for choosing the bases for segmenting a given market is the ability to trace sales and costs to the segments defined. Allocating sales and costs is the most stringent requirement and limitation of profitability accounting as used to support marketing decisions.

Among the many possible bases for market segmentation, the analysis can be accomplished using widely recognized geographic, demographic, and socio-economic variables.[7] Many of these, such as geographic units and population or income figures, provide known universe classifications against which to compare company sales and cost performance. Other bases of segmentation such as buyer usage rate, expected benefits, or psychological or sociological characteristics of consumers typically require research to match their distribution, directly or indirectly, with company sales and costs.

Given proper segmentation, separate products (or channels or other elements of the marketing mix) can serve as the primary basis for cost and revenue allocation. Knowledge of profit by segments then contributes directly to decisions concerning the product line and adjustment of sales, advertising, and other decision variables. The process is illustrated in the following industrial example.

A matrix system can be developed as part of marketing planning to partition segments for profitability analysis.[8] A company with lines of computers, calculators, and adding machines might first divide its market into territories as in the upper section of Figure 1. The cell representing adding machines in the eastern market might next be sorted by product items and customer classes. The chief product perference of each company class is noted by an important benefit segmentation within the cells of the lower section of Figure 1.

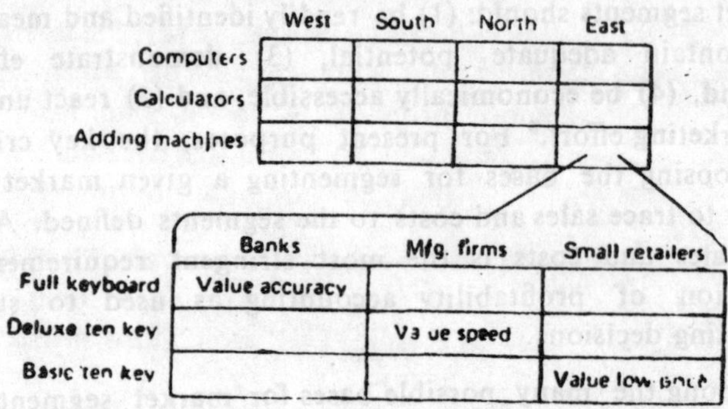

Figure 1. Matrix breakdown by products and segments

Since the segments react differently to product variations and other marketing activities, it is advantageous to isolate profit by product for each market segment. Using this information, the marketing manager can specifically tailor product policies to particular maket segments and judge the reaction of segments to increased or decreased marketing efforts over time. Decision adjustments and control of marketing costs interact to improve product line management directly and other decisions indirectly.

In theory, segment profitability analysis is worthwhile only where decisions adjusting the marketing mix add incremental profits that exceed the costs of the extra analysis. In practice, information concerning the profitability of marketing decisions has been so spare that the analysis is likely to be profitable where allocations to market segments are approximate and fail to approach theoretical perfection.

Marketing Cost Analysis

In its simplest form, marketing cost analysis relates the cost of marketing activities to sales revenues in order to measure profits. A profit and loss statement must be constructed for any marketing component (*e.g.*, product, channel) being analyzed. The approach consists of dividing the firm's basic costs (*e g.*, salaries, rent) into their functional categories (*e.g.*, selling, advertising). The functional category amounts are then assigned within the appropriate marketing classifications.

The actual form of the profit and loss statements will depend upon the nature of the company being analyzed, the purpose of the marketing analysis, and the records available. The form of statement will also depend upon the accounting technique used to assign costs to the marketing components under study. One might use a full-cost approach, assigning both direct and indirect costs across the marketing classifications on the best available bases. Alternatively, one might use a direct-cost approach and assign direct costs only, avoiding arbitrary assignment of fixed or overhead costs. Most marketing sources have utilized the full and direct-cost approaches

A third costing approach is better suited to the needs of the marketing manager and the requirements of analysis by market segments. Essentialy, it is an adaptation of the contribution approach to preparing financial statements.[9] Table 1 presents a simplified illustration of how the contribution approach can be adapted to break out product profitability for adding machines in the eastern market.

First, all of the variable nonmarketing costs have been assigned to products. These costs represent nonmarketing dollar expenditures which fluctuate, in total, directly in proportion to short-run changes in the sales volume of a given product. Similarly, variable marketing costs have been deducted to produce variable product contribution margins identical to those which would result from a direct costing approach.

The remaining marketing costs have been broken down into two categories—assignable and nonassignable. The assignable costs represent dollar expenditures of a fixed or discretionary nature for which reasonably valid bases exist for allocating them to specific products. For example, the assignment of salesmen's salaries in Table 1 might be based on Sevin's recommendation to use selling time devoted to each product, as shown by special sales-call reports or special studies. The marketing manager's salary could be assigned on the basis of personal records indicating the amount of time devoted to the management of each product. Product advertising would be assigned by reference to the actual amount spent on advertising each product.

The use of the actual dollar level of sales was purposely avoided in choosing the allocation bases for the assignable costs in Table 1. Horngren, among others, has stated that when dealing with fixed or discretionary costs. The costs of efforts are independent of the results actually obtained, in the sense that the costs are programmed by management, not determined by sales.

The non-assignable marketing costs represent dollar expenditure of a fixed or discretionary nature for which there are no valid bases for assignment to products. Consequently, institutional advertising has not been assigned to the products to avoid confounding the product profitability margins which would result from the arbitrary allocation of this cost. Since the primary purpose is calculating marketing related product contribution margins, the remaining non-marketing costs can be taken as a deduction from the total marketing contribution margin to produce a net profit figure for the firm.

Although the preceding example was purposely simplified, the framework is sufficiently flexible to handle different objectives and more complex problems. If the firm in Table 1 were

Table 1. Product productivity analysis—contribution approach

	Company total	*Full keyboard*	*Deluxe ten key*	*Basic ten key*
Net Sales	$10,000	$5,000	$3,000	$2,000
Variable Manufacturing Costs	5,100	2,500	1,375	1,225
Mfg. Contribution	$ 4,900	$2,500	$1,625	$ 775
Marketing Costs Variable:				
Sales Commissions	450	225	135	90
Variable Contribution	$ 4,450	$2,275	$1,490	$ 685
Assignable:				
Salaries—Salesmen	1,600	770	630	200
Salary—Marketing Manager	100	50	25	25
Product Advertising	1,000	670	200	130
Total	$ 2,700	$1,490	$ 855	$ 355
Product Contribution	$ 1,750	$ 785	$ 635	$ 330
Non-assignable				
Institutional Advertising	150			
Marketing Contribution	$ 1,600			
Fixed-joint sts				
General Administration	300			
Manufacturing	900			
Total	$ 1,200			
Net Profits	$ 400			

a single product firm, for example, the three customer classes (banks, manufacturers, and retailers) could easily be substituted for primary emphasis in place of the products. The analysis would differ only through variations in the treatment of fixed, variable, and assignable costs required by the new objective. That assignability changes with objective may be illustrated by the fact that product advertising costs can often be assigned to products but rarely to customer classes.

To aid in handling more complex problems, a discussion of common bases for assigning a wide range of marketing costs may be found in Sevin. In some instances, the approach can be further improved by application of mathematical programming to assign costs to the marketing components. Budgetary data and marketing lags could also be introduced to upgrade the analysis.

Costing by Segments

In particular, the framework of the contribution approach may be applied to costing by segments. Table 2 extends the product analysis of Table 1. Recall that the segments are partitioned by territorial, customer class, and product benefit criteria although the primary customer class names are used to identify segments in the table. Instead of tracing the sales of each product to all three customer classes, one simplifying device is to identify the primary benefit sought by a customer class as segment sales and to combine sales of the given product to the other customer classes as nonsegment sales. For example, sales of the full-keyboard adding machine to banks become segment sales, while sales to large manufacturing firms or to retailers are nonsegment sales. This device is appropriate where non-target sales are expected to be minimal; otherwise more columns can be added to the table.

Where sales revenues can be traced directly to customers, customer classes, and territories and where marketing costs can be similarly traced, the analysis is straightfoward. Where the less tangible benefit segmentation is used, sales analysis or marketing research must measure the degree to which benefits are related to each customer class. If sales analysis shows that banks purchase 75 per cent of the full-keyboard sales because they value accuracy while manufacturers and retailers account for the remaining 25 percent, both revenues and sales commissions mav be prorated accordingly. This allocation is employed in Table 2.

To illustrate a few marketing implications, it might be noted that over one-half of the full-keyboard profit contribution actually comes from nonsegment sales rather than from the primary target segment. The nonsegment profitability results in part from low personal selling and absence of advertising costs. An opportunity possibly exists in further promotion, perhaps to large manufacturing firms. Had the table completed the analysis for purchases of full-keyboard machines by manufacturers and retailers, the actual segment of opportunity could be pinpointed. If institutional or other possible sales proved substantial during further classification, a new segment of opportunity might be identified.

Quite obviously, the eastern banking segment has a low profit contribution considering the level of marketing effort expended. Table 2 deals with one sample area and product class, and a comparison with other area banking segments might prove enlightening. Perhaps marketing costs could be reduced in the eastern segment if sales were up to par. Or if sales were comparatively low, marketing effort (price, personal selling, advertising) could be reallocated to meet competition more effectively.

Similar analysis can be applied to the manufacturing and retailing segments of Table 2, and to the territories and products not incorporated in the present illustration. The advantage over standard sales analyses is that a profit rather than a volume measure is applied and that variations in marketing costs and sales response are taken into account.

Marketing Productivity Consumer Segments

The previous example has been simplified so that minimum tables serve to explain the technique. Segment analysis becomes

Table 2. Segment productivity analysis—contribution approach

	Company total	Full keyboard		Deluxe 10-key		Basic 10-key retail seg.
		Bank seg.	Nonseg.	Mfg. seg.	Nonseg.	
Net Sales	$10,000	$3,750	$1,250	$2,550	$450	$2 000
Variable Manufacturing Costs	5,100	1,875	625	1,169	206	1,225
Mfg. Contribution	$ 4,900	$1,875	$ 625	$1,381	$244	$ 775
Marketing Costs Variable:						
Sales Commissions	450	169	56	115	20	9
Variable Contribution	$ 4,450	$1,706	$ 569	$1,266	$224	$ 685
Assignable						
Salaries—Salesman	1,600	630	140	420	210	200
Salary—Marketing Manager	100	38	12	19	6	25
Product Advertising	1,000	670	-0-	200	-0-	130
Total	$ 2,700	$1,338	$ 152	$ 639	$216	$ 355
Segment Contribution	$ 1,750	$ 368	$ 417	$ 627	$ 8	$ 330

Non-assignable	
Institutional Advertising	150
Marketing Contribution	**$ 1,600**
Fixed-joint Costs	
General Administration	300
Manufacturing	900
Total	**$ 1,200**
Net Profits	400

complex as more than two or three criteria are used for partitioning and as additional criteria are considered for different classes of marketing decisions. A further example adds realism and extends the concept to a consumer situation.

A company that sells snowmobiles is likely to have some special channel problems. To control channel management, meteorological data permit primary and secondary snow belts to be mapped across the U.S. and Canada. Sales analysis or research could show how to allocate purchases among consumers in major metropolitan, city, town, and rural areas. Further analysis could determine patronage among department stores, automotive dealers, farm equipment dealers, marinas, and other classes of outlets. Sales to resorts for rentals might be included as a segment or analyzed separately. Finally, the several analyses could map sales into geographical units. Segmenting by snow conditions, population density, outlets patronized, and dwelling area and then allocating revenues and costs to the segments would point outlet selection and channel adjustments toword the more profitable outlets in favourable population and snow-belt locations.

By collecting and analyzing warranty card information, snowmobile purchasers could be classified as to family life cycle, social status, or other variables. This data would probe the profit potential of appealing to young families, selected social classes, or possibly even to hunters, sailing enthusiasts, and other outdoors people. Dates on the warranty cards would help adjust the timing of promotions in advance of the snow season or to balance the pre-Christmas advertising in line with purchase habits of its customer segments. Having targeted promotion on the basis of past data, current warrantly card information, and revenue and cost information, the profitability of each target segment could be determined.

Analyzing the profitability of advertising or price decisions involves special problems in tracing sales and costs. If segments have been defined on tangible bases, say area and dealer patronage, the difficulty might be overcome by setting up an experiment. Variations of advertising messages, local media, and possibly price would serve as treatments in segments matched to control other variables. Recording segment revenues and treatment costs would constitute a profit measure of selected advertising and/or price decisions. Experiments may thus be used with segment cost analysis to plan corporate marketing programmes.

Managerial Implications

Given responsible means of partitioning market segments, major elements of the marketing mix may be segregated for analysis using the contribution approach to cost accounting. An example has been employed to show how segment profitability can be measured for items in a product line thereby contributing directly to product management decisions. By analyzing the profit and loss statements for the costs of other marketing efforts, additional adjustments can be made in other decisions such as personal selling and advertising. A further example has indicated how channel and other marketing management problems can be similarly gauged by a profit measure for a consumer product and consumer segments.

Several major problems have to be met in applying costing techniques to market segments. One difficulty is choosing productive bases for segmentation, and limiting analysis to a manageable number of bases is another. Although some bases are obvious from experience, they remain product specific, and criteria for choice are not fully developed. Another major problem is obtaining data for the less tangible modes of segmentation, particularly data that permit assignment of sales revenues and costs in accord with each base used for segment definition.

Recognizing and solving problems, however, often leads to further improvements. For example, many of the behavioural applications to marketing imply use in segment analysis but are difficult to relate to other marketing variables on any basis other than judgement. As limitations of source data are overcome, profit accounting by segments may add to the marketing utility of behavioural advances.

Costing by market segments promises improvement in marketing efficiency by way of better planning of expenditures and control of costs. Upon documenting reasons for today's soaring marking costs, Weiss comments over and over that marketing costs are resistant to sophisticated cost a nalysis and that marketing cost controls [are inadequate in modern corporations.[12] Although not calculated to stem stuch pressures as inflation, cost accounting by market segments can control selling, advertising, packaging, and other marketing costs in relation to profit potentials. Perhaps even greater value stems from the potential ability to fine-tune product offerings and other marketing decisions to the requirements of well-defined consumer segments. As part of the material regularly supplied to marketing managers, market segment profitability analysis could easily become a key component of marketing information systems of the future.

NOTES

1. Wendell R. Smith, "Product Differentiation and Market Segmentation as Alternative Marketing Strategies," *Journal of Marketing*, Vol. 21 (July 1965), pp. 3-8; and James F. Engel, Henry F. Fiorillo. and Murray A. Cayley, eds., *Market Segmentation: Concepts and Applications* (New York: Holt, Rinehart and Winston, Inc., 1972),
2. Philip Kotler, *Marketing Management*, Second Edition (Englewood Cliffs, New Jersey: Prentice-Hall, Inc., 1972), p. 166.
3. Ronald E. Frank, "Market Segmentation Research: Findings and Implications," in *Applications of the Sciences in Marketing Management* Frank M. Bass, Charles W. King, and Edgar A. Pessemier, eds. (New York: John Wiley & Sons, Inc., 1968), p. 39.
4. Closest to the present analysis and perhaps the best summary of the state of the art is Charles H. Sevin, *Marketing Productivity Analysis* (New York: McGraw-Hill Book Company, 1965).
5. Robert B. Miner, "Distribution Costs," in *Marketing Handbook*, Albert W. Frey, ed. (New York: The Ronald Press Company, 1965); see especially pp., 13-17 and 23-32.
6. Martin L. Bell, *Marketing: Concepts and Strategy*, Second Edition (Boston: Houghton Mifflin Company, 1972), p. 185.

7. See William M. Weilbacher, "Standard Classification of Consumer Characteristics," *Journal of Marketing*, Vol. 31 (January 1967), p. 27.

8. See William J.E. Crissy and Robert M. Kaplan, "Matrix Models for Marketing Planning," *MSU Business Topics*, Vol. 11 (Summer 1963), p. 48. The matrix "targeting" treatment is also familiar to readers of basic marketing texts by E.J. McCarthy or G. D. Downing.

9. See Charles R. Horngren, *Cost Accounting: A Managerial Emphasis*, 2nd ed. (Englewood Cliffs, New Jersey: Prentice-Hall, Inc., 1967); and Ralph L. Day and Peter D. Bennett, "Should Salesmen's Compensation be Geared to Profits?" *Journal of Marketing*, Vol. 26 (October 1962), pp. 6-9.

10. William J. Baumol and Charles H. Sevin "Marketing Costs and Mathematical Programming," in *Management Information: A Quantitative Accent*, Thomas Williams and Charles Griffin eds. (Homewood, Illinois: Richard D. Irwin, Inc., 1967), pp. 176-190.

11. Richard A. Feder, "How to Measure Marketing Performance," in *Readings in Cost Accounting, Budgeting and Control*, 3rd ed., (Cincinnati, Ohio: South-Western Publishing Co., 1968), pp. 650-668.

12. E.B. Weiss, "Pooled Marketing: Antidote for Soaring Marketing Costs, *Advertising Age*, Vol. 43 (November 13, 1972), pp. 63-64.

13

Designing A Trade Fair Stand

BRUCE BENDOW AND GARETH JONES

DEVELOPING a suitable design for a trade fair stand and selecting an appropriate stand site can help achieve success in fair participation. For many countries, participating in trade fair and other types of exhibitions is the most important way of promoting exports, in terms of money, time and efforts expended, and potentially at least in terms of results. Many factors enter into exhibiting successfully, but design of the stand and the presentation of individual exhibits are certainly among the key elements.

It is obvious that an unattractive stand will give a bad impression to visitors. It may create or contribute to a poor image of the exhibiting country or its products, and it can make the job of selling much harder. An attractive stand can have the opposite effect.

There are also other ways that the design of a stand can held, or hurt, the results of exhibiting by making it easier, or

Bruce Bendow is ITC's adviser on trade fairs and commercial publicity. Gareth Jones heads an exhibition design firm in the United Kingdom. This article is extracted from a new ITC training pack, Exhibition Stand Design, harder, to talk with visitors, for example. Or by showing products to their best advantage or, conversely, by allowing them to appear uninteresting or be easily overlooked.

The stand designer therefore plays a very important role in the results of exhibiting. His task is not as simple as many people think, for his job is not merely to design an attractive stand but also to develop one that will help the exhibitor to achieve specific objectives. Not only may these objectives vary from one exhibition to the next, but so will the local conditions of the cxhibition location and the business and cultural environment of that country. The designer must take these factors into acount. And, of course, he usually has to do the job on a limited budget.

The designer must be able to rely on receiving appropriate support from his clients to do his work satisfactorily. He cannot do his job properly by working alone. He must be briefed and backed up by the exhibiting fism(s) or the project manager, who can explain to him the objectives of exhibiting, who understands and can obtain the information the designer needs to do his job, and who appreciates the problems and limitations facing the designer. In a developing country, the staff in a national trade promotion organization may often have this responsibility.

If designing an exhibition stand were purely an artistic exercise, it would be almost impossible to answer the question "What is good design?' In a way that would satisfy everyone, everywhere. Tastes and aesthetic reactions vary from country to country, from culture to culture and from person to person.

There certainly is an important aesthetic aspect to stand design. In some cases this aspect can be a very important one, arguably the most important. The existence of this aesthetic element is one reason why designing is not simply a matter of rigid formulas and pure technology, and why there will often be differences of opinion about a particular design.

Even on the technical level there is often more than one valid solution to a design problem for trade fair stands.

Furthermore, the question of cost must be considered. Spending more money does not guarantee a better exhibition stand, but it often can help. In judging a stand design, one must ask, "Is this the best that could be achieved with the money availables?"

Taking all this into account, it is clear that one should not be too rigid or dogmatic in judging stand designs. Nevertheless, there is a basic criterion that any stand design must meet if it is to be succeessful ("successful" in the sense of contributting to the success of the overall exhibition project). In addition to this basic criterion, there are a number of principles, or "golden rules", that, if followed, usually contribute to the success of a design.

The basic criterion that a stand design must meet is that of being functional. This means that the design of the stand, in all its verious aspects, must help the exhibitors to achieve their particular commercial objectives.

Another aspect of this functional requirement is that the design must meent the physical needs of the staff on the stand. For instance, they require enough chairs so that they can work effectively and also rest when necessary, they usually need a proper work surface and a place to store things, and so on. Accommodating these needs is closely related to the stand's function in commercial terms. People are more productive in a comfortable, efficient environment.

One of the problems that a designer of an exhibition stand often faces is that the objectives of exhibiting have not been specifically stated in the brief that is given to him. In many cases, the objectives have not really been thought out. Sometimes, one of the important services the designer can perform is to help his client to define what his objectives of trade fair participation really are.

There are a variety of possible objectives in exhibiting. Usually an exhibitor attempts to achieve a combination of goals, although some will be more important than others. Among the possible objectives of participating in a trade show are to:

1. Create a particular image of the country and/or company exhibiting. The specific impression aimed at might be, for example, "modern," "traditional," "rural," "industrial," "progressive," "solid and respectable," "business like" and so on. The impression being conveyed should, of course, reflect an overall marketing strategy.
2. Sell specific products over the counter to the public.
3. Take orders for products from trade buyers.
4. Introduce a particular new product.
5. Make and record a maximum number of new, qualified business contracts.
6. Maintain contact and promote goodwill with established customers.
7. Inform business visitors about the country's industrial capacity.
8. Promote investments.
9. Promote the country to the tourist trade.
10. Promote the country as a tourist attraction to the public at large.

Each of these objectives has obvious design implications. A stand set up to sell products over the counter to crowds of consumers will be very different from one designed to induce discussions with selected business contacts.

There are ten "golden rules" of good stand design practice:

1. Keep it simple. The more complex the design of a stand is, the greater the risk of confusing the visitor, and the lesser the chance of creating a clear, strong impact. Furthermore, a lot of clutter will make it hard for the staff on the stand to work efficiently. Stand construction should be kept as simple as possible, while assuring that the desired results can be achieved.

2. Minimize the number of focal points. Focal points in exhibition stands are features that attract attention. The choice of focal points should obviously reflect the objectives of exhibiting. Very often they will be specific products—new products being introduced, or the exhibitor's most important or most representative products. In other cases, an information stand or counter might be an appropriate focal point, or an audiovisual display that will draw visitors into the stand.

To maximize impact, there should be a minimum number of focal points—perhaps only one. Too many focal points divide the visitors' attention and tend to confuse and weaken the overall impression that the visitors take away with them. On the other hand, many stands make the mistake of having no focal point at all.

3. Establish a clear theme. The "theme" is the basic message or impression that the exhibitor wishes to convey about his organization or his products or both. The theme of a stand or of a group of stands can concern fairly explicit attributes of products, of a company or of a country; or it can express qualities of a less tangible kind. The theme, and the impact it creates, should be consistent with what the exhibitor really wants to say about his company and his products.

Exhibitor with large budgets have tendency to build prestige stands that may be very impressive but do not deliver a clear message. Designers of more modest stands make a similar mistake if they simply try to make an attractive or striking stand that does not convey a clear commercial message of help to promote the products.

Achieving a clear theme is partly a matter of using focal points, as mentioned above. It is also a matter of using appropriate colours, graphics and displays in a consistent way to make a unified impression.

4. Establish a strong identity. This is important for a number of reasons. A clearly identifiable stand is easier to find by visitors who are looking for it than one that does not have any distinguishing characterstics. It can leave an impression even on fair visitors who do not stop at the stand, triggering recognition at some later date. In the case of a national, collective participation by a group of individual exhibitors, a strong national identification can maximize the overall impact and help draw more attention to the individual stands than the stands could by themselves.

5. Attract attention. For a large, well integrated stand, attracting attention is usually not great problem, particularly if the stand is suitably situated in the hall. But it is not so easy to attract the attention of busy visitors to a small, shell-scheme stand located in the midst of many other small stands, halfway down an aisle. (A shell scheme is a standardized stand and furnishings provided by the exhibition organizer). A variety of techniques can be used, such as colour combinations that stand out, demonstrations, animated displays and so on. But whatever methods are employed, they should do more than attract attention. They should stimulate the interest of the type of visitor that the exhibitors are trying to reach. And they should harmonize with the overall design of the stand.

6. Design through the eyes of the target visitors. One of the primary functions of an exhibition stand is to make a calculated impression on target visitors. To achieve the impression desired, the designer must first of all know who the target visitors are. Then he must know or try to find out how such visitors react to various design elements. He must understand not only what these visitors will be looking for, but how such elements as colours will strike them, and how they already perceive the exhibitor.

7. Suit the design to the number of people expected. The designer should take into account both the number of visitors and the number of staff that the stand will have to accommodate. An overcrowded stand is inefficient and can discourage visitors. So can a stand that is too empty. The size of the stand is obviously a major factor here, and the designer may little to say about this. But he can deal with various elements that effect use of space, such as layout, the amount and kind of furniture, and the methods of displaying products.

8. Plan the traffic management. The exhibitor may want large numbers of visitors to flow freely through the stand. Or he may wish to attract many people, but to screen them before admitting only a small number inside. He may intend to only a small number inside. He may inted to record the name of every visitor, or only selected ones: or, on the other hand, registration might not be important at all.

The arrangement of the stand is crucial to managing the traffic properly, so the designer must establish at the outwet what sort of traffic flow the exhibitor wants.

9. Ensure that the stand is easy to erect and discount. The stand construction should be simple and straightforward enough to erect and discount in the time allowed. The build-up and take-down periods are usually set by the exhibition organizers. It is essential that the designer know this schedule before he starts to design.

10. Insist on a clear budget, and work within it. Working without a clear budget is a potentially dangerous situation for a designer. If the construction costs turn out to be exorbitant, he may be blamed. Therefore the designer should insist on having a precise budget, and should assure that he stays within it.

Conclusion: If there is a single conclusion that can be drawn from these basic principles, it is that a good stand design is harmonious. An exhibition stand is made up of many of elements-layout, lighting, colours, graphics, the merchandise displays, the furnishings and the structure itself. A good design blends all these elements so that they work together to help the exhibitors achieve their objectives.

Six basic steps should be followed in designing a stand:

1. Obtain complete information. Designing an effective stand, and doing it without a lot of false starts and revisions, depends to a great extent on having information that is as complete as possible, as soon as possible. This includes information about the exhibitors, such as their budgets, their objectives, their market activities, and position, how they want to project them selves, how many people they will have on the stand, and any special facilities needed, such as audiovisual displays, discussion or entertainment areas and so on. Graphic references are also important, such as examples of the exhibitors' logos and advertising.

nformation about the products is also needed; such as their number and nature, which should be featured and which characteristics played up, how the products look, if they are to be demonstrated and any special technical requirements.

Details must also be ascertained on the exhibition itself. The floor and site plans must be obtained, showing sercices, technical data and building regulations. Information on the shellstand schemes and the possibilities for, or required. It is likewise important to know what type of show it is the size and nature of the audience, who the competition is and how their stands tend to look.

2. Decide on stand size, shape and layout. Ideally, the designer should be involved in deciding on the size and shape of the stand, based on such factors as the number and nature of exhibits and the stand's function. In practice, however, the space is often booked before the

designer is involved. His first task, then, is to design a layout that will make the best use of the space available.

To do this, he will have to take into account the following factors:

The position and shape of the stand.

The specific space and display needs connected with the products of individual exhibitors.

The need for such facilities as discussion area, food and drink dispensing, storage, demonstrations, information centres and so on.

The expected number of people on the stand and the desired traffic flow.

3. Decide on the overall theme and impression. The theme should reflect the company or country exhibiting, the product and the marketing objectives. So should the specific impression that is to be created by the stand. The exhibitor should define the theme and the impression he sould to make for the designer. But all too often the exhibitor himself has not worked this out. It therefore falls on the designer to learn as much as he can about the company's or country's marketing situation and the image it already has in the market, so that he can help define what the stand's "look" should be.

4. Plan the individual design elements. This involves the colour schemes, the lighting, the display equipment and furnishings, and graphics—the physical elements of the stand. All of the information already mentioned above is needed to select and blend these elements effectively.

   The designer must also know about the physical properties of the products being displayed, so that he can choose the most attractive ways of showing them. The selection of the best type of lighting, for example, depends very much on the colour and texture of the products.

5. Work out the construction methods. The designer must keep in mind practical and economic construction methods as he designs the structural components.
6. Brief the construction contractor. Once the design has been approved, the designer should draw up detailed working plans and complete specifications. Usually the designer is also responsible for supervising fabrication of the stand components and on-site construction. Therefore he should have a thorough knowledge of construction techniques and a good working relationship with the contractor.

(A series of extracts from the training pack on specific stand design topics starts below. The training pack is designed for easy application).

Site selection involves finding the best answers to three questions:

How large should the stand site be?

Where should it be located-in which hall, and where in that hall?

What shape should it be?

The decisions taken on these questions are among the most important decisions affecting the designer's work, so he obviously should be deeply involved in making them. But for many exhibitions, the location and shape of the site and sometime even its size are dictated to the exhibitors by the exhibition organizer. In well established exhibitions, priority is given to the wishes of the exhibitors who have been participating repeatedly and to the ones taking the most space. Large national participations may be particularly attractive to fair organizers for their prestige value, and this may increase their bargaining power when negotiating for a preferred site.

Even if a trade promotion organization or other exhibitor cannot always choose the exact site it wants, it usually will have at least a limited choice in terms of size, and some options regarding the location and possibly the shape of the site. The expertise of a competent designer is especially important in selecting the site for a stand that will group a number of exhibitors under one national banner. Poor choices have often been made because the design implications were not understood.

Ideally, the designer and the project officer managing the participation should work together in the site selection process. For important projects both should actually visit the exhibition facility. If this is not feasible, they should obtain as much information as possible from a commercial attache or other representative about the exhibition facility and the sites available, This could be a valuable supplement to the information provided by the organizer.

Many factors must be taken into account in choosing the best site for the stand. In addition to the information from the field, much will be needed from the exhibitor or group organizer. These factors include details on the size, location and shape. These issues are very much interrelated, which often complicates the site selection process.

How much space should be booked? As mentioned above, the exhibition organizer may impose a limit on the amount of space that an exhibitor can take. Another limiting factor that is often even more important is the budget of the participants.

Apart from those two constraints, other elements that should be considered when deciding on how large a site is needed are:

1. Products: The space calculation generally starts with the products to be displayed—what kind will be displayed and how many of each. From this information a rough estimate of the space needed for displays can be made. Whatever idea the exhibitors already have about how to display the products will obviously

play a role in this estimate. Some products might be displayed on the wall; others might need display cases. A machine might not only take up a large floor space but also require space all around it for people to view it from different angles.

2. Exhibitors: The next factor to take into account is the number of individual exhibitors. A rule of thumb is to allow about four square metres of net stand space for each exhibitor having a representative on the stand. (Net stand space is space not occupted by exhibits).

   Adding the space needed for product displays to the net stand space given a rough minimum requirement of the space for each stand, and for the group as a whole (if it is a group stand).

   In practice, nine square meters would be the minimum for any individual stand, or individual booth or unit in group stand, and 15 square metres is quite normal for such a stand.

3. Visitors: The number and nature of visitors expected must also be considered. For large numbers of visitors, extra floor space should be allowed. If a small number of trade visitors is expected, less space for traffic would be required, but on the other hand, space might have to be set aside for discussion areas.

4. Activities: As mentioned above, if business discussions are envisaged, the basic space calculation must be adjusted for this. Other activities that will take place on the stand will also have space implications, such as demonstrations, a fashion show, or the operation of a central information or visitor screening desk.

5. Facilities required: A review of the product display requirements will have indicated any special, space-consuming needs, such as freezer chests, an audiovisual display, or a platform and gangway for a fashion show. Other facilities that should be taken into account in calculating space requirements might include extra

storage and lock-up areas and hospitality facilities, including a bar, a refrigerator, and cooking and washing-up equipment.

6. Size of competing stands: There is an obvious relation between the size of a stand and the amount of attention it receives. But this is relative.

A 25-square-metre stand would look imposing in the middle of a row of 9-square-metre stands, but it could shrink to insignificance if surrounded by 200-square-metre stands. It is important to check the sizes of the other stands that will be around the stand concerned before deciding on how large that stand should be.

14

New Perspective on Exports

R.F.S. TALYASKHAN

We generally think of exports as a series of business transactions involving the supply and shipment of various types of commodities and materials. This is, of course, true of 95 per cent of our export business. These exports are subsidised by Government through various incentive schemes and other measures, which induce manufacturers to export more, thereby earning foreign exchange for the country. It is a sad reflection of our times that these incentives are necessary. Despite higher productivity, we are still not in a position to export economically at world market prices, as any gains achieved by increases in efficiently are more than offset by the upward spiralling costs of materials and labour.

Even with these incentives, the time had come when India's traditional lines of exports such as textiles, tea, jute, cotton and coffee will be greatly reduced because of increasingly still higher competition from other countries in fields in which we were once supreme. To offset this trend, we have in the past few years, entered the field of non-traditional exports like manufactured goods and engineering products, but the latent fear of all manufacturers and exporters has been that those products may not be competitive enough in quality and price for sustained and continuous foreign exchange earnings. From

Advertising Club, Bombay.

a long term point of view, this fear should stimulate our exporters and manufacturers to greater efforts. We have, to think in terms of diversifying the aspects of our export trade and to tackle the problem from a wider perspective. The orientation of our thinking should, be flexible enough to recognise export outlets and opportunities which are not readily apparent on the surface.

One of the ways of doing this is to consider the feasibility of exporting components and parts to industries that are now being set up in developing countries. This is, in effect, a form of sub-contracting which could usefully be employed on such items as say, unfinished castings, forgings and stampings which could be machined and finished by the nascent industry in the developing country.

An extension of this sub-contracting principle can perhaps better be achieved by applying parts or components to subsidiaries or associates of overseas collaborators of Indian manufacturers, who may have started a joint-venture in a developing country. However, one must be realistic about this, as it is obviously not always in the interest of the overseas principal to allow an India-based Company to apply component parts to a third country where he can perhaps export more profitably. Nevertheless, mutual agreements can sometimes be worked out. For instance, the foreign exchange so earned by the Indian company can in turn be used to import components or raw materials from the parent firm. From a long-term point of view this approach may, in fact, turn out to be economically advantageous to the foreign Principal.

The logical extension of this type of collaboration may very well lead to the formation of tripartite joint-venture which perhaps has received serious attention so far. It may sometimes happen that, for political or balance of trade reasons, the stabilising catalytic influence of an Indian partner may be acceptable to all parties, whereas a straight-forward bilateral agreement between a foreign principal and the local entrepreneur in a developing country, might not receive the blessing of this Government. From India's point of view, it is, however, preferable to consider the setting up of direct joint-ventures in developing countries in Africa and West Asia where we can supply our own know-how and management skills.

Equity participation in these joint-ventures can only be made by providing indigenously manufactured machine tools and equipment, as to foreign exchange would be permitted to be sent out of the country. Nevertheless, there are, at this moment, some 35 to 40 joint-ventures with Indian collaboration, operating in various parts of the world. The majority of them are in Africa.

The advantages of setting-up such joint-ventures lie in the fact that profits can be made in the following way:

(a) We can derive payments in foreign exchange for know-how.

(b) We can obtain royalties on the products that are being manufactured.

(c) We can repatriate dividends on equity shares, and

(d) Last but not least, we can, for the next decade or so, hope to export component parts and materials to the industries that are being set up, thereby ensuring a steady source of foreign exchange earnings and continuous work for our factories.

The Ministry of Commerce was considering in what manner Indian entrepreneurs may benefit by way of import entitlements from foreign exchange earned through know-how, royalty and other such fees. That the Government of India is fully aware of the need to assist Indian parties undertaking collaboration or investments abroad was evidenced from the statement of Finance Minister, where he said:

"Some fiscal encouragement needs to be given to our industries to encourage them to provide technical know-how and technical services to newly developing countries. I propose, therefore, to provide for a concessional rate of tax on dividends received by an Indian company from a foreign company on shares allotted to the Indian company in consideration for supplying technical know-how or rendering technical services. This concessional rate of 2.5 per cent will also be charged on royalties, commissions, fees etc., received by an Indian company from a foreign company for supply of technical know-how and technical service."

Another avenue open for exploration is the possibilities of exporting our engineering and technical skills. Development plans for various countries particularly in Africa, will entail a more widespread use of project consultants as well as the employment of management personnel with experience. As an example, geogogical surveys water-well drilling programmes, irrigation schemes, dam construction, hydro-electric projects, air conditioning installations and the processing of agricultural products are projects which we, in India, are familiar with, having learnt our.

APPENDIX I

Note on India's Small Industry Exports

In many countries, small industries are responsible for a large proportion of their countries' foreign exchange earnings. It is not always possible to give precise statistics because there are often no precise definitions abroad of small scale industry as there is in India. Authoritative figures, however, show that in Japan, for instance, 67 per cent of that country's export trade is accounted for by small scale industries. It is probable that nearly 50 per cent of U.K.'s exports are achieved by what in India, would be classified as small scale industries.

In other countries, small scale units do export not because of Government compulsion or of financial incentives but because they find that, in the long run it pays them better to export their products than to sell them in the home market. One of the firms in the U.K. which makes highly competitive consumer products with 25 employees and a capital of about

Rs. 1 lakh, exported 80 per cent of its output simply because more profits were made by exporting than in the domestic market. Much of the world's trade is conducted through comparatively small importing merchants abroad and it is frequently found that these merchants prefer to deal with small manufacturers upon whom they feel they can rely for personal attention much more than on large producers. If the Indian manufacturer wishes to import raw materials and machinery, or wishes to go abroad for study or on holiday, or if his family want the benefits of imported items, then that manufacturer must help to earn the necessary foreign exchange. Just because he is classed as a small-scale industry does not mean that he can expect his biggers in industry to do all the work for him. There is really no reason why Indian small scale industries should not emulate their counterparts in other countries. A survey showed that, in general, the quality of products made in the Indian small scale sector was suitable for overseas markets and that prices, generally, were suitable also.

The main deficiency of Indian small industry is in the field of export know-how. Many small industries believe that all they need to know is at what prices competing products sell in overseas markets and to have lists of names of importers to whom they can just write a letter. Much more is needed; this includes knowledge of what products are most suitable for which overseas markets; how to present those articles properly in the way of sales leaflets, catalogues, and packaging. It also includes knowledge of how to price the articles in a way acceptable to the foreign buyer, how to write attractive sales letters, how to ship the goods and prepare the shipping documents in a way which will give the importer no trouble, and how to arrange payment.

Lessons from Japan[1]

1. Need for Marketing Strategy

The success of the Japanese export programme was due largely to the highly developed merchandising sense of Japanese business, large and small. This sensitivity to the needs of foreign consumers in terms of product, design, colour and quality does not seem to exist widely among Indian proprietors of small industry. These skills must be developed if Indian small industry is to compete in the world markets.

2. Strengthening of Distribution Channels—Export Houses and Indent Houses

The Export House system of Japan has been a major factor for the success of Japanese foreign trade. They provide the necessary facilities for thousands of manufacturers on a scale which no individual firm could develop. Indian small industries should establish Export Houses with sufficient capital and competent trained personnel. There should be no more than 12 Export Houses for all India, and they should operate on a regional basis, such as Madras, Calcutta, Bombay, Delhi and other commercial centres. They should be organized in such a manner that there are three departments dealing respectively with domestic sales, exports, and imports. There should be no competition among Export Houses in foreign countries. Indent Houses (large general wholesalers in major foreign commercial centres) should be used extensively in collaboration with Export Houses.

3. Direct Contact with Foreign Markets

The Japanese practice of having merchant vessels stocked with the products of small manufacturers and going from one market to another could be effectively used by Indian manufacturers.

4. Encouragement of Export Drive

The desirability of tax concessions, import privileges and other forms of Government subsidy for those firms which are contributing substantially to India's foreign trade should be examined.

5. Encouragement of Foreign Collaboration

The investment environment in India cannot be considered favourable when contrasted with countries such as Malaysia, and Brazil. The obstacles placed in the way of investment and foreign capital should be eliminated and a generally favourable environment created.

Factors Limiting Exports and Problems Faced by Small Industry

1. Internal Seller's Market

The sellers' market in India has been a major factor for the lack of export effort by business in general and small business in particular. Inferior merchandise is sold with little difficulty in the Indian market and the poor design and quality of this merchandise makes it difficult to sell them abroad where it has to compete with the products of countries who are more sophisticated industrially.

2. Heavy Tax Burden

A revision of the Indian tax system which would be designed to encourage export is highly desirable.

3. Poor Management of Small Units

General management in small industry is not competent to compete in world markets. One man control lack of delegation and administrative bottlenecks are evidence of this poor management. This situation is contrasted with the current Trends in small industry management in Japan, which includes greater use of consultants and the willingness to include non-family members at the higher levels of management.

4. Bottlenecks in Raw Materials

Small manufacturers have difficulty in obtaining raw materials and power. Small industries should be given greater opportunity to import the necessary raw materials when there is a reasonable certainty of their selling abroad and obtaining foreign exchange. The import entitlements currently provided by the government may be more extensive.

5. Bottlenecks in Technical Know-how and Semi-skilled Labour

The high rate of absenteeism among semi-skilled labourers, and the relative lack of technical skills which exist in the small sector are unfavourable factors.

6. Other Reasons for the Low Volume of Exports by Small-Scale Industry

(a) Lack of modern marketing techniques.

(b) Poor packaging and product design.

(c) Poor brand policy.

(d) Lack of knowledge of foreign markets by the small manufacturers.

Japanese manufacturers obtain prompt and adequate market information of all major foreign markets from JETRO (Japnese Export Trade Organization—a market research organization sponsored jointly by the Japanese Government and Japanese industry).

7. Poor Understanding of Cost Accounting

Many Indian products are not priced realistically in world markets.

Small Industries Having Exports Potential

These may be grouped into three major categories:

(a) Industries which had increased exports sales each year.

(b) Industries which may be considered to be progressive because of exports which increased as compared with previous years.

(c) Industries whose sales decreased in comparison with previous years.

Traditional items of India's export trade such as tea, cotton, jute, cashew, spices and mica, are excluded. Also those products which are mainly in the large scale sector are excluded.

(a) ***Promising Exports***

1. Oil cakes (including deflated groundnut meal)
2. Fruits and vegetables, fruits, fresh or dried
3. Groundnut Oil
4. Cotton piecegoods, handloom products
5. Coir manufacturers (excluding fibre and yarn)
6. Coir mats and mattings
7. Lemongrass Oil
8. Prawns
9. Bristles
10. Plants and parts of plants for use in dyeing and tanning
11. Animal casing
12. Canned fish
13. Sewing machines and parts
14. Candles, tubes and articles of inflammable materials
15. Umbrellas, walking sticks and similar articles
16. Palmarosa oil
17. Leather manufactures
18. Artificial leather

(*b*) ***Progressive Exports***

1. Goat skins and kid skins, undressed
2. Gums, resins
3. Lac
4. Carpets, floor rugs, mats and matting
5. Castor oil
6. Groundnut oil

7. Footwear
8. Handicrafts (such as artware)
9. Fruits
10. Vegetable oils (non-essential)
11. Household, utensils of iron and steel
12. Meat, fresh, chilled and frozen
13. Soap and other cleansing preparations
14. Plastic goods
15. Linseed oil
16. Cutlery, including table and kitchenware

(c) *Stagnant Exports*

1. Leather and leather manufactures
2. Hides and skins, tanned or dressed
3. Leather undressed
4. Bones for manufacturing purposes
5. Plant, seeds, flowers mainly for use in medicine or perfumery
6. Opium crude
7. Dressed and finished leather
8. Palm fibre
9. Sandalwood oil
10. Silver, platinum, gems and jewellery
11. Bidi leaves
12. Travel goods, handbags and similar articles
13. Coir fibre
14. Dry batteries

Industries which may be considered to have prospects for export trade includes the following:

Bristles
Canned fish
Sewing machines
Carpets
Vegetable oils
Footwear
Household utensils of iron and steel
Meat-fresh, chilled and frozen
Soap and other cleaning preparations
Plastic goods
Silver
Platinum
Gems and jewellery
Bicycles
Preserved Fruit and Vegetables
Industrial and scientific instruments
Machine tools

Studies of specific foreign markets by existing organizations in India that are concerned with small industry should be made. The Export Promotion Councils, Ministry of Commerce, Federation of Associations of Small Industry in India, and other associations with similar objectives could undertake these effects if they are backed by sufficient funds and provide with experienced personnel. Various trade associations can play an important role in promoting exports. Such associations, with the help of the Government can encourage standardisation of products, advocate a high degree of integrity among industralists, thus ensuring satisfactory dealings with foreign buyers. They can also encourage either voluntary or mandatory quality control system.

Use of samples in foreign markets through participation in foreign trade fairs by In ian manufacturers. Strengthening of existing export incentives—import entitlement—based on a company's export volume—ranging from 20 per cent upto 75 per cent of the rupee value of the exports are worth examining.

NOTE

Export Marketing Techniques of Japan's Small Enterprises

Japan is poor in natural resources which are indispensable for the development of the economy. Therefore, for many years, promotion of international trade has been one of the most important problems of acting the country which has been taking various measure for export promotion. There are some measures taken *exclusively* for the promotion of export of commodities produced by small business. Because of scarcity of necessary funds, most small enterprises find it difficult to get correct information and trends in foreign markets and also on developing a new market abroad. In order to make up for such handicaps of its small business and to promote their exports, the government takes the following measures:

(1) To find local products which are suitable for foreign tastes and modes and to improve their quality and design so as to meet foreign requirements, the government invites designers and other experts from abroad, who go around the country to give advice and guidance.

When it is necessary to improve the quality of those local products which are discovered by foreign experts, the government gives subsidies to their producers.

(2) A Japan Export Merchandise Fair is organized once a year to introduce and advertise products of smaller enterprises. The Government gives financial assistance for the opening of the Fair, Merchandise of superior quality selected at the Fair are to be displayed at special booths in the International Trade Fair which is held every year in the Tokyo or Osaka.

(3) For qualitative improvement of export products of smaller enterprises and to encourage trial production of new commodities, technical advise and other assistance is given to small business.

(4) Various measures taken by JETRO (Japan External Trade Organization), such as market research, advertising, intermediation of trade, consultation on foreign trade, have contributed much for the export small business products.

(5) As to financing, the Small Business Finance Corporation supplies plant and Equipment funds at lower rates of inerest (7.5 to 7.6 percent for enterprises which have concluded long-term export contracts or for enterprises which belong to designated lines of business and have given actual results of exporting more than 20 per cent of their total production.

(6) In order to facilitate borrowing of Operation funds by small business connected with export, some credit guarantee associations make guarantee commitment at lower rates of premium.

(7) As to taxation, extra depreciation is allowed on machinery and other fixed assets owned by small enterprises which have income through foreign trade. Besides, 1.5 per cent income through foreign trade transaction can be exempted from corporate tax when it is kept as 'foreign market development reserve.'

Packaging for Exports

Quality goods which are exported from India in excellent condition often reach their destination in a damaged state. They may be returned and cause considerable loss to the seller, or they may be retained to the disadvantage of the buyer. In either case, they give the exporter—and even the country of their origin a bad name. So acute was the problem that the Government of India has set up an Indian Institute of Packaging which concentrates on problems of packaging.

Packaging for the domestic market need not only be attractive; for export purposes it has to be strong and protective as well. Insurance studies indicate that about 80 per cent of the losses in respect of export cargo can be prevented by proper packaging.

Export packaging has three major functions to perform: protection against water and moisture, against breakage and against theft. Covering that is imprevious to moisture should be used to protect goods that are affected by water which can cause rust, stains, mildew, rotting, delamination, swelling or warping.

Breakage may be prevented by proper choice of container. Articles which do not fill the container should be braced, fastened, blocked or otherwise held in place to prevent interior movement. Great attention should be paid to inner packaging.

The container and the interior packing should be such as to absorb shocks and cushion external pressure. To prevent pilferage, new well constructed containers should be used made, of fibre board or nailed wooden boxes. The contents should not be described on the outside.

Costs can be kept down considerably by the use of the appropriate material. Indian packaging tends to be haphazard in the choice of material and their quality, and accordingly more costly.

Another factor to be borne in mind is that in some countries and for some items charges on imports may be levied according to the number of containers, so that a larger number of boxes will attract a higher levy. This can be an important cost item. Some governments have stringent regulations on the use of internal packaging material. Care should also be taken to ensure that packaging material does not contain anything offensive to religious sentiments.

While the world trade in fish and fish products expanded from over 5 million tonnes in 1954 to 15 million tonnes in 1963, India's exports fell from 25,000 tonnes to 17,000 tonnes. India's share in the world trade accordingly declined from 0.47 percent to 0.1 per cent. Similarly, world production of fish rose from 24.6 million tonnes in 1951-53 to 44.6 million tonnes in 1961-63, and canned beer should be quite as good as mackerel, sardine tuna. The quality of the product will be the deciding factor.

Processed foods are in very great demand in Switzerland which has one of the highest living standards in the world. Fish consumption (of all products, excluding crustaceans and molluscs) for 1964 was 23.86 kilos per inhabitant, and increase of 3.62 kilos over the 1963 figure of 20.24 kilos. The total consumption of fish and fish products for 1964 was around 136 million kilos. The per capita consumption of crustaceans and molluscs was approximately 2.30 kilos, and increase of 0.60 kilos over the 1963 figure of 2.20 kilos.

Frozen foods are becoming increasingly popular. Deep-freeze units for storage of frozen foods are available all over the country and commercial deep-freezes are installed in 2500 villages. Consumption of frogs' legs is probably in the region of 125,000 kilos per annum, of which only half is produced locally. Consumption has been rising, particularly in the restaurant trade which takes some 50 per cent of the domestic production. Imports of frozen frogs legs come mostly from Rumania, Czechoslovakia and France.

There is good scope for Indian exports, though transport costs from India are higher than from Eastern Europe. Canned prawns and shrimps are another important import item. Consumption has more than doubled over the last few years. About 25 percent of the volume of imports consists of shrimps. The rest is prawns. Shrimps, however, constitute 50 per cent of the value. India exported 17,000 kilos of prawns and shrimps in 1963, the highest so far; in 1964, there was a sharp decline.

There is also scope for the export of frozen shrimps to the U.S. Imports into California and Arizona of shrimps from India for 1968 were 10,22,921 pounds against 6,13,877 pounds during 1964. Imports of frozen shrimps (pickled and deveined) went up 15 times as compared with 1964.

Swill importers have complained that the prices of Indian timber are unusually high, though the quality is good. The main variety imported from India is palisander, of which 1,13,000 kgs, valued at 2,27,000 francs were imported in 1964. Much less expensive is Brazilian Palisander, of which Switzerland imported 1,81,000 kgs., valued at 2,08,000 francs. Swill importers also buy Indian timber indirectly from Italy. The Italians import is in large quantities and veneer it for local consumption and for export to foreign countries. Though Italian prices are high, the Swiss prefer to import it from Italy because they are certain of the quality. Indian exporters would do well to try and market veneered palisander, teak and walnut. The acceptable dimensions of sheets are 0.6 centimeters thick, 6 ft; or more long and as wide as possible. There is no Customs duty on the import of sawn timber into Switzerland.

15

Programming, Budgeting and Evaluation—Three Essential Management Functions of a TPO

CAMILO JARAMILLO

To achieve results that meet the needs of the country's foreign trade sector, a national trade promotion organization (TPO) should systematically plan and budget its promotional activities. Yet many TOPs give relatively little attention to planning a coherent programme of operations and to budgeting resöurces in line with the objectives of that programme. Evaluating the success of the programme activities is also seldom undertaken by TOPs as a matter of course, although such an exercise could often provide guidelines for improving future operations and optimizing the limited funds at the disposal of the organization.

Camilo Jaramillo is ITC's adviser on the institutional aspects of trade promotion. This article is based on a study that he recently wrote on the institutional and managerial aspects of a national trade promotion organization. (See also "Organizational Features of a National Trade Promotion Organization", *Forum*. October-December 1984, page 20).

To carry out programming, budgeting and evaluation effectively, trade promotion officials should understand the importance of these functions for the success of their work and attempt to overcome problems that may arise in undertaking these tasks. The discussion that follows identifies some of the potential problem areas and suggests possible approaches for overcoming them.

Only a few TPOs in developing countries have established the practice of drawing up an annual work programme. Instead most of them merely continue to carry out the same types of activities that they have undertaken in the past, with no clear indicaiion of how these relate to each other and of the objectives to be achieved through them. The TPO staff consequently devote most of their time to helping solve day-to-day export problems rather than working towards longer term trade promotion goals.

In some cases TPO may have a "work programme" in name, but in reality the programme consists of only a list activities, without specific targets. Emphasis is given to the number of activities to be carried out over the year, rather than their quality and their relationship to overall trade promotion goals of the organization.

For the small number of TPOs that have instituted programming as regular feature of their operations, improvements could often be made in the way in which the programme is frequently the result of adding together the individual plans of each department, which tends to lead to isolated and sometimes conflicting activities. Only a few TPOs have some kind of programming unit or team that can discuss the individual plans and succeed in harmonizing them.

In addition, many of the work programmes in operation have the serious defect of representing only the viewpoint of the TPO staff, without due consideration of the needs of the export community. There is a marked absence in most TPOs of working groups of any type containing representatives of the business sector and also of any attempt to make system inquiries among businessmen of their trade promotion requirements. Consequently in many cases the TPOs activities do not reflect the real needs of the export sector. For example "upstream" trade promotion activities (that is, export development work staring at the production phase) is usually not included in a TPO's programme.

Finally, many TPOs that have an annual work programme tend to abandon it when world market conditions change. They then start ad hoc activities of a temporary nature, instead of adapting the plan to the new circumstances.

A possible approach: To overcome these problems, TPOs in developing countries should establish some type of programming and budgeting unit within their organizational setup that can assist their management in identifying objectives and concentrating the institution's often limited human and financial resources on priority areas. The unit could be established either as a separate section or as a working group composed of the heads of the TPO's departments.

The unit could be responsible for providing the TPO's executives, as well as the rest of the staff, with short, medium and long-term objectives on which to focus their work. At the same time, it could harmonize all of the TPO's activities and thereby avoid ineffective and conflicting courses of action. By involving the export community in the discussions leading up to the preparation of the work programme, the unit could assure that its plans reflected the actual needs of the business sector. (ITC has issued guidelines on how to prepare an annual work programme, as well as programmes on a product basis, which can be obtained from ITC upon request).

The types of objectives set and the range of activities selected to achieve them will of course be influenced by the amount of financial resources available to the TPO and the degree to which these funds remain stable or can be increased from one year to the next.

TPOs can obtain the funds to cover their operating expenses from several different sources. The origin of such financing has

an important bearing on the continuity of the TPO's programme and on the dynamism of its overall activities.

Funds from the national budget: Financing through the annual budget of the ministry of trade or another official body to which the TPO is directly or indirectly attached is the most frequent source of funds for a TPO. However relying on financing from such yearly budgetary allotments has certain drawbacks, such as:

1. In many cases, the funds provided by the ministry are insufficient to cover all of the activities that the TPO should be carrying out.
2. Because it is subject to an annual allocation, which in many cases varies substantially from one year to another, the TPO is prevented from engaging in medium-term programmes.
3. In case of national budgetary difficulties, the TPO's funds may be among the first to be cut, since a high priority in the government's overall programme and it tends to lack the political backing that other sectors of the public service have.
4. In most cases, financing through a ministry's budget links the TPO staff to the civil service regulations, which may limit the possibilities to pay them satisfactory salaries and consequently to recruit the most appropriate type of staff for trade promotion work.
5. The funds allocated through the annual budget are based, in most instances, on past levels of expenditure. This prevents the TPO from working on a development programme basis and instead leaves it with the alternative of simply trying to justify the expenditure of a given amount based on previous outlays.

Specific allocations; TPOs are in a much better position if they have their own source of financing or at least when a substantial part of their budget comes from such a source, rather than solely from the national budget. Some of the alternatives include:

1. Levy on imports: In some developing countries a special levy has been established on imports to finance the activities of the TPO. The rationale is that the import sector benefits from increased exports, because it is usually the main user of the foreign exchange generated by exports; it can increase its import activities when additional foreign exchange is available.

In developing countries using very moderate. A levy, the rate charged is usually very moderate. A levy of around 1 per cent of the import value can generate enough funds to cover the TPO's basic activities. Compared with the customs duties usually in effect, the rate is not a burden to importers in most cases.* If the levy is adequately explained and justified, the import sector tends to accept it with the hope that the TPO's activities will generate the foreign exchange required for increased imports.

Certain developing countries that have used this type of financing have been able to put their trade promotion organizations on a solid financial footing.

2. Levy on exports: As an alternative to the above, some developing countries impose a tax on sector is the one that benefits from the TPO's services and it should therefore help finance them. There may be some justification for this reasoning. However in many developing countries it is difficult to impose a levy on an export product that may already by only marginally competitive in price. The amount of the levy, even if

* It should be noted that this method of financing export promotion activities would not be in conformity with the rules of the GATT if it led to import charges in excess of tariff concessions by a contracting party to the GATT. However many developing countries have not made tariff concessions in the GATT and others have committed themselves to maximum tariffs in regard to only a small portion of their imports.

moderate, might make the export price too high for the goods to sell on the foreign market. This is especially the case for non-traditional export lines.

In a few countries a compromise solution has been worked out, whereby a proportion of the rebates granted to exporters to compensate for internal taxes is retained by the authorities and transferred directly to the TPO to cover all or part of its expenses. Under this formula, the responsibility for financing the promotional activities still falls on the export sector, but the effects on export firms are more limited, since the benefits that the firms receive are reduced only in part.

The main advantage of applying levies on imports or exports as a source of financing is to guarantee a stable and permanent source of funds for the TPO's activities, thereby allowing it to programme its actions on a medium-term basis. Under such a system, a precise mechanism should exist to assure that the money collected reaches the TPO directly and is not simply incorporated into the government's overall revenues.

One relatively minor drawback with the levy system is that sudden drops in the total value of imports or exports, for one reason or another, might induce a similar decrease in the TPO's financial resources. This problem has occurred in certain countries using levies as a major source for the TPO's funding. However if the levy has been established at a high enough level from the beginning, most TPOs can accumulate sufficient reserves over time to allow them to overcome the difficult periods during the short term without drastically cutting back on their activities.

In some countries it may not be possible to implement a system of levies, since the fiscal regulations may prevent the imposition of taxes or levies for a specific end-use.

Charging for services: Charging for services is a source of financing that is frequently foreseen in a TPO's statutes. However this means of funding poses certain problems:

1. If there is a charge for a service, it means that some expense must have been incurred to generate that service. Therefore the charge simply represents an offset of expenses, rather than a source of financing for new or additional activities.

2. In most developing countries, particularly when export consciousness is not highly developed, export promotion services should be provided free, since charging for them will probably prevent exporters from using them. Until there is a real commitment to exporting, businessmen will tend to be reluctant to pay for foreign trade information and similar services.

3. To establish the practice of charging from the beginning of a TPO's operations could limit the use of a TPO's services to a great extent, because exporters might be hesitant to pay for services that are not yet well established. It might be possible to begin charging gradually, as the TPO staff gain experience and as the scope and quality of the services improve.

4. An activity for which charging is feasible is the sale of specialized publications. Publications sales could even generate some profit. However in the long run revenue from this source would probably represent only a minimal portion of a TPO's required financing.

For the above reasons, charging for services is far from the ideal solution as a source of finding for a TPO.

Contributions: Contributions to a TPO can be either voluntary or mandatory. (However TPOs are usually not the type of institution that receives voluntary contributions).

In some developed countries TPOs that are semi-private organizations with a regular membership derive a large portion of their budget from mandatory contributions by the export community. In these cases, the financial support required from the government is limited. Such a system can work well when the TPO operates efficiently and when the export community has confidence in quality of the services it provides.

For developing countries, however, especially those with relatively new TPOs, such an approach would probably not be very successful. If there is a need to contribute to a service organization, the business community will probably prefer to make its contributions to an institution in specialized product sector, which it may feel more closely linked to.

In conclusion, the ideal source of financing for a TPO is usually the creation of a separate specific source of funding, such as the levies mentioned above. However when this is not feasible, anequate provision should be made in the national budget to provide the necessary financial support.

Budgeting procedures: When an allotment from the annual ministry budget is the only possible source of funding for a trade promotion organization, which is the situation in a majority of cases, the budget authorities should be encouraged to overcome some of the drawbacks outlined above so that the TPO can benefit from an adequate volume offinancing for its activities. Some improvements that might be made include:

1. **Arranging for the TPO to prepare its budget on the basis of promotional programmes, so that it can have the responsibility for defining its work programme and then getting the necessary financing to cover these activities. By basing its proposals on marketing plans and programmes, broken down by product or sector, the TPO can incorporate all of the activities required to launch an export drive for a particular product. If these programmes can also be linked to specific national export strategies and objectives, the budget proposals will tend to meet with greater success than if they are drawn up without any reference to broader national policies and decisions.**
2. **Avoiding across-the-board reductions of funds in case of reduced financial resources. When sufficient resources cannot be obtained to cover the cost, a programmed activity should be entirely eliminated, instead of proportionately reducing the allocation to all areas, which would results in any activity.**

3. Determining the real needs of the TPO, including salary levels, to guarantee a high technical performance, and conveying these requirements to the budgetary authorities. Otherwise the TPO might have to limit its activities to those that could be covered with the resources automatically allotted throught the ministry, which might tend to cover primarily the payroll costs and only a few promotional activities.

4. Convincing the national budgetary authorities of the need to provide adequate and stable resources to the TPO. The argument cöuld be used that, considering the country's need to generate foreign exchange through export promotion and development, trade promotion activities should have priority and consequently be free from sudden and significant budget cuts.

Such measures should help to avoid the vicious circle that sometimes develops when TPO is not fully able to perform the duties assigned to it because of lack of resources, and the authorities in turn do not grant the required funds because they feel that the TPO has not lived up to expectations.

Evaluation is another key function for the effective operation of a TPO. However evaluation is not systematically carried out in most TPOs, even in many developed countries. One of the reasons is that no standard procedurce have been designed for evaluating trade promotion programmes and activities. (ITC is drawing up guidelines that could be applied to the evaluation of such activites, which will be available in the coming months.)

Two main problems arise in the evaluation of trade promotion activities: the lack of detailed up-to-date trade statistics and the absence of quantitative targets for the programmed activities. Although the total figures of foreign trade performance are usually available within a short time after the end of each calendar or fiscal year, these statistics are not sufficient for judging the effectiveness of an individual promotional activity carried out for a specific product on a particular foreign market. Export performance can therefore be analyzed only on a global basis in the short term, and, after more detailed statistics have been published, only for traditional product sectors. Further more, the absence of pre-established specific trade promotion targets makes it impossible to determine if a programme has been effective. In addition, many TPOs carry out a number of activities that are not included in their annual work programmes, which likewise cannot be evaluated against any predetermined yardsticks.

Another difficulty is that some trade promotion activities are by nature so general that they are difficult to evaluate in terms of concrete results achieved. Examples are efforts to improve the overall export marketing skills of the business community and to increase export consciousness in the country.

Certain more specific types of activities can be more esasily evaluated, and in fact are more frequently so analyzed by a number of TPOs. This is especially the case for trade fairs and missions. The evaluation exercise is usually based on standard questionnaires that are completed at the end of the particular event. But this types of exercise is indicative only of the preliminary results achieved during the fair or the mission and should be repeated at least a year later (which is done in a few countries) to produce more valid conclusions.

Other specific activities that could be evaluated but are usually not include two very costly ones—operating a trade information service and running a national trade representation service abroad. One of the reasons that these are no systematically reviewed them is taken assumption that these activities automatically produce satisfactory results. With adequate evaluation procedures, however, the performance of such services could undoubtedly be improved and savings could made in them in the future.

Many TPOs that have established some type of regular or systematic evaluation procedures could often improve this operation by focusing less on describing the way in which the programmes have been carried out and instead measuring their real impact on the specific export activity.

By the same token, they could give more consideration to cost-benefit analysis, which is an important tool for designing-future work programmes and preparing the budget.

In all of the different types of evaluation exerises discussed above, a TPO should keep in mind that the purpose of evaluation is not simply to criticize past activities but rather to identify ways in which future programmes can be improved. By determining why a given programme was a success or failure, a TPO's management can select the elements in it that could be incorporated in future plans because of their positive impact on the programme and, conversely, those to delete because they failed to produce the expected results.

In addition to evaluating the external promotional programme, evaluation of a TPO's internal staffing and organization is like-wise a necessary exercise. In many TPOs, staff evaluations are carried out on a yearly basis. However they are undertaken mainly to judge the persons' past performance, rather than determine his ability to undertake new activities. Furthermore, when personnel are assigned to new posts within the organization, those evaluations are not always taken into consideration. Also, evaluations are seldom made of a section, department or division as a whole, which might help the TPO's executives to decide on the changes needed in the internal organization to improve the overall performance of the institution.

APPENDIX I

Transport Problems in a Large Marketing Company

Hindustan Lever

In 1960 this Company had about 11,000 direct dealers. They issued 1,35,000 invoices. In other words, each of these dealers bought on an average twelve times in a year. Every one of these transactions involves them in a transport activity; many of them involve two, because often they mɔve their goods not direct to the dealer, but first from the factory to a depot, and then from the depot to the dealer. There are also several thousand tons of materials required for production moving their goods to factories located in different regions of India. In 1959, factories 85,000 tons of vegetable oils and 60,000 tons of oilseeds—their main raw materials—from various parts of India over the internal transport system; and of these about 10 per cent of the former and 48 per cent of the latter moved at company's risk, part or whole of the way and the rest, at the risk of the suppliers. Here, again, more than one movement is involved, first to the collection points and then to factories either directly or through suppliers.

With so many hundred thousands of movements to consider, the Company is deeply interested in everything that goes on in transport. First, the transport costs were in 19ↄ9, equal to nearly half the profits. They added up to considerably more than their proposed dividend; naturally, therefore, it is of the utmost importance to the Company that they should be as low as possible. Secondly, every ton of oilseed or oil, help the Company at the collection points for, want of transport or delay in transit, every case of *Sunlight* or tin of *Dalda* that is sitting in a railway wagon or a truck instead of in a consumer's

Hindustan Lever Ltd.

capital tied up, earning nothing. Of the total current assets of the Company one rupee in every five, represents goods in transit, or in a depot or factory awaiting despatch. Every rupee they can free by better organization or quicker transit, times it a rupee they can use elsewhere to serve the consumer and make a profit by doing something else. Thirdly, the methods of transport must suit the consignees, be they factories or dealers. It is no good getting goods to the destination cheaply if they arrive in the middle of the night and the consignee is required to unload straight away. It is no good getting in oil quickly to these factories if there is considerable leakage as a resuit, nor is it any good getting the finished goods to the dealer quickly if every for example, *Dalda* tin is dented, and every bar of soap bruised.

In achieving these objectives, they use every form of transport available, having regard to the nature of the product and its packing, distance, transit time, cost and convenience of consignees. Over the last ten years or so the Railways have done a commendable job in improving transport over their network, particularly in regard to the movement of raw materials in bulk and transport of finished products over long distances. However, they have made two main innovations in the movement of our finished products, namely transport and depots.

In 1950 their normal method of despatch of finished goods was by rail straight to the dealer, and as far as possible, in full wagonloads. This meant that they tied up a great deal of their own capitial, the goods spent an average of 21 days in the wagon, and in one year for example, they had Rs. 187 lakhs worth of manufactured goods at the factories because they got wagons very irregularly. It was common experience in those days that for several days they got no wagons and then had sixteen on one day. They also had to tie up a good deal of their dealers' capital. The man in a small town who had to take a full wagonload of vanaspati, might well find himself with four, or five months' requirements on his hands at once, and for this typing up of their dealers' capital they had to pay either in bigger discounts or in letting them make larger profits on stocks in their hands whenever they had to raise the prices.

The Company had become much more flexible. In one year about 50 percent of their despatches were made by road; another 2 per cent were made by Quick Transit Service, a service the railways simply did not offer then. Their average transit time has been reduced from the 21 days of 1950 to 5 days of 1960. At their then rate of sale, that meant they were saving perhaps Rs. 1½ crores of scarce capital. Moreover, they had much less damage. Road journey normally involves no transhipment, whereas rail transport involves transhipment whenever there is a break of gauge; and road journeys are door to door, whereas with railways, even though they have sidings, their dealers do not, so that there is always an extra handling at their railway stations. Finally, with road contractors, they are usully able, at a price, to get them to accept responsibility for damage; the railways were very chary of accepting responsibility, and their employees are correspodingly careless. When they make a claim on their road carriers, it is settled within days, and usually in full. When they make claims on the railways, it used take an average of six months before a decision is obtained and they do not recover more than half their losses. There has been an improvement in that the Railways had made the decision to accept carriers' risk for them. Indeed, as road competition had grown, the Railways had become more attentive to claim, and the Q.T.S. cause much less damage from heavy shunting than ordinary services.

With costs, the Company had less good fortune. Changing to the road had saved the company money on the short hauls, roughly speaking on all those below 300 miles, which represent about 80 per cent of their despatches from their distribution centres. From their Bombay factory to Poona by road, for instance is Rs. 6.50 per ton of *Dalda* from their Delhi depot to Ludhiana by road than by rail. And they are endlessly looking for economies in packing. Earlier, for instance, all their soap was moved in wooden boxes. Now 70 per cent go in cardboard containers, which are a quarter cheaper. If all this had to go in wood boxes, it would have cost the Company an extra Rs. 24 lakhs.

They had also been helped by the depots. They had fifty one. For a cost of Rs. 22 per ton, including the extra freight the break of journey involved, they gave two great advantages. First they could reduce their working capital. If they had to carry enough stocks at their Calcutta factory to be able to despatch to each dealer their toilet preparations all over India on just those occasions when the raiways had small bookings open, they would fill many more godowns at the factory with hair oil and talcum powder than they possessed and they would have still more capital sitting idle in railway wagons as the small consignments wended slowly across the sub-continent. Secondly, they could see to it that their dealers were more seldom out of stock. Their minimum toilet preparations order was Rs. 200. You could well magine that a dealer in Trunelveli who had to wait for Rs. 200 worth of preparations to get to him by smalls from Calcutta would be out of stock most of the time; or else, he would have to lock up an immense amount of capital by buying for months and months ahead of his requirements at a time; and if he does that, he has to put his margin up, which for the same consnmer price, means that the Company margin has to go down. If he has to add another 5 per cent to the price to make up for the fact that he is turning over his capital once in three months instead of once a month, the addition is equal the Company's profits; even in a good year it would be equal to much more than half in a bad year.

The depots were so placed about the country that they could always be served by full wagon or lorry loads, and then customers could be served from them, usually by road in the smallest of smalls, and within at the most a few days of the receipt of their order. The results was that both the company and the dealers could operate with less stock in the pipeline. The minimum pipeline stocks of vanaspati, for example, had been cut by some 2,000 tons, or nearly a third, over a three year period; this had led to a reduction of Rs. 40 lakhs in the capital invested in packed stocks spread between the Company and the wholesalers and a very large part of it was due to the depots. Because they permitted smaller individual orders, the depots make the *Company's whole distribution system* more efficient. When the Company had to send vanaspati in full wagon-loads, they could not have a separate wholesaler in a small town. He would have had to take perhaps a year's stock at a time. So the little towns had to be serviced from nearby bigger ones, which was always expensive and often inefficient. Now they could often serve these direct from the depot, even though they could only take a few cases at a time, and the number of their vanaspati wholesalers had risen from about 1,500 in 1956 to 1,780 in 1960, with all that meant in extra energy and initiative applied to the business. But all such savings get swallowed up, though they do not become any less important, by government's increasing use of transport as a means of taxation. Since 1950 *rail freights* had gone up from 14 percent depending upon the product and distance; the cost of diesel oil in Bombay had doubled from Rs. 1.18 to Rs. 2.34; an excise of 40 per cent has been put on tyres; that part of the cost of petrol in Bombay city which tax has gone up two and one-third times; the tax (Customs and excise) on an ordinary Mercedes Benz truck had increased from Rs. 2,070 to Rs. 5,070. We may put it in another way; a truck doing 35,000 miles in 1950 paid Rs. 1,500 in taxes of every sort; in 1960 it paid over Rs. 2,000 and still more on Inter-State movement. Naturally, the Company's bills had gone up with them.

They would have mind the extra taxes less if they were spent on the means of transport from which they are taken. The Company recognizes the great improvement which had occurred in the services provided by the Railways over the last decade. Wagons are usually more freely available, transit time have come down, railway officials of all grades are more helpful than they used to be. But enough had not been done for the roads. Key bridges were still missing, the lack of which reduces the value of huudreds of miles of National Highway. The bridge over the Chambal on the Bombay-Agra highway was ready in 1960 but no bridge at Dehri-on-Sone on the Calcutta-Delhi highway, or over the three great rivers between Calcutta and

Cuttack. Often essential parts of a through highway had still not been built; the Rs 10 crore bridge over the Ganga at Nokameh could not be used to full advantage because the authorities had still not built the few necessary miles of approach road on either side of the bridge. A bridge was under construction over the Brahmaputra at Pandu in Assam. In the master plan there was no provision for a river ghat near the bridge site, with the rosult that goods coming by water transport from the Calcutta will have to proceed beyond Pandu to Gauhati and come back by road to Pandu. Even where the Highways have been built, they are usually narrow, and often badly surfaced; frequently their bridges are weak and their foundations inadequate. There is only one adequate road in all India, the *Grand Trunk Road* from Delhi to the Punjab. The result is accidents and low load limits; both are dangerous both waste capital. Sometimes, the load limits are lower than even the bad roads make necessary. Thus Maharashtra has an average pay-load carrying limit of 130 maunds, whereas its neighbours, with no better roads permit 200 maunds; not only are freights in Maharashtra unnecessarily higher as a result, but also lorries have to reload when they get across the State border, with much consequent delay, damage and expense.

Not only were the allocations for road improvements too low, but there was no urgency about what was being done. Bridges take years to build. When a road is damaged, it takes months to mend. After the floods in Gujarat the railway line to Surat was mended in three weeks. The full restoration of the road took one year. Traffic was diverted involving an extra distance of 60 miles and often through the fields, formonths when the repair or improvement concerned could have been carried out in weeks; and every such diversion puts up costs, and uses up scarce foreign exchange, for going through the fields shortens the life of vehicle and tyres, and puts up the conrumption of fuel.

Most irksome of all are the rules governing road transport. The planners say that the country is short of transport, and that the provision of more rail capacity is one of the heaviest of all burdens on India's limited capital, about 20 per cent of the whole second five-year plan was being devoted to the Railways. One would have thought, therefore, that they would want to see the maximum use being made of those roads which exist, and the maximum relief being given to the railways by the use of lorries. In other words, one would have expected, if transport were properly planned, that there would be no restrictions placed on road transport beyond those necessarily imposed by the limitations on the avalability of trucks. So deeply were the railways and the road transport authorities rooted in the thinking of the 1930s. that restrictions were infinite, restrictions on the routes that could be plied, on the distances that coud be travelled, on carring goods from one State to another, on loads, on the use of trailers. One would think India had an immense superfluity of transport, and that the loads had to be rationed out to give everybody a living, regardless of cost, instead of transport being always on the verge of bottleneck and so expensive that every future addition to its costs is a serious matter; one rupee in every twenty of the company costs was on transport including handling.

Railways and roads alike have improved enormously over the last few years; The Company's transport department had considerable achievements to its credit, and both the Government and the carriers have shown so much responsiveness to new ideas. One should welcome the introduction by the Railways of a *Container Service* of the type they have in many foreign countries; this would be particularly useful in India where they would case the whole problem of transhipment at points where the gauge changes. Secondly, more attention should be paid to *Refrigerated Transport*, both by rail and road. The lack of refrigerated transport inhibits particularly the development of the fruit, vegetable, fish and milk industries, all of them admirable ways of improving both the income of the villager and nutrition of the townsman and all of them dependent for carriage over any distance upon refrigeration. We should be keen on *insulated wagons* for edible oils and for vanaspati; these do not require refrigeration but they would keep better if they could at least be insulated. Thirdly, the municipalities shouid be prompt in their refund of octroi on re-exports; one often has to wait months for such refunds; it takes six months in towns as big as Ahmedabad and Bangalore; sometimes a refund of terminal taxes cannot be got at all, as at Agra and Kanpur; and the Company had to close down an otherwise suitable depot in Gwalior because the Municipal Corporation would not refund the octroi on depatches sent outside the towns; we can see no reason why the inhabitants of one towu should be allowed to tax the surrounding villagers, or the inhabitants of other towns in this way. Fourthly, there is scope for improvement in the way vegetable oil is transported by sea. The Company uses country-craft to bring seed and oil from Saurashtra to Bombay, 13,851 metric tons of seed and 4,676 metric tons of oil were transported in this manner in a year. While the facilities provided by county-craft for movement of bagged material are reasonably adequate except during the monsoon, one cannot say the same about movement of oil. Shipment of oil in drums by country-craft or coastal steamer is an uneconomic method due to the weight of the drums transported and the losses which occur in transit. The cheapest way of moving oil would be in bulk, but there were no bulk handling facilities in Saurashtra ports nor are they adequate in the other ports. This is a problem which is tied up with the much larger problem of loading large quantites of oil into steamer for the export trade. In India's Plan targets for export of oil great consideration should be given to providing better facilities at the main ports for storage prior to loading and ultimate pumping from the storage tanks into ships' bulk tanks. The recommendations of the Masani Committee on Road Transport Reorganistion, which had been generally endorsed by the Transport Council was an important step. But the problems of coordination of different forms of transport formed the subject matter of further consideration by the Neogy Committee and now the Pandey Committee.

APPENDIX II

Problems in Distribution: Case Study

The Western India Chemicals Company was a large enterprise manufacturing and selling products of household consumption. The Company had been in the Indian market as importers almost from the turn of the century. As early as 1933, judging the market to have potential and wanting to be more competitive, the Company put up manufacturing units in the country. The distribution of their products was through sole Selling Agents situated in the port towns of Bombay, Madras and Calcutta. During World War II, a situation of serious shortage arose and, to ensure equitable distribution, the Company took over the marketing of their products, At the end of the War, its marketing set-up was crystallized around its three principal groups of products: soaps, vanaspati and cosmetics. The distribution system of the Company evolved in the fifties was naturally conditioned by the growing national economy.

The Company had two soaps and cosmetics factories and four vanaspati factories. When they took over their own distribution, they despatched all stocks directly from these factories by rail to traders in various towns.

In 1956, the Company developed secondary despatch points and by 1960 had five Company depots and fifty Clearing and Forwarding Agencies. The distinction between the two was that depots were staffed by Company personnel whilst C&F.A.'s were contracted out on a remuneration (average their Rs. 10 per tonne) on the tonnage distributed by the Agent. Simultaneously, from the mid-fifteis, the Company started using road transport for a proportion of their products until in 1960, 40 per cent of factory despatches and 90 per cent of secondary

The Western India Chemicals Company

despatches were made by road. They found road transport to be more expensive than rail for distances over 300 miles and that soaps were 15 per cent less expensive per tonne to carry than vanaspati on railways. These facts had two effects. (1) By 1960 nearly three-quarters of vanaspati primary despatches were made by road while almost all soaps primary despatches were made by rail. The Company's *transport expenses* went up in the case of soaps from Rs. 80 per tonne in 1956 to Rs. 100 per tonne in 1960 and in the case of Foods from Rs. 60 per tonne in 1956 to Rs. 80 per tonne in 1960. This development, despite added costs of despatch points and road transport, had five reasons. Firstly, capital. The Company could send by rail only large consignments which took a long time (anything upto a month) to reach destinations; the availablity of wagons was erratic and thus they piled up huge stocks which tied up Company capital. Secondly, damages. The railways had a cumbersome system for settling claims whilst road contractors were prepared to accept full responsibility. Thirdly, service to markets by road was more convenient (door delivery to trader) and in smaller consignments, more frequent (allowing the trader to cut the amount of capital he required to tie up in their business). Fourthly, expanding distribution of Company products to smaller towns which were not railheads could only be satisfactorily serviced by road. Fifthly, by despatching company stocks from within State boundaries, they were able to avoid the incidence of Central Sales Tax (1 percent of turnover).

The king pin of the Company's distribution system was the *wholesale stockist*. The goods are invoiced and despatched to the stockist; these goods are distributed by Company salesmen to the retailers in the markets; and further orders were booked from the stockist to provide for the expected demand of the market in the period following, until the salesman visited that market again and repeated the cycle of working. It was a central part of the wholesale stockist's terms of appointment that he maintained adequate stocks for the needs of his market, as judged by the Company salesman. Also, since credit was an important part of transactions in the bazar, the stockist provided judicious and necessary credit. In sum, he was the Company's agent in this town, continuously present to service his market with its products.

The Company salesman helped in ensuring the efficient movement of stocks from despatch point to consumer. He booked orders from wholesalers according to the needs of particular markets, forecasting demand as best as he could. He redistributed the wholesaler stocks to retail outlets in the town, making about 30 calls a day and spending 80 per cent of his working time on this part of his job. In doing retail redistribution, the salesman ensured that each retailer carried as high stocks as would be commensurate with the retailer's off-take; displayed his products adequately to achieve consumer attention; and put across to the retailer the advertising points behind his products, in an attempt to inform and influence the retailer so that in his turn the retailer may persuade consumers. The salesman also took pains to see that this distribution system worked as smoothly as possible, attending to any trade complaints. He provided leadership to the stockist in the organisation of the stockist's business concerned with the distribution of their products. An example of the last activity was be his supervision of the distribution which the stockist does on his own in between the salesman's visit, which the Company refer to as feed-back as to the trends concerning the Company's own products and competitor's products in the market.

The Company's salesman were led and supervised by Sales Managers. The country was divided into four regions, each under the charge of a Regional Sales Co-ordinator; who was a part of the head office marketing team led by the Marketing Director. The other part of this marketing team consisted of Brand Managers reporting to a Marketing Co-ordinator. The sales and marketing parts of this team worked in close concert to evolve and recommend marketing policy to the Board of the Company.

This was the broad pattern of distribution common to the three product groups of the Company.

The Edible Products Groups business was large, 40,000 tonnes or Rs. 10 crores a year. The business was centred around vanaspati which were in various packs under the same brand name. *Savad* had 40 per cent share of the vanaspati packed market and with their bulk pack *Ganesh* had 10 per cent share of the loose market. The total vanaspati market was expanding at 5 per cent per annum, the bulk/loose packs expanding at a somewhat faster rate. The Company felt that with growing purity and quality consciousness, Savad had an important role to play in the future.

The Company's Distribution was conditioned by the fact that vanaspati is a perishable item of daily consumption. It was thus essential that the goods go out into the markets quickly, that they are distributed to individual retailers at short and regular intervals and that be sold out to the consumers within three months of production.

The Edible Products Group had taken to road transport as it ensured that the stock reached individual markets within two weeks. 75 per cent of primary despatches and 90 per cent of secondary despatches were done by road. Transport costs were 3.1 per cent of turn over, and had gone up by 33 per cent since 1956

The Group covers a total of 3,500 markets with a population of 80 million; 2,400 markets with a population of 75 million in the urban sector representing 95 per cent of the urban population, in the rural sector, they covered 1,100 markets with a total population of 5 million, about 1.5 per cent of the entire rural population. The Group salesmen visited 1,20,000 outlets.

The Company had three types of markets: Standard, Development and Future. Roughly one-third of its markets were in each category. They had full wholesalers in their Standard markets to whom they paid a commission of 4 per cent on turn-over. They had always followed a strict monopoly system for wholesalers, having one per town, in view of the importance of proper redistribution and rotation of stocks. They had subwholesalers appointed by main town wholesalers in Development markets, whose remuneration was from the wholesalers and was about 2.5 per cent. They had a host of Future markets, worked either by the wholesaler or sub-wholesaler where they had no local representative, which were visited periodically by these parties. In this case, the Company paid actuals in terms of transport and expenses, which came to 2 per cent of turn-over.

The discount of 4 per cent paid to the main town wholesaler covered all costs of sub-wholesaler and the Company paid an extra 2 per cent for the 7 per cent of business which the Future markets provided. The net return to the wholesaler on investment per annum varied between 25 to 30 per cent before tax. Both wholesalers and sub-wholesalers were supplied stocks directly from Company depots/C. & F.As. They had to maintain adequate stock levels to feed the markets, they were in charge of proper rotation of stocks; they redistributed to all individual retailers once a week at their own expense and they provided adequate credit to the retail trade.

The Company salesman visited all Standard and Development markets once in four weeks and carried out the distribution to individual retailers. He supervised all the other working of the wholesaler; he was also in control of Future working and tried to cover each Future market twice a year. The Company employed 80 salesmen and their total expenses came to 1 per cent of turn-over.

This Group's aim was to promote towns from Future working to Development Towns and on to Standard markets. At the same time, its Future working ensured that its goods reached the markets on the rural fringe at no extra cost to the consumer and at small cost to the Group. Its salesmen could only cover regularly the Standard and Development towns which formed two thirds of the total towns covered and gave 93 per cent of the business. Their visits to Future markets were irregular and at long intervals. The Group appreciated that wholesaler working of Future markets was by no means the ideal solution and was constantly reviewing new methods of servicing such markets. The group was also conscious that its sales organisation could perhaps handle a longer price list than it was doing in 1960 without any or appreciable increases in cost. This could show interesting possibilities in the context of growing demand in towns in the allied fields of packaged convenience goods.

The *Detergents Group's* business was 60,000 tonnes or Rs. 12 crores a year. Soap is an item of mass consumption and a semi-necessity in economic terms. Soaps are used in even the remotest villages and it was estimated that half the total consumption and about one third of the money spent on soap was in the rural sector. The Company had almost 10 per eent share of the market which was growing at 7 per cent per annum, somewhat faster than its brands. Competition was on the increase particularly from small units outside the organized sector of industry. Vigorous distribution played a crucial role in maintaining tonnage and achieving expansion. The Detergents Group relied rather more on rail primary despatches, since soaps had a greater keepability than Foods and promptness of primary despatches was not quite so important, 60 per cent of primary despatches and 10 per cent of secondary despatches were by rail; transport costs were Rs. 100 per tonne, up 25 per cent since 1956, or 5 per cent turn-over.

The Detergents Group covered the entire urban population of the country and visit all 2,500 towns. They also covered 2,000 villages or 15 million rural population, nearly 5 per cent of the total. The group salesmen called upon 1,50,000 retailers in the country. The Group estimated that perhaps 20 per cent of their products were ultimately consumed in areas outside their distribution cover.

They had two types of markets, Standard and Jeep. Each Standard market had one or more appointed wholesaler depending on the size of business. Traditionally the Group had booked direct orders from a large number of parties. This led to unhappy competition in the Wholesale sections of the trade and redistribution to retailers suffered. Accordingly, they moved towards a monopoly system in the late fifties which had ensured a regular supply of goods to the retail trade, and adequate margins to the Wholesalers. Wholesalers received a remuneration of 4 per cent of turn-over and had a 25 per cent net return on investment. The Wholesaler maintained reasonable stocks at all times, and redistributed stock at regular intervals to the retail trade. Salesmen and the smaller ones at twelve-weekly intervals. There were 120 salesmen covering 1,800 standard markets and they cost 1 per cent of turn-over.

The Group developed Sales Jeeps in the early fifties to enable them to extend coverage in the rural sector. Essentially, the Sales Jeeps did two things: they carried stocks to markets which did not have resident wholesalers to provide stocks locally, and they carried salesmen enabling them to work two or three small markets in a working day—markets which could not provide a full day's occupation for the salesman. Since the Jeeps operated in the smallest towns and the largest villages, they carried a pricelist which was only half as long as the Standard salesman's list, in view of the fact that there was little market there for washing powders. One remification of this was the thought in the Company that the Jeeps could perhaps handle additional products without increasing costs or lessening efficiency. By means of the Sales Jeeps, the Group were covering 2,700 markets with 20 Jeeps, giving 10 per cent of the Soaps business at a cost of 6 per cent of turnover. It was apart of the objective of the Jeep operation to appoint suitable wholesalers, and to develop such markets to Standard markets in due course, thus enabling the Jeeps to go deeper into the countryside.

Further, expansion of Jeeps from this position seemed unlikely, as over the years, the more potential small towns were put on to the Standard markets coverage and the volume of business in the extension towns did not justify the inherently high cost of the Jeep operation. The volume of business was becoming increasingly difficult to come by in the context of rising costs. It was increasingly difficult for the smaller markets which could be added on to Jeep coverage to provide this business at the same cost. The Group was considering alternative methods of further extension of distribution. A cheap and simple method of getting stocks to the villages was being sought. It was felt that perhaps the wholesalers would play their role here.

The *Cosmetics Group* had two principal components. One was toilet soaps—they had a popular priced toiler soap (HAMARA), and three pramium priced toilet soaps. The other was cosmetics properly speaking—skin, hair, shaving and dental preparations. The soaps component of the Cosmetic Group provided a turnover of Rs. 1.3 crores (of which its HAMARA gave a net sales value of Rs. 1 crore); the cosmetics part of the Group gave a turnover of Rs. 90 lakhs. HAMARA had a reasonable (15 per cent) share of its market whilst the cosmetic lines, a very small (2 to 5 per cent) share of their respective product fields. Both toilet soaps and cosmetics had been hardly expanding at all in late fifties.

The Cosmetics Group covered about 1,800 towns with a population of 50 million. Depending on the importance of the markets, the frequency of visit of their salesmen ranged from 16 to 4 in a year. Like the Detergents Group, they operated through redistribution stockists to whom they gave 4 percent discount. Although the Cosmetics Group salesmen called on 80,000 retail outlats, only HAMARA was sold to all these outlets; cosmetic lines were sold only to 10,000 outlets. Cosmetics Group salesmen used HAMARA as a hook to get retailer buying and then tried to extend the distribution of cosmetic lines. As the distribution figures showed they have had only very limited success in this direction, and Group itself was having some reservations as to how far this mere extension of distribution for sophisticated cosmetic lines was either practicable or desirable. Outside their coverage, the Cosmetics Group solicited business through mail by sending circulars to the Detergents Group traders in about 2,500 markets with a population of 15 million—and thus obtained 4 per cent of their business.

The Cosmetics Group's business was small, and despite higher margins than the other two Groups, the Group found it difficult to maintain a marketing overhead of 75 salesmen, 15 supervisors, 8 sales managers—totalling a net selling cost of Rs. 20 lakhs. Nevertheless, the Company felt that the Group had a small share in a lucarative and expanding business, and if it was able to increase this satisfactorily, that investment would be worth-while. For expansion, they had a number of new lines and brands as projects to be developed. As far as distribution was concerned, they felt that only one product—HAMARA—needed expended width. For other cosmetic lines, they were already going to about 70,000 retailers who provided a negligible amount of turnover.

What changes would you recommend in the distribution system of Western India?